L A
JUSTICE

ROBERT L. VERNON

to, Katie Mastain
Bob Vernon
Jan 8, 2014

LA JUSTICE

ROBERT L. VERNON

ISBN: 1-4609-4842-4
ISBN-13: 9781460948422

To our children,
Pam and her husband, Steve; Bob and his wife, Kristen;
our best friends
and the parents of our most-prized treasures,
our grandchildren

Acknowledgments

This book could not have been done without the help of many people. I want to acknowledge here, with deep gratitude, their contributions to my life and work.

Esther, my wife and best friend. Much of the material in the book is hers. She patiently endured.

Dr. James Dobson, who got the whole thing started.

Bobby Phillips, director of Hume Lake Christian Camps, a good friend who inspired me and gave me encouragement and counsel throughout this project.

Fernando J. "Nick" Najera, my training officer, who gave me my love for police work.

Mary Helen Ayala, my first and last secretary. Her professionalism and loyalty have been a great encouragement to us. She also assisted in the research for this book.

Larry Weeden, for his superb editing job.

Al Janssen, for his help as publishing director and idea man throughout the process.

Larry Fetters, Dave Powers, Len Huntshammer, and Dan Koenig for being true partners during the last hard year.

Daryl Gates, a good boss who allowed me to lead.

Nancy Thomason, for her devotion to the children of the projects, who gave me the story of Eric.

Bob Vernon, Jr., who gave me good professional counsel.

Hume Lake Christian Camps, for providing the setting for much of the writing project.

George Morrison, who gave me good insight.

Captain Tim McBride, a true professional who executed the plan.

Stan Chambers, a committed and honest journalist.

Lieutenant Mike Hillman, a cop's cop who was prepared.

The men and women of the LAPD who sincerely want to protect and serve.

The staff of Focus on the Family, for their superb support and pursuit of excellence.

CONTENTS

INTRODUCTION

As I considered writing this book, I asked myself, "Does the world really need this book? Is this effort absolutely necessary?"

After nearly 38 years of service with the Los Angeles Police Department (LAPD), I retired in mid-1992. As I left, I felt a heavy burden weighing me down. I had seen many changes in L.A. over those years: the family unit breaking apart; greater unhappiness, violence, and crime; the city I've loved and protected in danger of becoming corrupted; leaders of strong, good character being attacked for their positive, moral influence on society.

Now I feel like a person standing outside a building that is catching on fire. I see people on every floor who are mostly unaware the building is burning. I cannot keep silent. I feel driven to shout, "Fire!" I'm compelled to sound the alarm, to do what I can to quench the flames. They can't be allowed to spread. For the danger isn't just to my family and my city—we're all caught in a cultural crisis. Your family and your city are at risk, too.

How does a corrupt city become clean? How does a clean city become corrupt? What are the causes of social unrest and family breakdown? What makes the youth of a society become "moral flatliners"—dead to any sense of right and wrong? A study of Los Angeles helps to answer those questions, because in many ways L.A. is the nation's trendsetter. It is a microcosm of the United States switched onto fast-forward. By looking at what's occurring there now, we get a preview of what's likely to happen in the rest of the country within five years.

For half a century, L.A. has been relatively free of corruption (as big cities go). But that wasn't always the case. In the 1930s, it was rife with corruption. From the mayor's office to the police department, under-the-table payoffs and other forms of graft were the order of the day.

In the late 1930s, a few brave citizens formed a committee and cleaned up city hall. A number of brilliant reform measures were enacted. The LAPD was cleansed as well, and the new chief of police was insulated from improper political influence by being given the "heat shield" of civil service protection.

In the decades that followed, L.A. was unusual among the nation's large cities with its professional, clean police department and comparatively corruption-free city hall. To be sure, there were isolated "independent contractors" who tried their hand at graft, but they were usually caught quickly and dealt with appropriately. L.A. was a good place to live.

During those years, the LAPD acted as a watchdog. If city officials became involved in illegal activity, the department took action. L.A. had a reputation as one of the few large cities with little or no organized crime influence.

One of the LAPD's primary weapons against corruption was its intelligence operations. Two intelligence divisions kept the criminals at bay. The Organized Crime Intelligence Division (OCID) kept the Mafia and other classic organized-crime barons out of town. The Public Disorder Intelligence Division (PDID) made terrorist groups and other subversive organizations ineffective. But times have changed.

Things began to get worse when Tom Bradley became mayor in 1973. In the first budget he controlled, he started reducing the size of the LAPD; this was *before* Proposition 13, California's tax limitation initiative, forced local governments to cut back a lot of civil services. The department dropped from more than 7,400 officers when he took office to a low of just over 6,700 in 1980—while the city's population was growing dramatically.

Bradley also led the move to eliminate community relations officers in 1978 because the police and local communities had grown too close for the comfort of some politicians. The neighborhood watch meetings were seen as a potentially powerful political action network.

I'm not sure about the motives of each and every member of the movement to weaken the police, but I believe I know their goal—to make the LAPD a second-rate, ineffective police department; to remove the teeth of the watchdog.

To pull that off, the enemies of the LAPD had to do two things. First, the department's highly effective intelligence operations had to be neutralized. Work on that began in the 1970s and continues today.

The infiltration of criminal gangs and other dangerous groups is now nearly impossible. That's one of the primary reasons the LAPD had little or no warning about the preplanned nature of the Rodney King riots in April 1992. It's shameful that at the same time the public cries for more help and protection, the politicians have crippled the police.

The second step in pulling the teeth of the watchdog was to gain control of the top management of the LAPD. Kick out the professional leadership. Eliminate those who still believe the department should police the illegal acts of everyone, including the investigation of politicians when necessary. (The audacity!)

Prior to the King incident, L.A. politicians tried twice to change the city charter to make the police more subject to political control. Both times they failed. The voters resisted returning to the system of the crooked 1930s, choosing instead to keep the political heat shield for their chief of police.

Then Rodney King provided the right event for the manipulators. Their plans were ready and were put into effect immediately. The mayor appointed a close ally, Warren Christopher, to do the job. (Right after the King incident, one of the persons later appointed to the Christopher Commission was overheard saying, "Now we've got what we needed. We can make our move now." The individual overhearing that comment later communicated it to my lawyer.)

In my opinion, the Christopher Commission was not interested primarily in getting to the facts or diagnosing the problems. Rather, the hidden agenda was to drive Chief Gates from office, change the city charter, and neutralize the watchdog function of the LAPD.

In June 1992, the city charter *was* changed, and the police chief's civil service protection was stripped away. I believe the people of L.A. were outraged at what they were led to think was a racist, brutal police department. They voted for the magic word *reform*, which had been wisely but misleadingly attached to the ballot measure. What they unwittingly did was to turn back the clock to the 1930s.

The referendum also put several other changes into effect. Since the real reform of the late 1930s, the police controlled those enterprises that are prone to corruption. Adult book stores, massage parlors, bath houses, amusement arcades, and adult entertainment bars were regulated under police commission permits and police enforcement. But a little-known portion of the new charter moved that important permit function to the city clerk's office—and closer to the influence of city hall.

How does a good city turn bad? Keep your eye on L.A. and you'll have your answer.

But this book is about more than the problems of Los Angeles. Just as our cities are in crisis, so are our other cultural institutions. Perhaps none is in greater danger than the most important institution of all—the family. Sifting through the rubble of American dreams, root causes of the crisis become apparent. The riots, gang warfare, racial unrest, crime, and violence all point to five basic problems. But facing the problems head-on brings hope. I had to write this book.

Robert L. Vernon
November 1992

PART 1:
THE MANY FACES OF
INJUSTICE

1

A LIVING NIGHTMARE

SIMI VALLEY—Four Los Angeles police officers won acquittals Wednesday in their trial for the beating of black motorist Rodney G. King, igniting renewed outrage over a racially charged case that had triggered a national debate on police brutality.

Hours after the verdicts were announced, angry demonstrators torched buildings, looted stores and assaulted passersby as civic leaders pleaded for calm. Gov. Pete Wilson deployed the National Guard at the request of Mayor Tom Bradley.

So began the lead story in the *Los Angeles Times* of Thursday, April 30, 1992. The day before had been the start of a living nightmare for the city I love and served as a police officer for more than 37 years. But I had been out of town that day and so was one of the last Angelenos to learn about the verdicts and the terrible riots that followed.

As the rioting began on Wednesday, April 29, I was sitting on a plane, returning to the city from a business trip. The Friday before had been my last day as assistant chief of police for Los Angeles, and I wondered what was happening in the department.

Having been a cop for so many years—number 2 man in the department for the last 7—and loving every minute of it, I was having trouble adjusting to the idea of retirement. The department had become my second family, adopting me as a 21-year-old, training me, and teaching me principles of discipline and commitment. I had learned from the best what it meant to be a real cop and a good partner. I had started as a "harness bull" (a uniformed footbeat cop), did my time in a radio car in the inner city, and worked as a detective in south-central Los Angeles. I had specialized as a Juvenile Narcotics detective and learned much about why kids take the wrong turn in life. I had paid my dues on the street. I grew nostalgic, lost in a variety of emotions.

As we neared Los Angeles International Airport (LAX) at about 8:30 P.M., I was vaguely aware that the plane used an unusual landing approach. We seemed to stay higher than usual passing over the city, and we swung wide over the Pacific before making our final approach from the west. Just 15 minutes before, I would learn later, 18-year-old Louis Watson had become the first fatality of the riots, shot to death at, ironically, the intersection of Vernon and Vermont avenues.

Once we were on the ground, I decided to stop off at the police substation and say hello to the officers working there. It was hard to break the tie; I still felt like one of them. Walking under the elevated restaurant that's the most-recognized part of the airport, I turned west toward the substation. It's located in a row of utility buildings in the center of the horseshoe formed by the terminals.

When I got there, I opened the door and asked for a "buzz" to go past the small reception area. Three airport officers were present, but no one wearing the LAPD uniform. "Hi, I'm Chief Vernon," I said. "Where is everyone? Do we have some type of special operation going?"

"They were all called out to help with the riots," came the answer. "All off-duty officers were called in at 7:00. We're backfilling the positions here temporarily."

"The riots? What riots?"

"You haven't heard? The King verdict came in this afternoon. The officers were found not guilty. I guess there are some big-time disturbances going on in South-Central."

What I said next was, "I was afraid of that. Well, I'd better get home quickly and see if the chief needs me. Do you know how big it is?"

What I felt was, *How bad might it be? Are we going to have another Watts tragedy on our hands?*

"All we know is what we see on TV," the officer replied, "and it doesn't look good there. Chief, I don't know where you live, but you'd better not go through South-Central, or even downtown L.A."

"Good advice. See you guys later. Thanks for giving us a hand."

Giving us a hand. I had cleaned out my office and said my good-byes the previous week, but I was still "on the books," using up earned vacation days and subject to recall by Chief Daryl Gates. I jumped in my car and headed for home and my uniforms.

As I drove north on the 405, I listened to the radio. It really was a riot—had been since 5:30 P.M.—with crowds in the streets, people being pulled from their cars and beaten, businesses being looted, buildings being set afire.

Before I got home, angry mobs would descend on City Hall and Parker Center (police headquarters), as well as the Times Building, where they would do thousands of dollars of damage to the ground floor. Before I got home, Mayor Bradley would declare a local state of emergency, preparing the way for Governor Wilson to call in the National Guard. Before I got home, at least three people would be dead.

My only consolation as I drove in the night was the knowledge that this time we were ready. In the Watts riots of 1965, we had been taken by surprise. I was there. As a lieutenant of 2 whole weeks, I had been sent to the Watts substation with nearly 20 men—half of my watch. I had seen the lack of organization and preparation. Largely because of that, we now had a tactical manual with an entire chapter covering what to do in a riot.

Included were statements of policy, strategy, and the specifics of forming a split force—one part to handle emergency calls and the other to be deployed in the riot zone. The manual had been a source of questions for many promotional exams since its inception, so all those in positions of leadership would have it practically committed to memory.

Only a few weeks before, on April 10, I had met with all 5 bureau commanding officers (or their designees), as well as the 18 station commanders who report to them, for specific riot preparation. (We had done the same thing at staff meetings for several months.) The details of our plans were discussed. All present were given handout materials to help them in implementation. They were warned of a forthcoming emergency response audit, and the audit was ordered on April 20, to be completed by the 24th. Since that meeting, we had conducted daily drills, city wide, to practice our tactical alert procedures. I had no doubt we were ready; this time we should be able to minimize the human and property loss. (For more about these plans, see chap. 14.)

Forty-five minutes after leaving the airport, I pulled into our driveway. The lights were on in the kitchen. I wondered if Esther, my wife, was aware of what was happening; I guessed she was. At the least, she would have heard from our daughter, Pam, who is married to an LAPD sergeant.

My mind was racing. We were scheduled to leave at 7:00 the next morning for Fort Lauderdale, Florida, from LAX. I felt certain those plans would change.

Esther met me at the back door. "Am I ever glad to see you!" she said. "There's a riot going on."

"I know. I just found out at the airport."

"I was afraid you wouldn't know and would drive right through it. You're not going in, are you? Remember, you're retired."

"I'm ready if I'm needed. I've been anticipating this one. We do have plans, but the chief may want me to make sure they're carried out."

I threw down my bag and headed for the phone. A few minutes later, I was talking to Captain Dan Watson, the commanding officer (CO) of the Emergency Command Center, known as the ECC. "This is Vernon. I just got back into town. I guess we've got a riot on our hands. I'm ready to come back in if the chief needs me. Can you get to him?"

"Will do, Sir. Hold on, and I'll see if I can get an answer." He was back on the line in a couple of minutes and said the chief thought they had the situation under control, so I wouldn't need to come in.

I hung up and tried to pack for Florida, but my heart wasn't in it. I turned on the TV and saw some of the violence and destruction. It didn't look as if things were even close to being under control. In fact, before the day was over, more than 500 fires would be set—1,000 by Thursday night—and scores of people would be hurt, including 1 firefighter shot in the head.

I was frustrated. Early reports said the police were slow to respond and seemed unorganized. A TV anchorwoman, looking at the violence with no officers in the area, said, "I can't believe the cops are looking at this and not doing something."

How can this be happening? I thought. The plans were clear. The "tac" manual set out the procedure. We were to have a split force—one to respond to life-threatening emergency calls, the other to serve as the riot-force. The affected area was to be controlled by one of three strategies: "linear strategy, sectioning, or cordoning." At the April 10 meeting of my commanders, I had emphasized sectoring as best for a large riot. The area affected was to be divided geographically. Sector commanders would take their teams and *stay* in their areas. The strategy was clear—gain control as quickly as possible, and don't leave.

I was confident the men and women at the front-line level were ready and willing to do just that. Yet the record later showed it took the police more than three hours from the time of the first call to establish control at the intersection of Florence and Normandie, where the riots began.

The problem must be in the leadership, I concluded. It seemed as if I were watching another police department, a paralyzed and weak organization, not the proud and effective force I had served.

I felt helpless. I began trying to figure out what could have gone wrong with the implementation of our plans. It was no secret there were factions at the top of the department. Since the King incident, certain high-level officers had become more interested in their careers than in obeying orders. And since Chief Gates had announced his retirement, some viewed him as a lame duck. Being seen as his ally, I, too, became a target—one whose orders should be ignored if possible.

All my training and instincts and concern for the city and the department made me extremely anxious to see more of what was going on. I *needed* to go to the ECC, even though it was now nearly 11:00 P.M. I picked up the phone, called in, and asked to speak to the highest-ranking officer available. Commander Jimmy Jones, one of the most talented and hardworking members of the executive staff, came on the line.

"Hi, Chief, this is Jimmy Jones," he said. "How can I help you?"

I explained my earlier call and my travel plans for the next day. "Jim," I concluded, "I don't think this is going to go away easily. I'm willing to come in and push back my retirement date. But I need to know within the next few hours."

"Chief, I agree with you. This is not going to be contained tonight or tomorrow. This is a big one. Let me see if I can get an answer for you. Hold on a minute."

Two or three minutes later, he was back: "Chief, they say go ahead with your plans. You shouldn't come in."

"Well, I don't feel good about this. Look, will you promise me that you'll personally talk with Chief Gates and tell him my concerns? Once I get on that plane tomorrow, it will be tough to turn things around if he changes his mind."

"You've got my word, Boss. I'll talk to the chief myself. But I think there may be a staff officer or two that has reasons for not wanting you here."

Rather than feeling better about things, I felt worse. Was someone giving the chief bad advice? Why would other officers not want my help in an emergency situation? My feelings intensified when I looked at the TV again and saw a replay of an incident in front of Parker Center. A large crowd burned a guard shack and broke windows at the front door. *Why haven't they declared an unlawful assembly?* I wondered. *There doesn't seem to be any attempt to gain control.*

In one view of the front of the building, I could see a deputy chief of police and at least one police commissioner watching events unfold. The commissioner was saying it was wise to tolerate the property loss rather than force a confrontation that would probably cost lives.

"You don't know what you're talking about!" I shouted at the TV image. "That's like saying let's start a little forest fire! You can't have a limited riot!"

I felt my wife's hand on my back trying to calm me down. I lowered my voice and said, "Don't they realize that if they allow people to destroy police headquarters, they're telling them they have the right to do anything they want? It doesn't make sense." Perhaps the answer to the overall lack of police action was starting to appear, but I would need more information before reaching strong conclusions.

The city was in flames. The police didn't seem to be responding the way they should, at least in parts of the city. And here I was retired. I did not sleep well that night; I kept hoping Chief Gates would call.

The next morning, Esther and I drove to LAX. For some reason, my offer to help had not been accepted. As we drove in, black smoke filled the air. The sun was shining on L.A. that day, but not breaking through at ground level. Our flight left just a few minutes after 7:00 A.M. From the air, the city looked even worse, and I felt more sick and helpless than ever.

As we prepared to land in Florida, Esther said, "I think it's providential that Chief Gates didn't ask you back. It was a no-win situation for you. You would have ordered swift, strong action, and while the deaths and injuries might have been far fewer than what actually happened, you still would have been blamed for any injuries. Whether the action was seen as too strong or too weak, you would have taken the heat."

Upon arriving in Fort Lauderdale, we drove to Turnberry Isle Country Club, a stately resort built in the classic Spanish tradition, where my meetings were to take place. After assigning us to a suite, the registration clerk handed me a note from our daughter saying it was urgent. We hurried to our room and called; it was 6:00 P.M. on Thursday, April 30.

Pam quickly assured us the family was fine but said my former secretary, Mary Helen, had called to say the chief's office needed to reach me. I hung up and punched in the number of my office. Mary Helen said Chief Gates had changed his mind and wanted me to come in. I had her transfer the call to his office, where I spoke to his secretary, Mary Miller.

"He asked you to do what, Bob?"

"Mary Helen said he asked me to come help deal with the riots," I responded.

"Well, that's news to me, but then things are pretty hectic right now. You might try calling directly to the ECC." It was unusual for the chief's secretary not to know about such a request. But the ECC was across the street from Parker Center in a bunker built to withstand a thermonuclear blast. Gates apparently was too busy to keep his staff across the street informed. This was a bad situation.

I called the airport and learned that the next flight I could catch wouldn't get me back to L.A. until 24 hours later. Then I called the ECC with the information. When the chief heard how long it would take me to get back, he again told me to stay put. "The National Guard is on its way, and we're getting things under control."

Feeling down, Esther and I went to dinner. When we came back afterward and turned on the TV, my mood only got worse. By this time, the savage beating of white truck driver Reginald Denny was becoming a focal point. The 11:00 P.M. newscast replayed the video at least three times. "Stop those guys!" I yelled. Out of habit I shouted orders at an imaginary squad of officers, directing them to stop the senseless violence.

Of course, no one heeded my commands. But my wife calmly reminded me there were people next door who could hear me. I quieted down.

I was sickened, not only by the merciless and senseless attack, but also by the comments being made about the LAPD. For some reason, the police appeared unwilling or unable to respond to such dire needs for help. The picture being painted was shameful. The department I loved and had been so proud to serve now appeared impotent and apathetic.

News reports over the next few days told of similar riots and looting in other cities. The fabric of our culture seemed to be unraveling. I began to think deeply about what was happening. What were the causes? Were there any patterns? What did the future hold for our nation and its families?

Someone has said, "As go the major cities of a nation, so goes the nation." If that statement is true, and I believe it is, our country is in serious trouble. Something is very wrong in Los Angeles, and something is very wrong in America. But what could we learn from the ashes? How can we prevent similar disasters in the future? How can despair be made to give way to hope? I needed to know.

Meanwhile, the rioting was in full swing. What was it really like? What was actually going on? How many people were involved? Where were the police in those first critical hours? The people who were there, who experienced the horror, can tell the story best.

2

SNAPSHOTS FROM THE RIOTS

Describing a riot with impersonal statistics doesn't begin to convey a true sense of what occurred. The best way to get that is to see it through the eyes of the people who were there. So in this chapter, we'll look at some "snapshots" of what happened from the perspective of the men and women of the LAPD.

April 29, 1992, 9:00 A.M.

The officer working the public counter walked into the watch commander's office at the 77th Street police station. Clipboards with wanted bulletins and recently issued orders hung from the wall behind the sergeant, who had two five-year service hash marks on his sleeve. The office looked cluttered but was actually organized. They were doing the best they could with a 1920s-vintage station.

"Sarge, I'm getting some weird calls," the officer said. "I didn't think too much about the first one, but then I just got this second one. I was writing up the first for your log when the second came in."

The sergeant frowned. "What is it, some kind of bomb threat or something?"

"No. This guy says, 'Look, cop, by Saturday you guys will know who Eight Trey are.' Then he hangs up. I get the distinct impression he means the 83rd Street Gangster Crips are going to try to pull off something soon."

"We can't afford to shine this on," the sergeant said. "I'll inform the captain's office. Get out the station defense plans." Both the sergeant and the officer knew the Eight Trey Crips are a dangerous gang, responsible for many brutal murders.

"Yes, Sir." The young officer spun around and headed back to the reception area to pull out the defense plans.

The sergeant talked it over with the other supervisors on the watch and also brought the detective CO in on the threat. For more than a week, some of the local gangs had been threatening to form a truce and combine their efforts to attack the police. Officers reported seeing graffiti on several walls announcing their public commitment. The graffiti had the LAPD initials with a red line through them—the symbol of death. Underneath the initials was the number 187—the California Penal Code section for murder.

Officers did not take those threats as idle harassment. Usually when the gangs publicly announce their commitment to a "contract," they carry it out.

April 29, 1992, 1:15 P.M.

The media and the public were notified that the jury in the trial of the four officers from the King incident would be "coming in" with a verdict. The mobilization of police resources should have started immediately. At 3:15 that afternoon, local radio and TV stations announced that the officers were found not guilty on almost all charges. The jury had deadlocked on one charge against one officer, and a mistrial on that charge was declared.

The night-watch lieutenant at the 77th Street station reported for duty about that time, and he decided to hold over the day watch. He asked the day-watch sergeants to go out in the field and sense the mood on the streets. The sergeant with two hash marks on his sleeve got the keys to his car and drove out of the back parking lot.

Less than a block away, he got his first reaction. Two young black women shouted at him, "Look out! Here comes a cop! He can do anything he wants to and get away with it."

But generally, although he did see some anger and frustration, people seemed to be controlling their emotions. One black man waved him down and gave him a leaflet being distributed by members of the Revolutionary Communist Party (RCP). The man didn't agree with their suggested action; the leaflet's headline read, "There's no justice in the courtroom—it's right to rebel!" It encouraged anarchy with such phrases as: "The system is the problem, and mass armed revolution is the solution. . . . The outcome of this trial must not be decided in the courtroom. It must be decided in the streets. . . . Make your rage serve by getting ready for the one and only real solution—proletarian revolution."

The sergeant drove around getting more impressions. He could see hostility in the eyes of some young people, but no threatening actions were being taken yet. Then, just when he was ready to return to the station and report his findings, he heard an "officer needs help" call at Florence near Raymond streets—Eight Trey Crip territory. He decided to respond, and when he arrived, the officers were taking a few young, black males into custody. Two white males had driven an old Cadillac into the area. The young blacks had attacked the car with baseball bats, shouting "Rodney! Rodney! Rodney!" It was a few minutes after 4:00 P.M. They transported the victims and suspects to the 77th Street station.

A relative calm still held over south-central Los Angeles. Between 4:00 and 5:00 P.M., only sporadic incidents of attempted looting were reported. The 77th Street, Southwest, and Southeast police stations reported only four of those crimes in addition to the incident at Florence and Raymond.

At that point, approximately 838 field police officers were on duty across the city. That number, although a small percentage of the department's total of more than 7,000, is actually more than is normal at any given time. Bear in mind that a police department has to provide 24-hours-a-day, 7-days-a-week, 365-days-a-year coverage, allowing for factors like court appearances, sickness, vacation, and regular days off.

In my opinion, the turning point in the day's events came when Mayor Tom Bradley held a press conference at 5:00 P.M. In his speech, Bradley said:

> Today the jury told the world that what we all saw with our own eyes was not a crime. Today that jury said we should tolerate such conduct by those who are sworn to protect and serve. My friends, I am here to tell the jury, "No, no, our eyes did not deceive us. We saw what we saw, and what we saw was a crime. No, we will not tolerate the savage beating of our citizens by a few renegade cops." . . . I understand full well that we

17

must give voice to our great frustration. I know that we must express our profound outrage—our anger. But we must do so in ways that bring honor to ourselves and our community. We must not bury the gains we have made in the rubble created by destructive behavior. We must not endanger the reforms we have achieved by resorting to mindless acts. We must not push back progress by striking back blindly.

I believe those words were unwise. Just reading them doesn't reveal the intensity and hostility they conveyed to the city. His statements were made with much emotion and fervor. He should have known emotions were already running high. That wasn't the time for inflammatory rhetoric but for the calming words of a statesman. Many people undoubtedly stopped listening when they heard their mayor state that "we must express our profound outrage—our anger." They took his words as permission, as a signal, to do what irresponsible activists had encouraged and predicted—"take it to the streets."

Seven minutes after Bradley concluded, rioting broke out. Whereas during the hour preceding the speech only 4 crimes had been reported in the South Bureau quadrant of the city, during the hour following 28 were reported. The rioting and looting spread rapidly from that point on. In the half hour between 7:00 and 7:30, 75 looting-related crimes occurred in those same 3 police areas.

April 29, 1992, 5:21 P.M.

An "officer needs help" call was broadcast at Florence and Normandie streets. The Eight Trey Crips were at it again, striking cars with baseball bats. A young officer described the incident:

"When I arrived, I saw 6 officers trying to arrest 2 gang members. A crowd was gathering. Within a few minutes, there were nearly 100 people in front of us and probably twice that many behind us. The crowd in front started pelting us with rocks and bottles. It was chaotic.

"Other police units arrived. A sergeant directed a skirmish line be formed. We gathered on the east side of Normandie and started our movement. It seemed as though we were about to get some measure of control. Then the lieutenant [Moulin] showed up and ordered us to withdraw. I thought we could handle it, but maybe he saw something I didn't. When we started to withdraw, it got real scary. Then, when we were out of there, I expected to go back in with more troops, but we were ordered not to go back in.

"We were ordered to the command post at 54th, between Van Ness and Arlington. During the first 15 minutes, some sergeants and a lieutenant had organized 5 10-person squads of officers. In my opinion, we could have gone back in and gained control, but we just sat around for more than 2 hours. There didn't seem to be any organization. I saw 2 commanders and 2 captains there. They seemed confused."

A tactical alert, the most basic of UO (unusual occurrence) reactions, was not called until approximately 6:00 P.M. Such an alert revises dispatching policy, making officers available for deployment to the emergency. That indecision cost the department valuable time in responding to the riots.

April 29, 1992, approximately 6:00 to 7:30 P.M., the command post (CP) at 54th and Arlington/Van Ness (an RTD bus garage)

Three hours had passed since the public announcement of the jury's verdict. *Confusion and indecisiveness* best describe the next few hours at the CP. Although two captains and two commanders were present by this time, the watch commander of the 77th Street station still appeared to be in charge. An incident of that magnitude is clearly above the level of responsibility of a watch commander. Someone of staff officer rank (commander or deputy chief) should have assumed control. Eventually, frustrated lieutenants and sergeants began giving missions to platoons and squads on their own initiative.

The Webster Commission, headed by former FBI and CIA Director William Webster and assigned to assess the LAPD's preparation for and response to the riots, explained, "Observers report that there did not appear to be an established chain of command at the command post for much of the first night. There were many high-ranking officers present, but no one stepped forward to give direction to the hundreds of officers there who were waiting for assignments.... As a result, the Field Command Post became a sort of 'black hole' into which police officers from all over the City were poured, but out of which few were deployed on the first night"(pp. 110, 109).

By 6:30 P.M., the field force had increased to 1,050 officers and supervisors.

The fire department received its first reports of riot-related fires between 7:00 and 7:30 P.M. Three fires were called in during that period. Within another hour, an additional 31 structure fires were reported. When firefighting crews came under violent attack by crowds of rioters, the fire command determined it would not be safe for its units to respond to calls without police escort. Firefighters were then formed into strike teams, each headed by a battalion chief, that were ready to go by 8:40 P.M.

The police CP did not provide police escort, however. A fire department battalion chief and several captains finally walked into the Metro section of the police CP and begged for help. They said the top brass of the CP had refused to provide escort. So the Metro supervisors assigned their Tactical Support Elements (TSEs) and rescue elements to support the firefighters. The fire department brass remained with the Metro supervisors to coordinate their efforts.

The number of incendiary-set fires increased rapidly. Between 7:00 P.M. and midnight, the fire department received more than 500 calls regarding buildings on fire. Many officers have reported to me that due to the almost simultaneous eruption of fires all over the southern portions of the city, he felt there was the strong possibility of a conspiracy on the part of some group or individuals.

April 29, 1992, 10:00 P.M.

A D platoon element moved east on Vernon Avenue shortly after 10:00 P.M. By now the elite Metro Division had formed its forces into rescue and TSE units. The D platoon is that group commonly called SWAT. This particular unit was conducting probes into the most hostile areas of the riot zone. A V-100 armored personnel carrier, manned by four officers, led the column. The next vehicle was a Chevy Suburban containing a lieutenant with eight SWAT officers. Two Metro sedans, each with four more SWAT officers, completed the strike force.

A Metro TSE was also in the area to support the D platoon column should they need it. A TSE is made up of 14 riot-trained officers, including 2 grenadiers (equipped with 12-gauge shotguns) and two countersniper marksmen (equipped with AR-15 military rifles).

The role of D platoon was to assist at "hot spots." Most of their activity that first night was offering some protection to the brave, unarmed firefighters. Now they were driving down Vernon for the second time, trying to find the crew of some

FLAMES
TOWER OVER A
POLICEMAN ON
THE SECOND DAY OF
THE RIOTS.

←WOMAN

UNABLE TO WATCH
THE BURNING OF
HER CLOTHING
STORE.

↑A LOOTER

PLEASED WITH HIS
PRIZE.

↗STOCKING

UP ON CLOTHES,
THREE WOMEN
TAKE ADVANTAGE
OF THE CHAOS.

RODNEY KING
(CENTER, IN SWEATER)
PLEADS FOR AN END TO
THE RIOTING AT AN L.A.
PRESS CONFERENCE ON
MAY 1, 1992.

RAISING
A PROTEST OUTSIDE
PARKER CENTER
FOLLOWING THE
VERDICTS ON
APRIL 29, 1992.

POLICE
TURNED OUT IN
FORCE AFTER MANY
BUILDINGS HAD
BEEN SET ABLAZE.

A CALIFORNIA
HIGHWAY PATROLMAN
AMIDST THE BURNED
REMAINS OF SOUTH-
CENTRAL L.A.
➔

LOOTERS
CARRY OFF A
TELEVISION WHILE
OTHERS WAIT THEIR
TURN.

ATTEMPTING
TO RESTORE ORDER,
POLICE GUARD A
GROUP OF HAND-
CUFFED LOOTING
SUSPECTS.

REPAIRING
THE DAMAGE—AN L.A.
CLEAN-UP CREW A FEW
DAYS LATER.
↗

↑THE INCIDENT THAT STARTED THE BANDWAGON ROLLING.

←BOB VERNON WITH TELEVISION NEWS REPORTER STAN CHAMBERS, WHO BROKE THE RODNEY KING STORY.

abandoned fire trucks. The first time they had been unsuccessful, so they had supposed the firefighters had somehow made it to safety. A check with the fire department CP, however, revealed the crews were still missing. They would give it another try.

A lieutenant in the Suburban was directing his column toward the abandoned trucks. A red glow in the smoky sky told them some new fires were just beginning to flare up. "Seems like there's a pattern developing here," the lieutenant said. "As soon as we put troops and fire equipment into a location, they firebomb another building not too far away."

"Yeah, Lieutenant, we're constantly playing catch-up here," an officer said. "These gang bangers know what they're doing all right. This is not a spontaneous riot. This is irregular warfare. Someone clearly had a plan. You can see the pattern in the sequence and location of the fires."

An officer in the back seat interrupted the conversation. "Hey, Boss, dead ahead. There's the two fire companies, but I still don't see any firefighters."

"Pull over," the lieutenant ordered. "Tell everyone to watch for an ambush. I don't like the looks of this."

The four vehicles separated and pulled to the curb. The officers quickly but carefully jumped out and moved silently toward the trucks. They moved from cover to cover, all alert, all looking for the first muzzle flash from a sniper's rifle.

The setting was eerie. The only sounds were distant sirens, far-off small arms fire, and the snapping and roaring of flames from a nearby business. The fire trucks sat in the middle of the street. Some of the hoses were strung out in the street, not yet connected to a fire hydrant. The trucks had been peppered with 40 to 50 high-velocity bullets; the paint was blown away in a 3/4-inch radius around each hole.

No firefighters were in sight, though it was hard to see much farther than across the street. Smoke filled the air. The disciplined officers of the strike force didn't talk. They looked to their leaders for direction as they deployed properly with cover, not grouped together. They almost formed a large circle, an area they could defend with an effective field of fire.

The lieutenant instructed, "Keep your cover." Then he shouted, "This is LAPD. We are police officers. Any firefighters around here?"

Silence. Then, after a few seconds they heard, "LAPD, we need some help. We're firemen. We're in the green house two doors east of our trucks."

"Stay there. We'll come to you."

The lieutenant pointed toward one of the sergeants and ordered, "Move your squad carefully toward the house. We'll cover you."

The sergeant nodded silently, then moved quietly along his squad, giving direction. They leapfrogged cautiously up the street as the acrid smell of smoke and fire filled their nostrils. If the firefighters had been forced to abandon their trucks, some danger was present, or at least had been.

As they approached the house, the front door opened slightly. The officers nearest the house identified themselves again. The door opened wide, and a firefighter in his call-outs, including his helmet, stepped into view and walked quickly toward the officers. A look of great relief covered his face.

During the next few minutes, the firefighters' harrowing story came out. They had responded to the fire. Upon arrival, before they could begin working, they were confronted by black gang members. The fire captain continued: "This guy stuck some kind of assault rifle in my face. I think it was an AK-47. He said he would blow my head off if we tried to put out the fire. I thought me and my crew had bought it. We were helpless. We're not armed. For some reason, the guy with the gun took my radio. They apparently want to know about our plans and activities. The Hispanic people in this house gave us refuge."

They were lucky. None of them was hurt. That night, another firefighter was not so fortunate; he was shot in the face. He's still partially paralyzed, but at least he survived.

That stolen radio would turn up about 24 hours later. Friday evening, April 30, an LAPD officer got off the Harbor Freeway at Florence Avenue and turned east on his way to work at the 77th Street station a few blocks away. Just as he turned on Florence, a black gang member started shooting at the officer. Unknown to the gangster, a sheriff's deputy had also exited the freeway on Florence. He was on his way to work at the sheriff's Firestone substation.

The deputy stopped his car and intervened. The shots of the gang member missed; the defensive shots of the two off-duty officers did not. The stolen radio was found on the gangster's dead body.

April 29, 1992, 10:15 P.M.

Another officer tells this story: "I was somewhere near 114th and Western. I'll never forget the moment. We were there to protect the firefighters, who had an impossible job. It was like some type of horrible bad dream. The air was cloudy with smoke. The only light was from the flames and the emergency lights. There was this nightmarish orange glow, dimmed because of the smoke. It was hard to breathe. At points, the flames from both sides of the street were meeting in the air, forming a hellish tunnel.

"I was standing there in 2 inches of water. A couple of dark figures splashed through the water about 50 feet from me. They weren't firemen or cops. A few seconds later, someone capped a few rounds [fired some shots]. I never saw the muzzle flashes. Maybe they weren't shooting at me. I couldn't believe it was real. It was like I was in some weird futuristic movie where all social order is gone. It didn't feel like America."

April 29, 1992, about 11:00 P.M.

Rioters had firebombed a store between 112th and 114th streets on Central Avenue. Across the street, on the east side of Central Avenue, are the Jordan Downs housing projects. Hard-core gang members have conducted a reign of terror there, controlling the projects for the last several years. Anyone opposing their drug dealing and other criminal activities has been beaten and killed.

Several companies of firefighters responded to the call. The store was beyond saving, however, so the firefighters were doing their best to save a church and other nearby structures. Two TSEs from Metro's C platoon had rolled with the fire department units. Sergeant Roger Blackwell, in charge of TSE #6, deployed north of them. He was concerned about the close proximity of the housing projects and the gangs. He wanted everyone on the alert, but he also wanted to demonstrate confidence and strength.

"Okay, you guys," he told his troops, "you know where we are. Don't go nodding off, but don't get the 'whip eye,' either. We can handle it." He spoke with a low but firm voice. Inside he was probably tense, but he didn't show it. His men were watching, and his calm demeanor was contagious. They settled into their positions, their eyes scanning the perimeter.

23

The second squad, TSE #4, under the direction of Sergeant Rich Beardslee, had deployed to the south and was moving north on Central Avenue. Both TSEs were commanded by Lieutenant John McCrillis and Sergeant Grady Dublin, his assistant. The firefighters had just hooked up their hoses to the hydrant on the northeast corner of 114th and Central when they came under fire. The rapid fire and loudness of the blasts left no doubt—assault rifles.

Sergeant Beardslee spoke calmly but with his well-known command presence: "We're under fire. Let's get out of these cars and get cover—now!" The driver skidded the car to a stop, and all four doors popped open, the men scurrying for cover. Beardslee gave hand signals to the following cars before he thought of his own safety.

Lieutenant McCrillis and Sergeant Dublin immediately responded to TSE #4's position. Dublin had been a member of Metro for more than 20 years, and the lieutenant wisely gave him tactical control of the incident. All of Dublin's experience was about to be tested again. His thoughts focused on keeping his people alive and yet completing his mission. He thought aloud as he shouted, "Sounds like shoulder weapons. Keep cool. Let's identify their fire positions. Talk to me if you see their locations."

Dublin's men followed his hand signals and began deploying to a tight perimeter. Soon they had a secure perimeter with a 360-degree field of fire.

Metro cops work regularly on a crime task force. They perform traditional police duties in those areas of the city where crime waves erupt. But they train constantly for the extraordinary. Thus, although they now faced death, they knew this was their business. Somehow, in spite of the normal reaction of fear, each one was eager to do his duty.

Officer Mike Damanakis tightened the grip on his AR-15 and squeezed off three quick shots. "There, just north of the second building; two muzzle flashes," he said.

Flame spat from the muzzle of Officer Mike Daly's rifle. "There's another position south of that one, about 30 yards," he said.

It was soon apparent that this was an ambush. Incoming fire came from multiple sources. High-velocity slugs exploded chunks of plaster, concrete, and brick from the buildings behind them. They were in the street and under the lights, in the middle of what seemed like a war zone.

"Let's get those lights out!" a sergeant shouted. Two of the riflemen soon had them out. "Okay, that's better. Now let's settle down. Remember, disciplined fire control." The firefight was to last more than two hours.

Sergeant Dublin keyed his Rover (a special police radio with citywide communication capability). "R 20 Charles, R 20 Charles to Metro CP. We are in a firefight at 114th and Central. We are pinned down. Send D platoon elements. We are pinned down."

Lieutenant Tom Lorenzen, the officer in charge of D platoon, broke in. "R 10 David to 20 Charles, copied that last transmission. We're coming, but it's going to take some time."

"20 Charles to 10 David, roger," Dublin acknowledged. Then he said to the man next to him, "We're on our own for a while."

Several more incoming rounds whined off the sidewalk a few feet north of them. Both Damanakis and Daly were busy keeping the fire positions just east of them worried with carefully placed shots. There wasn't much talking, just the sharp blasts of the rifles, followed by the metallic ring of the ejected brass on the pavement.

"Where's that latest stuff coming from?" Dublin asked.

"Up north from our positions, Sarge," someone answered.

Dublin keyed his Rover again. "20 Charles to 70 Charles, we're getting some fire now from positions north of us. Can you give us any help?"

Sergeant Blackwell, nearly two blocks north, answered quickly. "70 Charles, roger. We'll try."

Officer John Puis turned to Blackwell and said, "Sarge, Jim and I can try to flank them. We'll stay north of them and go east."

"Okay, give it a try, but take care. There's lots of guns pointed at us right now."

Officers John Puis and Jim Moody, both trained in countersniper tactics, moved out, careful to keep away from any back light. The street lights were out, as were most of the lights in the buildings. The only background light came from the flames, though that light was getting brighter as the fires spread. The firefighters were seeking cover as well. They were as much a target as the police—perhaps more.

Puis and Moody crept from car to car and building to building. They stayed north of the housing projects and the snipers' positions, moving east. Over their midnight blue LAPD uniforms, each wore heavy-duty, camouflaged, military body armor. They also wore the new U.S. Army ballistic helmet. Their movements were

25

labored under the extra weight.

Soon they were crouched behind a six-foot cement block wall with a small, wrought iron fence mounted on top. Two shopping carts sat next to the wall.

"Hold this cart steady," Puis whispered. "I'll have a look over the wall." He slung his rifle over his shoulder and carefully climbed into the cart, his movements slowed by the heavy body armor. He raised his head over the wall cautiously and saw two figures gliding swiftly along the north edge of the housing project building closest to them. Both were carrying some type of rifle. They were flanking TSE #4 at 114th and Central, moving north of them but south of Puis and Moody. The two figures stopped, crouched, and began firing toward TSE #4.

Puis raised his "Aim Point"-equipped AR-15 and dialed in on the heavy muzzle flashes. (The "Aim Point" is a sighting device that places an artificial dot on the target and adjusts for distance and elevation, greatly improving accuracy.) He squeezed the trigger repeatedly. A near-white flash of flame shot out of the muzzle each time. Ejected brass casings rattled around the cement wall and walkway. Soon the bolt on the rifle flew open; a 20-round magazine was empty.

Puis climbed down from his position, and he and Moody ran farther east. Here Puis could look around the end of the wall. A combat veteran, he knew that shooting twice from the same position could get a man killed.

"Give me another mag," Puis said. Moody passed him another 20-round magazine. Puis crouched in his new position and again dialed in on muzzle flashes coming from a second location. Within a few seconds, he had laid down a 12-round burst of fire. The hostile fire stopped abruptly. The two officers waited a few minutes, but there was no more shooting from this location.

Soon the D platoon element arrived with the V-100. They drove the armored vehicle to the area of Puis's targets. One body was recovered, and bloody evidence indicated at least one other sniper had been wounded and crawled away. Two additional bodies were recovered in the morning light, and in the locations where TSE #4 had seen gunfire the night before, they found large groupings of empty shell casings. There had been at least ten hostile fire locations. It had been quite a battle.

April 30, 1992, 7:30 P.M.—second day of the riots

A lieutenant and a sergeant were rushing northbound on Vermont Avenue to assist squads of officers trying to suppress looting. As they approached 24th Street in their plain radio car, the sergeant said, "Hey, Boss, look at the liquor store on the corner."

The lieutenant swung his eyes in the direction the sergeant was pointing. He saw that the metal grating designed to protect the front door and windows had been bent, making a small hole.

"Looks like an ant hole," the lieutenant responded. "Look at them crawling in and out. Let's take 'em."

They pulled their car across the street, parking it facing the Korean-owned store. Then they jumped out and grabbed a couple of looters trying to leave. The thieves had their hands full of bottles, and one dropped a half-gallon jug of whiskey.

"Open the trunk and get the box of flex handcuff cords," the lieutenant ordered. "I'll stand here by the hole and not let anyone else out until we get some backup. There's a bunch more in there, by the sound of things."

They cuffed the first two looters, and the lieutenant broadcast a request for assistance with multiple arrestees. Then he took out his ballpoint pen and marked his police serial number on the arms of the suspects. They wouldn't be able to rub it off with their hands secured behind their backs as they were.

"This way we'll know which arrestees are ours when we get to the field jail unit," the lieutenant explained. The sergeant drew his pen and started marking the looters he helped out through the hole.

An RTD bus soon pulled up. Metro Lieutenant Mike Hillman had asked bus drivers at the CP at 54th and Arlington to volunteer for this hazardous duty. Many agreed to accept the mission. They loaded 19 arrestees taken from the store onto the bus. A couple of detectives were also on board to give the driver security for his unscheduled run.

There's little disagreement about what occurred during the first few hours of the riots. First, in south-central Los Angeles, the focal point seemed to be Florence and Normandie. Although acts of looting occurred in various parts of the city, the activities at that location were unique. The crimes there were primarily directed against people. Property damage and looting were secondary. But in the rest of the city, riot-related crimes were primarily directed against property.

Second, most officers experienced in assessing the size of crowds estimate that between 20,000 and 30,000 people were involved in the riots. Probably fewer than 500 attacked people and started the fires. The remainder were opportunists who joined in the looting. Realizing there are more than half a million people living in that part of the city, it can be said conclusively that a very small percentage of the residents were involved. Thus, painting the residents of south-central L.A. with the broad brush of "violent anarchists" is extremely unfair. Most were not involved in the riots and did not support them.

Third, in several areas of the city, the rioting was controlled almost immediately. In the Foothill area, for example, where the original King incident occurred, the department's riot plans were used with great success.

Most significantly, all accounts support the fact that the officers at the operating level in all police areas were ready and willing to do their job. The patrol officers and their field supervisors demonstrated their strong desire to take whatever action was necessary. And when they were allowed to do so, they performed courageously and effectively.

In other words, the failure to respond rapidly to the crisis seemed to be a paralysis of *leadership*. Something had occurred with some of the top brass to bring them to a point of vacillation and indecisiveness. They appeared unable to provide proper command.

The LAPD had been known for years as the epitome of a professional police organization. Now a big question mark hung over it. During a major catastrophic event, the leadership had failed. What had gone wrong?

A series of events occurred that will answer those questions. Many little-known facts, revealed in this book, will shed light on what's occurring in Los Angeles. An understanding of those facts will help us see what will happen *throughout our country* in the not-too-distant future unless swift corrective action is taken. In my opinion, the L.A. phenomenon offers a rare glimpse into the future.

In this book I want to explain my role in the events that became known as the Rodney King incident, explore the political climate that dramatically changed life within the LAPD, and examine the forces at work that produced the riots and let them get out of control.

In addition, we need to take a look at the bigger picture. As a professional police officer for almost four decades, I've seen enormous changes in the culture and values of the city I love. As I reflected on my experiences and those changes, I began to see an explanation for what has happened. I also realized where our hope lies as a society if we're ever to move beyond violence and injustice.

3

RODNEY KING
STEPS INTO HISTORY

On Sunday, March 3, 1991, shortly after midnight, the following radio broadcast was made by an LAPD dispatcher:

"All Valley Bureau units—special attention Foothill area units—the CHP [California Highway Patrol] is in pursuit of a light-colored vehicle, westbound on the 210 freeway from La Tuna Canyon. The vehicle is being driven at speeds in excess of 90 miles per hour. It is failing to yield to red light and siren. The vehicle is now entering LAPD jurisdiction. Any unit that can assist, please identify."

With that routine beginning, a police pursuit of a drunken driver late on a Saturday night/early Sunday morning, one of the most traumatic events in recent American history got under way. I and the rest of the world wouldn't hear about it until the next day.

At 6:45 on Monday morning, March 4, the Southern California climate was still too cold for shorts and a T-shirt. I was wearing my Parker Center running outfit. I opened the back gate and walked down the driveway to the street. At the sidewalk, I turned right and started my ritual jog. Three and a half miles would take me about 32 minutes. Definitely not a competitive pace, but a vital part of my "keep Bob Vernon alive" program. Coping with the schedule and tensions of being assistant chief of the LAPD made such a program mandatory.

Chief Gates was attending a major cities chiefs' meeting in Miami, leaving me "on the hotseat"—acting chief of police. Running on the horse trail just west of the Rose Bowl, I thought about my schedule for the week. It looked pretty benign at that point. *But in this business,* I reminded myself, *the schedule has a way of filling up. Still, chances are, nothing too unusual will happen.* In a city like Los Angeles, however, being the person with final authority, even in the short term, adds a certain feeling of anticipation and soberness.

I glanced up at the seven-thousand-foot peaks of the San Bernardino Mountains and thought: *It's good to be alive; good to be able to jog; good to see the misty shadows in the high valleys, the granite outcroppings near Mount Wilson peak.* I shot up a quick prayer of thanks.

I needed this time of wake-up, exhilaration . . . and diversion. Most of the time, even during off hours, I was depended upon to make tough decisions—the ones the people below in the hierarchy either didn't want to or couldn't make. Then there was the tough duty of informing a young mother and her children that their husband and daddy had just been killed; the middle-of-the-night phone calls when you knew, before you picked up the phone, that you were about to be "on duty," that whatever you said in response to the information you were about to be given would probably change the lives of several, maybe many, people. Some decisions involved deploying officers "in harm's way," and you knew that during the next few seconds, depending on what you said, someone could lose his freedom . . . or his life.

In spite of the tension, though, I loved the challenge. I found myself looking forward to those times when Chief Gates handed over the reins and left town. I had that feeling now, even looking forward to "Black Tuesday." That's what Gates called the day of the weekly police commission meeting. The five commissioners, appointed by the mayor, act as an outside board of directors. They set the broad policy of the department and give the chief his overall direction. Those meetings had become more controversial during recent years and, at times, flat-out confrontational.

I arrived back at home and got ready for the day. Thirty minutes later, I parked my take-home city car in the underground garage of Parker Center. The navy blue T-bird didn't really look like a police car unless I popped the emergency lights up into place. A 48-channel Rover radio in the convertacom allowed me to operate in all 18 police areas of the city. More than half my time, however, was spent here at headquarters, still known by criminals as the "glass house."

I exited the elevator on the sixth floor and walked directly around the corner and into my office at 9:15 A.M. I greeted my staff with a jovial "Roll call" to make fun of the fact I was 15 minutes late. Mary Helen had wanted me in at 9:00 sharp this morning. I followed that with: "Whose turn to make the coffee?"

Five of us worked out of the three-room suite. Mary Helen Ayala, my executive secretary—the best in the city—ran the office from the center reception room across from Lieutenant Sergio Robleto, my adjutant. To the right, Sergeant Huntshammer shared an office with Mary Helen's assistant, Danielle Jimenez. My office was on the left.

Being adjutant to a chief officer is a tough job. An adjutant is an aide who executes the directives of his chief. He reviews the boss's correspondence and prepares letters of response or calls the correspondent. He reviews staff work and prepares memos for the chief's signature. He regularly contacts the officers reporting to his chief, passing on the boss's insight and orders. Those officers are much higher in rank than he is, which means he has to possess great tact and diplomatic ability.

I asked Sergio if there was anything noteworthy on the 24-hour logs, and he replied, "No, just the usual: seven homicides, a couple of gang drive-bys, and . . . like that."

We're in pretty bad shape, I thought, *when we all accept seven homicides as business as usual.*

Mary Helen followed me into my office.

"Sir, Chief Kroeker and Lieutenant Mike Markulis from O.S.B. Homicide need to see you about some warrants they plan to serve tonight. I've squeezed them in at 1400 hours (2:00 P.M.), just before Lieutenant Hillman at 1430 hours (2:30). He wants to bring you up to date on the abortion protest demos. Commander Morrison has to see you first thing this morning. I think it's about an audit his office did. You know how he is—wouldn't say much. But he's in a 'high hover' about something."

"Okay, have him come in at 1000 hours (10:00 A.M.). That will give me enough time to plan my day—*what's left of it.* Is my luncheon with Brewer still on?"

"Yes, at that favorite spot of his on West Jefferson."

Jesse Brewer had just retired as one of my peers. For the last couple of years, he had served as the assistant chief in charge of the Office of Administrative Services. I had known him for more than 25 years and valued him as a friend. He had been of particular help to me during my first area command in Venice during the early 1970s. He had also reported to me as the deputy chief over south-central L.A. prior to getting his third star. I had strongly urged Chief Gates to give him that promotion (technically a pay-grade advancement given at the sole discretion of the chief).

As I had expected, the day was already filling up. Commander Morrison at 10:00. As chief of staff, he rarely asked for an immediate appointment unless he needed one. If it was urgent, though, he would be camping on my doorstep.

George Morrison is the kind of professional you need in such a key position: complete integrity; knows how to keep his mouth shut; has plenty of contacts both within the department and throughout the government. Slightly over six feet tall, with a full head of salt-and-pepper hair, a ruddy complexion, and a heavy but well-trimmed mustache, he could be cast in a movie as a British army officer from the 1800s. His athletic build, military bearing, and strong gaze are intimidating.

For the next 30 minutes I reviewed paperwork, including some statistics on how our 5 bureaus were managing their overtime money. We had 4 months to go in the fiscal year, with slightly less than $4 million left in the account. Yet we were spending well over a million a month with no reserves. I would have to put the brakes on the spending somehow.

I summoned Sergio into my office and discussed my schedule for the day. I also asked him to draw up a memo to the five deputy chiefs commanding the bureaus, tightening the screws on the overtime allotments. He already had one in the making. Sergio was one of those perfect aides who anticipates the direction of his boss.

At 9:59 A.M., Morrison arrived. He briefed me on an internal audit his Inspection and Control unit had performed. The audit had disclosed some performance deficiencies within several divisions. After discussing it for a few minutes, he handed me a prepared report in the standard format. All I needed to do was read the section titled "significant findings" and then review the "recommendations" section. After initialing the recommendations I agreed with, I would give the document to Sergio, who would see that appropriate steps were taken for implementation. We called it "completed staff work."

Then Morrison said, "Chief, I think you know that you and the boss have a few staff officers who are not what I would call loyal."

"Yes, I know that, George."

"I guess we're all a bit ambitious or we wouldn't be where we are, but some of these guys are something else. They must smell blood since the media and a few politicians have taken shots at both you and the boss."

For the last several years, certain politicians and the media had criticized Daryl Gates. They had described the department as too aggressive and militaristic under his leadership. They were unhappy with his "Hammer Task Force" strategy against the violent gang members. As his director of operations, I had also been the subject of criticism.

"You're right," I answered. "We have a few people who are more interested in their own agenda than in the welfare of the department and this city."

"Well, it's not for me to tell you what to do, but if I were you, I would be very careful. I know you probably hate to operate this way, but you should be documenting everything of significance. In the future, it may become very important to be able to prove you issued certain directives or made a specific policy decision."

"You're absolutely right—I do hate to operate that way. But I probably should be more aware of protecting the record."

"Look, Chief, you and I were brought up under Chief Parker, who taught us to do a professional job and make decisions based on what's right. But we both know there are certain people across the street in City Hall who want this department to be politically controlled so they can do what they please."

"And there are a few over here wearing a star or two who are willing to play ball as long as in the process they get their share of power."

"You said it, Chief."

"I know, George. But just remember, the vast majority of the officers working the street feel the same way you and I do. And for that matter, so do most of the staff officers in the executive suites."

George had said as much as he felt he should. I was warned. As he stepped out the door, I leaned back in my chair and thought, *How did it happen? Just a few years ago, everything seemed to be on the right track. Plenty of political support from the city council. Oh, we've always had a few detractors who seemed to have an antipolice agenda, but the majority came through when we really needed them, as long as what we were doing was right.*

Ever since Tom Bradley had been elected mayor, the police commission seemed to be dominated by people with a basic mistrust of the department. But even most of them had been willing to learn about us, to keep an open mind, to revise preconceived ideas if the facts led them in that direction. Now things were different. From my viewpoint, the commission seemed to be purposefully assuming an adversarial relationship.

The city council had changed, too, becoming increasingly controlled by people who tended to see us as part of the problem rather than part of the solution. There were still a few who considered straightforward law enforcement a top priority, but often it was difficult to get sufficient votes to overcome the apparent plan to "bring down the Big Blue Machine."

I first became aware of the move against us just before the 1984 Olympic Summer Games here in L.A. The issue was police intelligence in the light of terrorist threats, and the movement to destroy the department's intelligence-gathering capability brought together a powerful coalition. Many well-meaning groups and individuals concerned about the possibility of illegal "police spying" joined forces with some not-so-well-meaning groups, including Marxists and the Revolutionary Communist Party.

Since that first somewhat successful campaign against the LAPD, much had happened. Now here we were with a police commission that often did not seem to support our efforts.

Two hours later, I was walking with Jesse Brewer toward our cars in a restaurant parking lot. The food had been great, and our conversation had been cordial and enjoyable. I had asked his advice about several matters, including a difficult personnel issue. I had also asked, "Jess, now that you're retired, do you have any candid criticism for me or the department? Is there anything you think we should be doing differently?"

"Not really," he had responded. "Nothing worth talking about."

"Are you sure? I'd really like to know what you think."

"No, I can't think of anything."

As we left the restaurant, I told him, "I'll be at your retirement dinner, of course, but I wanted to take this opportunity to personally express my appreciation for being able to work with you these many years. I also want you to know I want to remain in touch."

"Thanks," he said. "I'm sure our paths will cross."

As I drove back to Parker Center, I reflected on our luncheon conversation. As usual, Jesse Brewer had shown all the marks of a kind man, an honest man, a true gentleman. He had given his counsel generously as a colleague and friend. I had always considered him one of "the good guys"—one of the best, in fact—and was proud to have served with him. I was looking forward to honoring him at his retirement dinner.

Unknown to me at that moment, Jesse Brewer would be appointed by Mayor Bradley to the police commission within a few weeks and would then become one of the strongest critics of the department and, particularly, of me. I cannot tell you how shocked and hurt I was when that happened.

The 2:00 P.M. meeting with Deputy Chief Mark Kroeker and Lieutenant Mike Markulis was interesting and important. Markulis ran the South Bureau's homicide unit. His detectives investigated nearly all the homicides that occurred in the four police areas in what's commonly referred to as south-central Los Angeles: Harbor, Southeast, 77th, and Southwest. Those stations house most of the officers working that portion of the city.

As the meeting got under way, Kroeker said, "Boss, Mike's troops have put together quite a series of murder investigations, involving some hardcase gang bangers. He's got a handful of arrest and search warrants. We plan on serving them at O'dark thirty [an LAPD phrase describing the early morning hours just before dawn] tomorrow morning. Some real bad actors are involved, all armed. We plan on using SWAT to help us make the entries."

Kroeker laid out the plans, Markulis jumping in every now and then with some of the fine details. Kroeker was a young 48, tall, blond, with a trim runner's build and talent that would put him in the executive suite of any corporation. It was good to have men like him shouldering the heavy responsibility of this type of assignment. As a deputy chief, he wore two stars and commanded well over one thousand uniformed troops and detectives. His quadrant of the city had by far the most violent crime and a large share of the street gang problem. He had been assigned this command a few weeks before and had obviously jumped in with both feet.

Mike Markulis, or "Big Mike," was the epitome of the professional cop—35-plus years of experience and still in one of the most demanding jobs in the department. Most murders happen at night, so guess how he spends a good portion of his evenings. And in his spare time he's a college professor.

The plan was good, the precautions well taken. They had covered all the bases. All I had to do was compliment them on the good work so far and their excellent preparations for tomorrow. Kroeker was right, I needed to be in on this one. There would be plenty of opportunity for trouble, and it was newsworthy, too. They would hit nine locations simultaneously. I had them notify Lieutenant Nixon from our press relations unit, and I made a note to call the president of the commission at the proper time. Basic principle here: Nobody likes surprises, especially the boss.

A little later, while reviewing several monthly progress reports from the five bureau commanders, I was interrupted by Mary Helen. "Chief, Lieutenant Nixon needs to see you now. He says it's hot."

"Okay, have him come right down."

Fred Nixon was number one assistant to then-Commander Bill Booth, the department's press relations officer. Nixon handled most of the routine contacts with the media and occasionally the heavy stuff when Booth or Chief Gates was not available. At 38 years old, he had wisdom beyond his years. I consulted with him regularly on my dealings with the media. I also tapped into his insight regarding the black community. His cultural roots, coupled with his technical expertise and wisdom, made him a valuable colleague.

Nixon walked in and came right to the point: "Hi, Chief. I hate to bother you, but I don't think this can wait. Your friend Stan Chambers from Channel 5 called. He says they have a videotape of a police incident that happened in Foothill area yesterday. He indicated they'll be airing portions of the tape on their 'News at Ten' tonight. He thinks you need to see the tape as soon as possible."

"Fred, I've known Stan Chambers for many years. If he thinks I need to see the tape, I need to see it."

"Chief, I don't think this is going to be a good one. He said something about the video showing a police beating. I'm sure he'll want you to make a comment about it as acting chief of police."

"Get it right away, Fred. We'll take a look and then decide what comments, if any, I should make."

Less than 30 minutes later, he was back holding a videotape box in his hand. "Do you want to view it here in your office?" he asked.

"Can't be done, Fred. All I've got here is the old department-issue machine, made for training tapes."

"No problem. It's a VHS, and I've got a VHS machine in my office." He paused, appeared to be thinking something through, and then said, "On second thought, we probably shouldn't be viewing this in my office for the first time. The media corps are in and out quite often."

"Wait a minute, I'm acting chief. The boss has one in his office. Let's take it down there."

We started down the hall toward room 619. The chief's office is sandwiched between two adjoining offices. One is shared by his executive officer and a receptionist. It has comfortable furniture and reading material and is used for receiving public and other nondepartmental visitors. The other office, 619, is where the worker bees swarm while waiting to see the chief or conducting business with his staff.

Mary Miller, the chief's executive secretary, was also the keeper of the gate. It was not wise to walk past her desk, which was strategically situated just in front of the door to his office. I rarely demanded immediate access or walked in on the chief, and then only when I knew that both she and he would understand the necessity.

After greeting her and explaining we needed to use the chief's VCR, Nixon and I walked into the office. Built in 1954, it was the only paneled office in Parker Center. A 12-foot conference table sat in the middle of the room. Four upholstered swivel chairs banked each side. The chief worked from one end of the table. Just behind his chair was a small telephone table against the wall. The idea was to force himself to not "bottom drawer" any documents that needed action. This arrangement put all the paperwork either in his briefcase or on his secretary's desk.

Against the south wall of the office, a built-in sideboard housed a video monitor and VCR. We pulled out the drawer with the tape deck, and Nixon popped in the cassette. I had already pushed the power button on the monitor.

The screen flashed the images of several police officers in the street in front of a squad car that had our markings. It appeared to be at night. They were hitting a large black man multiple times with their batons. The man was moving around on his hands and knees. The blows and some kicking continued. The violence appeared to have gotten out of control. I was holding a mug in my right hand, and as soon as I realized what was happening, I slammed it on the conference table, spilling some coffee.

"Holy cow, Chief!" Nixon said.

"What is this, Fred? Where and when did this happen?" I knew I needed to remain calm and professional, now more than ever, but I was stunned. We needed to get all the facts as soon as possible, and I needed to stay objective to do my job, yet I felt as if someone had just slammed a fist into my gut. I had no doubt the scene on this video would do tremendous, lasting damage to the badge I had always worn proudly.

"I think he said Foothill area. I'll make some calls and get you more information, quick like. Chief, this is bad news—big time."

"Freddy, if this is what it appears to be, this is what the chief's enemies have been waiting for. This may be a thermonuclear bomb."

We stepped back into room 619. Nixon headed for the door. I turned to the chief's adjutant, Lieutenant Russ Leach, and said, "Russ, get Captain Moore up here on the double." Maurice Moore was the CO of the Internal Affairs Division (IAD). Rodney King had just stepped into history.

My mind was racing. The decisions I would make over the next few minutes and hours would be far reaching. I had been taught a basic axiom long ago: If you make decisions based on expediency or political concerns, you'll be wrong most of the time. If you make decisions based on principle—on what you sincerely believe is right—it will later be adjudged just and fair.

I knew what I had to do: Get all the facts and let the chips fall where they may. I had to get a thorough and honest investigation started immediately. I had about six hours before the tape would be seen by a few hundred thousand Angelenos, including many police officers. Time was of the essence.

I was sitting at the desk of one of the secretaries. I picked up a pad of desk memos and began making a list of people I needed to reach as soon as I took my first steps of action. Chief Gates was at the top of the list.

The door of 619 swung open with force enough to knock down anyone standing in its way. Maurice Moore thrust himself into the room. He was carrying a yellow legal tablet, and his eyes were wide with anticipation, but he still managed to deliver his familiar smile. "You called, Sir ?"

"Yes, Maurice. I'm afraid this is going to be one of those nights when you really earn your money. Come on into the office. I want to show you something."

He followed me past Mary's desk and into the chief's office. I got the video ready to run again and said, "Maurice, watch this carefully. I want to get as far as we can on investigating this incident before the ten o'clock news tonight."

I punched the play button. The images flashed on the screen once more. This time it seemed to take longer. My mind registered more blows. I glanced at Moore, who seemed transfixed. His mouth dropped slightly open.

"Where did you get this, Chief ?" he said. "Are these our men? When and where did this occur?" He looked dismayed and frustrated and clearly didn't like what he was watching any more than I did.

"They're ours all right. I have Fred Nixon verifying the date and location right now, but I think it's going to be the Foothill area. Look, I want you to get on this code 3 [which literally means red lights and sirens blaring; used here to mean "top priority"]. Take as many men as you need, and get right with it. If you need any resources you don't have—anything—just let me know and you've got it."

Moore looked toward the north wall of the office. It was glass from about four feet up. The sky had grown dark since lunchtime. Rain pelted the window with a fury, and a lightning bolt flashed across our view just behind the federal building. "Okay, Chief, you got it," he said. "I'll get to it first thing in the morning."

"Maurice—" I said.

"I know, I know. Just kidding. It's raining out there, Chief. Remember we're not used to rain here in L.A. But you'll have your investigation well on the way by ten o'clock tonight. And a darned good one, too."

"Look, Maurice, I know this goes without saying, but integrity is the name of the game. Seize as much evidence as you can. Identify the concerned officers. Round up as much of the paperwork as you can, including supervisor and watch commander logs. In general, do the professional job IAD does best. This may be the most important investigation you'll ever lead. Got it?"

"Yes, Sir, and you know we'll do our best."

Beginning at that moment, IAD began one of the most thorough and expensive investigations in its history. An IAD inquiry is one of the most comprehensive and well-documented investigations performed by the department. All witnesses are interviewed, and verbatim statements are recorded. Physical evidence is collected and thoroughly examined. In this case, the involved officers' uniforms, shoes, and equipment would be scrutinized. All the relevant original paperwork was also seized. Even simple accusations of misconduct require many hours of investigation and reporting, and this one went far beyond simple. Thousands of hours of work would be done, resulting in a report several inches thick.

Internal discipline proceeds independent of criminal prosecution. Even when officers are acquitted of criminal charges, they're often found guilty by a departmental board of rights. Those hearings are similar to military court martial proceedings.

Accordingly, IAD investigations are not welcomed by officers. Most of them recognize the necessity and importance of these penetrating probes, but being the subject of one is uncomfortable, to say the least.

Officers under criminal investigation have the same rights as all other citizens. For example, they may refuse to answer questions under provisions of the Fifth Amendment to the Constitution. In an IAD probe, however, those rights do not apply. An officer must respond to all questions or face additional charges of insubordination. Detectives from IAD are often referred to as "head hunters" since the results of their work may cost an officer his or her job.

A few minutes later, I was back in room 619 after viewing the tape several more times. I had allowed a few of the chief's trusted staff to watch it also. A silent gloom had settled over the office. I sat staring into space, thinking. Then I spoke my thoughts.

"This is going to be bigger than Eula Love [a case in which police shot and killed a female assault suspect as she threw a knife at them; the incident resulted in intense scrutiny of the department and a comprehensive revision of its shooting policy]. This will have a major impact on the department. We'll be reacting to this incident for a year—maybe longer."

"You really think so, Chief?" said Lieutenant Leach.

"No question about it. This is going to be the beginning of a major undertaking by those who want to get rid of the chief and control the department. We may have just handed them the issue they've been waiting for—on a silver platter."

Little did I know at the time how prophetic those words would be, how much change would occur in the department, the city, and my personal life over the next few months.

4

THE BANDWAGON
STARTS ROLLING

An hour after first seeing the tape, I was back in my own office. I had briefed my staff on what was happening. Chief Gates had been notified and would be on the next plane back to Los Angeles. (He arrived around midnight.) I had also informed the president of the police commission and the mayor's office. At this point, Channel 5 apparently had an exclusive on the video, but they would no doubt be sharing it with other news agencies following their initial broadcast. After consulting with Fred Nixon, I decided to call Stan and give him a statement.

Before doing that, however, I had another important call to make. Deputy Chief Ed Gomez was the CO of California Highway Patrol officers in Southern California. Nixon had discovered that some of his officers had been involved in the incident in some way. At that point we suspected they started a vehicle pursuit that had culminated in the arrest. One of Gates's staff had tracked Gomez down and now had him on the phone.

I explained the video's contents and added, "The bad news for you is, I've been told some of your officers are involved." Then I told him he could contact Captain Maurice Moore of our IAD for further details when they became available, and I promised to send a copy of the videotape.

After ensuring the investigation was well under way, I grabbed my briefcase and hurried to the underground garage. I flipped on the car radio and quickly scanned the news stations. Nothing about the story was on the radio yet. By this time, I had been informed that the incident actually started at approximately 12:30 Sunday morning. I wondered why I had been kept in the dark until Monday afternoon—and then had been notified through a newsman. *That Chambers really has integrity,* I thought. *He didn't have to give me a six hour "heads up" on the story.*

I arrived at home 30 minutes later, at 6:45 P.M. I had done a lot of thinking as I drove. It was no secret that the mayor and several members of the city council wanted Chief Gates out. Some of them and several special interest groups had been calling for his resignation for a few years, asserting the department had become too confrontational under his leadership. They needed an issue that would coalesce various groups and individuals while at the same time eroding the support he had. I was certain they would use this incident to full advantage toward that end.

Chief Gates had announced he would retire after the 1984 Los Angeles Olympic Games. Although he had changed his mind and remained, his departure was viewed by many as imminent. People within and without the department began posturing to fill the power vacuum. Two deputy chiefs were often seen entering the mayor's office and meeting with other politicians.

As I turned into our driveway, I felt the familiar calm I always experienced upon arriving at home. Esther had made our home a place of refreshment and peace. When I got out of the car and walked across the patio, I felt a hundred miles from the problems of the office—until the phone rang.

Esther and I married young, she at 18 and I at 21. One of the reasons our love has grown over the years is our partnership in everything. She is interested and participates in my life, and I in hers. When I knew in advance that I was facing an unusual schedule or stress point, she was aware of it. She gives me the encouragement and support I need. She entertained business guests in our home and attended various police functions with me. Community people told me she was my greatest asset. Every night we debrief each other. I'm convinced this sharing is one of the reasons I seemed to weather stress so well and, at times, even appeared to thrive on it.

Vashti, our Siberian husky, met me near the back door. Then Esther and I discussed what I had learned that day and the possible implications as she put the finishing touches on our dinner. As a cop's wife, she never knew exactly when I'd be home. Dinner had to be prepared in such a way that taking the step of no return began after a phone call advising her of my ETA (estimated time of arrival) or when the car rolled up the driveway.

"We know how certain politicians will react to this," she said, "but what about the general public?"

"I don't really know what happened out there," I answered, "but I can tell you this: The video looks bad. I'm a cop. I'm disturbed by what I see. My guess is most people will be deeply troubled—many outraged. That's why it's so important to get to the bottom of this and get all the facts out in the open."

"Are you going to make any public statements? I think you should. The people should know you've got IAD out there doing their thing."

"My gosh! I forgot! I was going to call Stan Chambers. I'd better give him a call right now."

It took several minutes to get through various operators and staff people at KTLA, but soon Stan was on the line. "Hi, Chief," he said. "Thanks for calling."

"Stan, you're the one who deserves the thanks. You're a real pro. With your advance on this one, I was able to get IAD out there several hours ago. I owe you."

"Chief, I'm just trying to do what's right. Listen, do you mind if I start a tape rolling?"

"No, I don't mind. Start the tape."

He then described the videotape's contents for the tape and concluded by asking, "Chief, do you have any comments about this incident?"

"Yes, Stan. I have viewed the videotape you provided. I have verified that a Mr. Rodney King was arrested by officers of our Foothill area in conjunction with officers of the California Highway Patrol. The arrest took place in the early morning hours of Sunday, March 3. After viewing the videotape, I have ordered an investigation by our Internal Affairs Division. As always, we will conduct a very thorough investigation and, as the saying goes, let the chips fall where they may. We will demand integrity throughout this process."

"Thank you, Chief Vernon, acting chief of police." Then Stan turned off his recorder and surprised me a little when he said, "By the way, I talked to the mayor, and he said he was pleased to learn you were taking swift action. He also said he was sure you would do a professional job."

I thanked him again for giving us a chance to get a thorough investigation started, and I pondered the mayor's comment. As Chief Gates's director of operations and someone seen as a Gates loyalist, I knew I wasn't Tom Bradley's favorite cop. But regardless of why he had given me the apparent vote of confidence, I was determined to live up to it.

At five minutes to ten, Esther and I were in the den to view the way the incident would be covered on Channel 5. We spend most of our waking hours in the house either there or in the kitchen. Our den isn't large, but it's comfortable. Besides the TV and a leather set of sofa, two club chairs, and my favorite recliner, the only other piece of furniture is Esther's American oak side-by-side. She has our few family heirlooms displayed in the shelves behind the curved glass door: for example, my father's steel helmet from World War I, a set of early American rhythm "bones," and a handmade doll from Esther's relatives.

When the "News at Ten" began, the Rodney King incident was the lead story. We watched as the action shots of the encounter filled the screen. Seeing the incident once more, hearing the journalists describe it, and knowing hundreds of thousands of other people were also looking on gave me that punched-in-the-gut feeling all over again.

"Oh, Bob!" Esther said, "Do you think there's more to it than what we're seeing? Can there be any justification for that type of action?"

She was voicing the questions I had been asking myself. But I responded, "Esther, one thing I've learned over my 37 years in this business is that you don't rush to conclusions. You have to get all the facts. Obviously I'm troubled by what I see or I wouldn't have started an IAD investigation."

During the next 48 hours, we would all view portions of that tape scores of times. One station actually used it as a "break" in and out of the commercials on its news program. Any doubts I had about the far-reaching impact of the video were buried under the avalanche of showings on local TV.

The Rodney King incident was at the top of the news programs, talk shows, and practically every other media agenda for the next several days. We received communiqués from many foreign countries, individuals, and organizations that were following the story.

The demand for Chief Gates to resign or be fired was picked up immediately. Groups and individuals that in the past had remained silent or even supported him this time thought his resignation was necessary. Members of the chief's own Community Forum asked him to resign. That group met monthly with him and was made up of representatives from such respected organizations as The Urban League, the NAACP, and various church denominations. The difference was evident. The King video graphically showed several white officers striking a black man repeatedly with clubs.

The hurt, disappointment, and initial anger were understandable, especially when it was revealed that at least one of the officers involved had made racially derogatory comments earlier, on his car computer. On the same night as the King incident, a transmission from the car of Officers Laurence Powell and Timothy Wind (two of the four tried in the King affair) referred to a domestic dispute in a black household as "right out of *Gorillas in the Mist.*" That was a movie about African gorillas—a clearly racist remark.

An unidentified officer sent back, "Ha, ha, ha, ha. Let me guess who be the parties."

The people of L.A. and the entire nation were shocked. The vast majority support law enforcement. We all desire order and peace in our communities. The LAPD has enjoyed a reputation as one of the top professional police agencies in the world. Yet, the images of the video were unavoidable. How were people of good faith to resolve this paradox?

The black community was no exception. My years of police experience have taught me that it is perhaps the most supportive of the police of the many ethnic communities in L.A. For example, the black community has several groups organized specifically to back the police. These groups include the South-Central Clergy councils, several women's support groups, and business support groups known as Boosters. The Booster groups financially uphold the various youth activities led by the police.

Voting patterns also bear out the black community's support of the LAPD. For the last several decades, ballot issues backing the police have received the highest approval there. Many groups talk a good line of support. The black community has put its money where its mouth is. The people there have demonstrated their support.

But their concern over this incident was also strong. Was this case typical of an endemic problem in our department, or was it an isolated kind of conduct that would not be tolerated but condemned?

Along with people of good faith came the sharks, opportunists with hidden agendas who started a "feeding frenzy." They seized the initiative and promoted their selfish interests. Their desire was not to pursue truth but to confuse, inflame, and provoke. Jesse Jackson came to town and joined Congresswoman Maxine Waters in a demonstration where they demanded Gates's resignation. Jackson was quoted by the *Times* as saying, "This in no aberration. This is a history of behavior fostered by police headquarters." Waters exhorted the crowd to "keep the pressure on Gates to resign."

In this setting, it would be difficult for the department and the chief to respond. Any attempt to be objective, to bring forward all relevant facts, would be perceived as a cover-up, rationalizing, and defensive. The chief had his work cut out for him.

The media, of course, were interested in getting a statement from Gates as soon as he returned to the city. Usually I wasn't eager to have him come back into town when I was acting chief, but in this instance I realized he needed to be in charge. I was at the office before 7:00 A.M. to give him a briefing. Captain Moore from IAD accompanied me to give his insight and the status of the investigation. I gave the chief an overview, explaining how LAPD got involved in the pursuit started by the CHP. Moore brought us both up to date on what his investigators had been doing throughout the night.

After Moore was dismissed, Gates and I discussed his dilemma. We had a cordial relationship but were not close; during my 12 years as his assistant chief, we had lunch together once. He's a private man who rarely reveals his personal feelings to others. Now I could see he was visibly troubled by the event and the impact it would have on the department. He loved the LAPD, and he told me he was deeply concerned about its future. He acknowledged he needed wisdom to do and say the right things over the next few hours and days. Then he put his thought process into words.

"Bob, I am shocked and sickened by what I saw on that tape. I know I must say something about that. On the other hand, I don't want to be blamed for somehow tainting any criminal or administrative action that will follow by prejudging the case."

I understood his concern. Any judgmental statement he made at that point could be used by attorneys to argue a violation of due process. He was between the proverbial rock and hard place. Over the next few minutes, I tried to help him think through the various things he must consider. Rather than give advice, I tried to stimulate his thought process by making statements and asking questions.

He was sitting in his usual spot at the end of the long conference table. I was sitting to his right. Directly across from me and to his left, we had a view of the northeastern part of the city. On a clear day, you could see the San Bernardino Mountains.

As I glanced out the window, I remember thinking that this was a departure from most of our other meetings here. Daryl Gates had remarkable resiliency. We had discussed many crises around this table, and he had always been confident, seemingly unaffected by the many media assaults. But this time was different. I could see he knew it, and it bothered him. This event caused him to open up with more of his deep feelings. He talked about his concern for the welfare and morale of the many men and women of the department. We discussed the delicate balance of supporting them and yet not condoning what appeared to be misconduct.

Captain Moore had told us our information at that point was much too sketchy for a conclusive opinion. The chief would be making the final decision about any internal discipline. In that regard, he couldn't make a public statement of guilt or innocence until all the facts were gathered and formally presented to him. On the other hand, certain politicians and other leaders were demanding he immediately condemn the officers publicly.

We also faced the problem of putting the alleged misconduct into perspective. Several individuals asserted that this incident demonstrated the LAPD was rife with racist and brutal cops. We knew all the data refuted that. Of the 300,000 arrests made annually by the department, less than 1 percent result in any citizen complaint whatsoever. Furthermore, force is used in less than 1 percent of all arrests. Our dilemma was how to preserve the reputation and morale of the mass of men and women who professionally discharge their duties and at the same time reaffirm our strong position against racism and brutality.

The LAPD struggles with the same problem as all private companies and public organizations: It recruits from the human race. Of course it has bad cops. It disciplines and fires bad cops. It sends law-breaking cops to prison. No one despises a bad cop like a good cop. The challenge is to properly and fairly identify the bad cops and not paint all the good ones with the proverbial "broad brush."

In his desire to walk that tightrope, Chief Gates chose to say of the incident publicly, "Even if we determine that the officers were out of line, it is an aberration." I'm sure he did that based on his knowledge of the facts and his sincere desire to support his troops. Certain people interpreted that choice of words, however, as indicating a desire to "stonewall" any scrutiny of the police. Some even said he was condoning brutality and racism, that it was departmental policy. They overlooked the rigorous investigation already under way, our commitment to discipline and prosecute if appropriate, and our willingness to open the department to examination.

As the saying goes, hindsight is 20/20. Perhaps a simple statement like this would have sufficed to ease the tensions: "The LAPD has zero tolerance for racism and brutality. We are investigating this incident and will take appropriate action, including internal discipline and criminal prosecution, if the facts so indicate." But who knows what the reaction would have been? Even such a simple and straightforward statement can be manipulated and given a "spin" by those who are more concerned with their own agendas than with the truth.

On Thursday, March 14—a little more than a week later—a special police commission meeting was called. Normally the meetings are held in a room that seats a maximum of about 50 people. But this meeting took place in the auditorium on the first floor of Parker Center, which can hold several hundred. The room was "state of the art" when it was constructed. The walls are covered with specially designed wooden planks designed to enhance acoustics. Seated in the last row, you can hear a whisper from the stage. Originally, it was a multipurpose facility. Security doors backstage open into the adjoining jail. A large metal screen can be dropped down and fastened to the floor at the front to allow show-ups of felony suspects.

The special meeting was advertised to allow public comment about the King incident. Congresswoman Waters, who represents portions of the city, had arranged testimony by some of her constituents. Several community activists were present. A total of more than 100 citizens and at least 50 media people crowded the front of the room.

I decided to monitor the meeting, entering the room from a door on the right side of the stage. As I walked down the stairs into the alcove next to the stage, I could hear shouting and screaming. Several officers were standing in the alcove and just inside the door, in the auditorium. I saw one of the chief's security people, Gene Arreola, and asked, "What's going on, Gene?"

"It's a fiasco, Chief," he said. He pointed to the commission members and Chief Gates, who were sitting on the stage at two long folding tables. The president had asked for a covering to be draped to the floor from the front of the tables to offer some modesty for the commission secretary and the female commissioner, Arreola explained. One of the commission staff had brought the standard snap-on covering from City Hall. It was royal blue.

But Danny Bakewell from the Brotherhood Crusade had objected to the color, apparently associating it with LAPD blue or the "thin blue line." He demanded that it be taken down. He eventually got the crowd excited; then he ran up on the stage and began trying to pull the covering off. The commission gave in to him and was now having the covering replaced with a roll of butcher paper. "Out of sight, huh, Chief?" Arreola concluded.

I listened to various people come forward and offer testimony. The basic theme was to denounce the department as a racist organization and to bash Daryl Gates, calling for his immediate removal. One black lady who attempted to voice support for the department was shouted down and not allowed to speak.

Over the next few days, the theme was repeated in the media as they covered various protest meetings. Simultaneously, an organization was formed to support the department. A rally was planned for Sunday, March 24, 1991, at the police academy. The chief would be honored. The lines were beginning to be drawn. The city was being divided.

Within the department, the same thing was happening. The directors of a black organization of police officers issued a statement in support of Chief Gates. The paper said in part:

> OJB [the Oscar Joel Bryant Foundation] does not condone those actions [King incident], nor does it believe this is "Business as usual." During recent weeks, there has been a call for Chief Daryl Gates to resign. Many community-based groups, along with individual members of the community, believe this is the answer to the "King incident" and other

alleged acts of excessive force. If Chief Gates should be blamed, then the Board of Police Commissioners, Office of the Mayor, and the City Council should also be held accountable. Chief Gates, during the past thirteen years, has provided strong leadership to the finest law enforcement agency in this nation. A reputation of this nature cannot be earned from substandard performance.

A few days later, certain members of that organization who objected to the statement asked for a special plenary meeting of the membership to discuss it.

Many high-ranking officers of the department were atypically silent. I started receiving advice from both outside friends and members of the department to not identify too closely with Gates. Some felt he could not recover from this "hit," that he was on his way out. People told me that if I was interested in continuing my career, I should distance myself from him. But the lessons on loyalty I had learned from my father pulled me in a different direction. (More about that in the next chapter.)

During this time of tension, I received an invitation to participate in the "Support the Chief" rally at the academy. I learned that if I agreed to go, I would probably be the only chief officer on the platform. Chief Gates was being deserted by even his highest-ranking subordinates. To stand alone behind him would put me at odds with my peers and make me a target of everyone who wanted to get rid of Gates. The atmosphere was like that on a sinking ship, with all hands running for the lifeboats. I had a difficult decision to make, one that could cost me my career.

5

THE BANDWAGON PICKS UP SPEED

They called him Roy. His full name was LeRoy Vernon, and he entered the world in 1895, the last of nine children born to Levi and Beulah Vernon. Levi was a wheelwright in Lima, Ohio. He fashioned wheels for the big wagons and coaches that were still being used to "Go west." When he was eight, Roy went with his married sisters to the Ozark Mountains of Arkansas because his mom and dad were experiencing hard times and could not provide for him.

Some of the family moved west to the promised land of California, settling in Los Angeles. Soon they established themselves and convinced Levi and Beulah to follow. Times were good in L.A. in 1910.

Within a year, Levi and Beulah wrote to the family back in Arkansas, asking them to please put Roy on a train and send him out. They were doing well, and Roy would have a better life with more opportunity in L.A. He was 16.

The Vernon family had a house in the Boyle Heights area of the city. The day Roy arrived, most of them walked down Brooklyn Avenue to the train yards by the Los Angeles River. They were happy to see him—and surprised. He had grown to more than six feet tall. His trousers were "high water," his legs sticking out at least eight inches below the cuffs. And he had a large revolver strapped on and tied down. They took the alleys and back streets home to avoid the police!

Roy worked as a house painter for one of his uncles for a couple of years and then enlisted in the Army. He became a member of Company C, Eleventh Machine Gun Battalion, of the Fourth Division. They shipped out to France with the American expeditionary force in World War I. His company suffered severe casualties. He was wounded and gassed at the battle of Chateau Theirry, and for the rest of his life he would have a chronic cough.

At the end of the war, Roy returned to civilian life and went back to painting until 1922. That was the year his life took a dramatic turn that would eventually affect my life as well as his: He joined the LAPD and for the next 20 years was a patrolman. Roy Vernon was my father.

In the movie *The Untouchables,* Sean Connery played a tough, honest, Irish street cop in a corrupt Chicago Police Department during the heyday of gangster Al Capone. Connery's character refused to go along with the crowd, to take payoffs from the Mob and look the other way at criminal activities. As a result, he was never promoted. He was still walking a beat late one night when FBI Agent Elliott Ness (played by Kevin Costner) found him and recruited him to help fight Capone. Eventually the Connery character was killed by a Capone assassin because of his commitment to integrity.

I don't know how accurate the movie was, but my dad was that kind of man. He was an honest cop in a police department that for many years was corrupt. He believed in principles. More importantly, he *lived* them.

During the 1920s and early '30s, Los Angeles had a lot of dishonesty in city government. If you were willing to compromise, you could buy a list of the answers to the city promotional examinations. "Bag men" in the police department picked up the graft. Many sergeants, lieutenants, and higher-ranking officers got their share of the "take." But Dad told me a sizable percentage of the force was honest.

The corruption came to a peak in the late 1930s. Frank Shaw was mayor, and his brother was his assistant. Practically all of city hall was in his hands. Buying influence and position was so apparent that the public became disgusted. A few brave citizens banded together to stop the abuses and betrayal of the public trust. Clifford Clinton, owner of Clifton's Cafeteria, formed a committee named C.I.V.I.C. Its purpose was to kick out the corrupt leaders and bring about changes in the law that would deter corruption in the future.

The struggle was not without danger. Clinton's house was bombed. A police lieutenant was later found responsible for the attack. When politicians control the police department, the situation can become extremely dangerous.

The reform movement was ultimately successful, however. In 1938, Frank Shaw was recalled. Fletcher Bowren, an honest judge, was elected mayor on a reform ticket. The city charter was revised to insulate the police department from the absolute control of politicians. The chief of police was given civil service protection. He could perform his job without having to worry about political interference. He could be fired or disciplined, but only after cause was established. He was given the rights of a civil service hearing to appeal any crooked political action. Any attempt to improperly influence the chief or frustrate lawful action by the department could now be stopped.

William H. Parker was a young lieutenant in the department during these events. He wrote most of the proposed changes in the law. Section 202 of the city charter has been recognized by many as a work of genius. It provides not only the necessary protection for an honest chief, but also a fair system of discipline for the rank and file. Parker's wisdom and integrity as expressed in section 202 would bring a new professionalism to the LAPD. (Appropriately, this significant change in the law and city policy would one day contribute to Parker's becoming chief of police.)

A difficult transition began. Arthur Hohmann was appointed chief of police. One of the higher-ranking officers with unquestioned integrity, he brought about sweeping change. He reorganized the department and reemphasized education and training. He also supervised the design of a new badge that is still proudly worn by LAPD officers and used as a standard by many departments.

Not everyone appreciated the rapid shift of direction and methodology. Hohmann's tenure was accompanied by controversy. He stepped down in June 1941 and was succeeded by Clemence B. Horrall, another insider. Horrall continued the effort to clean up the city and the LAPD but was not completely successful. He resigned in June 1949 after a prostitution scandal.

Years of dishonest leadership had allowed the tentacles of corruption to burrow deep. It would take extraordinary measures to root it all out. The whole system needed a vigorous shakedown. A rugged, no-nonsense leader was required to "kick rear ends and take names." To do the job, the city hired William A. Worton, a hard-bitten Marine Corps general. He brought firm discipline, spit and polish, and strong leadership to the organization.

During his brief tenure, Worton quickly identified those who could be trusted with important responsibility. He promoted Parker to deputy chief in May 1950 and gave him the task of organizing a new Internal Affairs Bureau. Morale improved rapidly. Worton had accomplished his mission in 14 months and set the stage for continued development. He stepped aside in August 1950, and Parker began his remarkable and historic 16 years of leadership. He was to become a legend in law enforcement and would rocket the LAPD into international prominence. He in turn selected a young officer named Daryl Francis Gates to be his driver and aide.

William Parker clearly understood the duties of a successful leader. He knew he had to build a strong organizational culture to affect the behavior of its members. During his first few years, he began to construct that culture. He had the gift of oratory, and he used it. He preached the principles of professional law enforcement. He seized the initiative, using every opportunity to explain and illustrate the values he believed in. He talked about integrity, discipline, commitment, and loyalty. He inspired people both within and without the department to "buy into" and share his values.

The values of the organization translated into rules and procedures. During the next decade, the LAPD manual was written. A special unit at the Training Division Police Academy was formed. They published Daily Training Bulletins that were used during the roll call period. Officers were taught from these bulletins and given personal copies.

The developing rules and regulations were tough and demanding. Parker ran a tight ship. Uniform inspections were conducted every day, and overweight cops got "fatman letters" that demanded they lose weight. His premise: Sharp-looking troops behave sharp. Professional conduct was required both on and off duty. An LAPD I.D. card was better than a check guarantee card, because everyone knew Parker required integrity regardless of the setting. His IAD became the model for enforcing internal discipline. Formal education and career-long training became essential for promotion and desirable assignments.

A vast majority of the troops accepted the rigorous requirements of the new culture. *They understood the principles behind the rules.* There was excitement in the air. Police work was becoming a profession. A price had to be paid, but the rewards were great.

My father witnessed the beginning of the change. He completed his 20 years of service and retired in 1942. Understanding the significance of what was happening, he encouraged my own interest in law enforcement. I joined the LAPD in 1954.

Roy Vernon was also a man who taught and modeled principles. He, like Parker, recognized that changing behavior must begin by influencing a belief system. He spent much time with me, his only son. He rarely called me by my name; most often it was "Pal." He took me fishing, hunting, camping, touring, shopping. We talked a lot. I understood what he believed. I saw a consistency between what he taught and his behavior. In other words, he had integrity.

During the early years, he was not a churchgoing man. He believed in God. He had clear concepts of right and wrong. He accepted the existence of absolutes. But his religion was not expressed in the then-contemporary way.

One afternoon soon after joining the LAPD, I was on patrol in the Lincoln Heights area. I was assigned to a one-person radio car, unit 11 L 93. My radio "beeped" three times, indicating a hotshot call.

"All units in the vicinity and 11 L 93 . . . 11 L 93, a 211 silent at the uniform store at Mission and Workman, across the street from County Hospital. Handle the call code 2."

I was less than a mile from the call at Griffin and North Broadway. I flipped on my amber lights and turned the car around, now heading southbound on Griffin. I was just accelerating when I spotted "Nick" Najera on his three-wheel motorcycle. He had apparently heard the call and was preparing to roll also. Since a 211 is an armed robbery, I thought it wise that we team up and go in together. He had the same idea and was waving me down and pulling over to the curb. I quickly screeched to a stop, and he jumped into the right front seat.

"This may be a good one, Bob," he said. "Today's the county payroll day, and a bunch of the employees cash their checks at that store."

"Okay. We've got a good chance. We're right on top of it."

We had just crossed Main and were heading for the railroad tracks when we saw trouble approaching. "Watch it, Vernon," Nick shouted, "a train is coming!"

The red lights were flashing and the bell was ringing as the crossing gate dropped across the tracks. The freight train came into view.

"Don't try it," he said. "I don't want to die."

"Don't worry, I don't duel with trains."

"Turn right and parallel the tracks. He's not going that fast. I think we can beat him to Mission with room to spare."

I turned the car east and raced on the dirt right-of-way along the tracks. As we approached Workman, we were next to the engine and gaining on it. A motorist, southbound on Workman, had stopped at the tracks. There was no gate at this crossing, just the lights and bells. He seemed fascinated by the scene he was viewing. A police car was racing the train. Then his car started creeping forward. The room between the front of his car and the tracks shrunk before our terrified eyes.

"We're not going to make it!" Nick said.

I hit the brakes in a panic lock skid. We weren't going to stop in time. It was either the train or the car, and I chose the car. We hit him in his right front panel. No one was injured, but we were out of commission. We didn't make the call. Two cars were damaged. To add insult to injury, the call turned out to be a false alarm.

A sergeant was sent to the scene to supervise the investigation of our accident and conduct a personnel inspection. He ended up chewing me out and recommending discipline for my poor judgment. He also criticized me for picking up Nick, since he was working a special detail. At the time I did a lot of rationalizing and would not immediately accept the criticism of the sergeant.

After work, I dropped by to see Dad. I told him about the TA (traffic accident) and my frustration and anger with the sergeant. He explained a principle I had heard before about submission to authority and loyalty: "Bob, you need to step back from this and look at it objectively, if you can. I know you had the best intentions. I think the sergeant believes you had good intentions. But in the kind of work you've chosen to do, intentions are not good enough."

"Okay, Dad, I can accept that, but the whole way he handled it was wrong. He chewed me out in front of other people. And I think he was wrong about my picking up Nick."

"Right. Let's say he could have handled you better. You may also have a point about teaming up with Nick. But remember he's your sergeant and your boss. As long as he doesn't ask or order you to do something illegal, immoral, or unethical, you owe him your allegiance and loyalty."

"What if he's wrong, Dad?"

"If you think your boss is wrong, you owe it to him to tell him so. That's part of loyalty. But remember, he's the boss. If, after you give him your opinion respectfully, he still holds to his position, go with him—unless you have one of the three exceptions."

"Wait a minute. You're saying go along with an idea or action you think is not the best unless it involves a violation of a principle?"

"That's the way I see it. When it comes to matters of preference, we've got to go along with proper authority. Someday, you may be in a position of rank in the department. Will you want the officers working under you to follow you, respect you, and like you only if they agree with you on every issue? I don't think so. I think you'll want their submission, loyalty, and friendship even when you goof. No one is perfect, you know."

Those were wise words. To be honest, however, I didn't enjoy hearing them again, especially at that moment.

On Tuesday, March 19, 1991, I walked into the chief's back office in room 619. Gene Arreola, one of his security people, greeted me and asked, "Are you going to the rally for the chief on Sunday at the academy?"

I had been vacillating, not wanting to cross this bridge. Yet I knew what the answer had to be. Loyalty was the issue here. Daryl Gates was not just my boss; he was a good one. He had never asked me to violate a principle. He loved the department and had tried to follow in the tradition of his mentor, Chief Parker. I didn't always agree with Gates's positions or style, of course, and I knew that attending the rally could be career suicide. But our differences were matters of preference, not principle, and in the end, my dad's lessons on loyalty won out over all other considerations.

"Yeah, Gene," I answered, "I'll be there. You can count on it."

"Great. Here, let me pin this on you."

He jumped to his feet and reached in his pocket, out of which he pulled a blue version of the "yellow ribbon" lapel pin. He stuck it on my lapel. I was committed.

On Sunday, March 24, church got out at noon. Esther and I drove directly to the academy. The facility is located in the southeast section of a beautiful park just a few miles from the Civic Center. The park bears the name of the Elysian family that gave it to the city many years ago.

Just north and a bit west of Dodger Stadium, the academy is nestled in a valley of the foothills that eventually become the Hollywood Hills as you travel west. When you're in the valley, it's hard to believe you're so close to the high-rise superstructure of the city. Tall pine trees and beautiful fern gardens establish the setting of an exclusive country club. The academy's red-tile roofs and multiple arches give it a California mission flavor. It was originally built in the early 1930s, mostly by the tax-free labor of selected prisoners called *trustees*. Much of the material used was also acquired at little or no cost. The beautiful, three-feet-thick walls, for example, are made of pieces of concrete redeemed from streets or sidewalks repaired by the Department of Public Works.

We entered the park from the Stadium Way turnoff of the Golden State Freeway. It was a beautiful day. Several pick-up soccer games were being played in various grassy areas. We noticed the jacaranda trees were just beginning to push out their lavender blossoms. *Early this year,* I thought.

The entrance to the academy was blocked with sawhorse-type barricades. Several volunteers were controlling traffic. I stopped my car and said, "Hello, I'm Chief Vernon. I believe we're expected."

"Yes, Chief. I recognize you," one of the volunteers said. "As you can see, we have a good turnout, so we're restricting most cars from this area. But there's a spot reserved for you. I just want you to know that I appreciate your standing with the chief. Not too many of the top brass are here."

We drove up to the flagpole in front of the firing range, which was built in 1932 for the Summer Olympics. The facility was given to the police department afterward.

We parked and walked past the café toward the parking lot, where a lieutenant approached us. "Chief," he said, "we've got a pretty good crowd out, especially for a Sunday. We have a place reserved for you on the platform. By the way, Chief, you're the only chief officer I've seen here except Chief Booth. I wonder what's going on, Sir?"

"Others may be arriving yet. How many people do you think are here?"

"At least four hundred, maybe more. We've got a whole contingent of the media here. All the local stations, and the wire services, too."

We walked down the steps by the revolver club store. He was right. At least 400 were assembled on the parking lot, along with a battery of at least 15 television cameras.

We made our way through the congestion on the makeshift stage to our seats. They were right next to the seats designated for the chief and his wife. Sima, or Sammy, as she likes to be called by friends, is a flight attendant for United Airlines. She's a striking brunette, with flashing brown eyes and a bubbly personality to match. She's one of those rare people you feel you've known for years ten minutes after meeting her. When they arrived a few minutes later, she was pleased to see that Esther had chosen to come with me.

The rally got under way. George Putnam, a local TV and radio personality, was the emcee. He got the crowd wound up by uttering such statements as: "This is an outrageous attempt by the ACLU to take over our city." "Tom Bradley and his henchmen are behind this attack on our chief." "Our chief stands for integrity. What do the politicians stand for?" and "This is the best police department in the world, led by the best police chief in the world." I remember thinking, *He's a master of sound bites.*

Several other speakers took the podium, most of them predictable in their support for the chief and the department. Then came a shocker. Gloria Allred, an attorney known for supporting feminist causes, was called to the platform. I was amazed.

Ms. Allred spoke from her position as a civil libertarian. She apparently wanted to maintain an image of consistency. She seemed to think it inappropriate for the mayor and others to demand the chief's resignation or firing until due process was fulfilled. But halfway through her pitch, she shifted over to her standard liberal remarks, and the audience began to grow uneasy. I heard a few boos. A couple of people shouted, "Sit down!"

After a few other speakers, I was called to the podium. I defended the men and women of the department from the unfair broad-brush indictments some were hurling. Charges like: "L.A. cops are brutal racists." Those accusations hurt when you know from personal experience that well over 90 percent of the officers are not so—that they're caring, committed professionals who go out every night and day, trying their best to do the job right.

Then I turned my attention to Chief Gates. I voiced my support for his commitment to the profession and all the people of the city. I expressed my opinion that the King incident was being unfairly used by vested interests; that politicians like Mayor Bradley and Councilmen Michael Woo and Zev Yaroslavsky wanted to grasp control of the department; that in order to do so, they would have to get rid of Chief Gates.

The crowd roared its approval. Later I was interviewed by the media. I expected some fallout, but I didn't think it would happen so soon. During the next few days, certain community leaders demanded the chief's removal. Congresswoman Maxine Waters (never a police supporter), community activist Mark Ridley-Thomas of the Southern Christian Leadership Conference (now a city councilman), and John Mack of the Los Angeles Urban League led the charge. Then it happened.

About a week and a half later, at 10:30 A.M. on April 4, we had just finished a chief's staff meeting in the 618 conference room. Across the hall from the chief's office, it's set up for both staff meetings and press conferences. The room gets a lot of use. On the four walls is an array of pencil etchings of previous chiefs, including Roger Murdock, William Parker, Thad Brown, Tom Reddin, and Ed Davis.

Chief Gates stopped me as we left the meeting. "I guess Mary has told you," he said. "The commission wants you and I and Dave Dotson down in the commission conference room at 10:45."

"Yeah. I'm ready to go. Do you know what's going on?"

"Not really. Maybe they're going to fire me."

"You think so—seriously?"

"You never know. Things are pretty wild around here lately. But if they try it, they had better know what they're doing."

We walked down the hall toward the elevators. I stuck my head in my office and told Mary Helen where I would be. When we got off on the first floor, some newsies were sniffing around.

We walked into the reception office of the commission staff. Assistant Chief Dave Dotson joined us. We stepped into the hall just outside the private commission conference room. That room is small and has a conference table about ten feet long, with three upholstered swivel chairs on each side and one at each end. Traditionally, the commission president sits at one end, the chief at the other. On the inside wall are shelves to house a VCR, a few other necessities, and a coffee maker. Next to that are mugs with the commission logo and a box of oatmeal and chocolate chip cookies, the kind I can't resist.

Someone came out of the room and invited the chief in, telling Dave and I to wait outside. We went a few steps back into Commander Peirsol's office. The receptionist said she would call us when they were ready for us.

It was about 15 to 20 minutes, but it seemed like an hour. Dave and I wondered what was really happening. I had gotten a glimpse into the room when the chief went in, and as I waited I thought, *It seemed as if the commissioners were somber. But that could be my imagination.*

Finally the door to the conference room opened. Chief Gates came out walking briskly as usual. He slowed down as he passed Dave and me, who by this time were standing.

"Good luck, you guys," he said. "I've just been suspended."

Suspended? How could they do it? There were no charges—no hearing—no due process.

I was shocked, still thinking about the implications, when one of the commissioners said, "Dave, come on in. We want to talk to you first. Bob, we'll have you come in later."

Dave followed the commissioner back into the conference room. The chief exited the office into the main hall and ran into a bank of reporters. I was standing alone. One of the secretaries walked up to me and asked what was happening. I told her, and she began to weep.

Another ten minutes went by, again seeming like an hour. The door opened, and I was invited in. When I had taken a seat, the president spoke. "Chief Vernon, we have just relieved Chief Gates from duty. He will be on suspension for 60 days. We have decided to appoint Dave acting chief of police. We know you're senior and have confidence in you, but we have appointed Dave. We know you will give him all the support he needs."

"Yes, Sir. I understand. Be assured I will support Dave."

That was it. They had removed Daryl Gates, but I couldn't understand how or why. I didn't like what was going on. I'm always bothered by a lack of integrity. For people who proclaim their interest in civil liberties, they were sure walking all over those of Daryl Gates—suspended without any charges or hearing.

Normally, I would have been appointed as the acting chief of police by virtue of my position and my seniority over Dave Dotson. There was a certain sting to being passed over. It was clear I didn't fit into their plans. But frankly, I was pleased I didn't. This was a forecast of things to come. Dave Dotson was known as being more in line with their liberal perspective. He and I got along professionally, but we certainly had opposing views of the world in general and of how to do police work in particular.

In the outside hall, the media had stopped the chief. He told them straightforwardly that he had been placed on involuntary suspension. When asked for a reason, he was quoted as saying: "I don't think there was a good explanation for it. At least, if they have one, it was not explained to me."

Several officers were in the hall when he made the announcement. Detective Charles Press, coffee cup in hand, said, "It's the greatest injustice I have ever heard about in my 26 years as a law enforcement officer. The mayor is practicing political prostitution. . . . It's a joke. Mayor Bradley ought to resign."

Another cop blurted out, "Moscow, L.A. That's where I live. I don't live in America."

A reporter shoved a mike in the face of another uniformed officer, asking him what he thought. "I'm not in a very good mood," he answered. "I don't think you'd like what I have to say."

But as Gates left a few hours later, he said, "I'll be back." And he was. Arguing that Gates had been suspended without cause, his lawyer threatened to sue the city. The city council met in closed session for four hours to discuss the issue, finally deciding to back the chief because he was likely to win a lawsuit. Council President John Ferraro called the ten to three vote that essentially reinstated Gates "more a victory for due process than it was for Chief Gates," but the result was that just a few days after the suspension, he was on the job again.

The battle wasn't over, however. It had just begun. And soon the flak would be heading my way, too.

6

THE ATTACKS
GET PERSONAL

An outside consultant with expertise in dealing with disasters and other negative events had volunteered his services to the LAPD. He had analyzed corporate response to events like the Tylenol tampering case and the Union Carbide tragedy in India. Chief Gates had invited me to sit in while he gave his insight. We were gathered around the end of the conference table in the chief's office. The perspective he gave was thoughtful and credible.

First he outlined some of the common reactions that occur after a catastrophic event: (1) Shock and even denial. (2) A lack of information. *What really happened?* (3) Escalation of events. (4) Intense outside scrutiny. *Form a committee to study it.* (5) A sense of loss of control by the concerned agency or individual. (6) A resultant siege mentality. *It's us versus them.* (7) And often the last stage before complete breakdown—panic. (8) Then decisions are made based on survival rather than long-term impact.

Much of what he described had already occurred, at least to some degree. He understood the subject. We listened.

"What you guys need to do is hire Red Adair," he concluded.

"Hire Red Adair?" The chief looked puzzled. I just listened.

"When a big oil company has one of its wells on fire," he explained, "what do they do? They hire Red Adair.

"They usually hold a press conference with the burning well in the background. Then they introduce Mr. Adair. Everyone knows him. He's the most effective oil well fire extinguisher in the business. Then he gets in a helicopter and 'chops' off toward the burning well, and that's the end of it. Except it's not quite that easy. Often it takes days, weeks, or even months to put out oil well fires. But once Red is hired, most everyone is satisfied. Why? Because the oil company has done everything it possibly can. It has taken the ultimate step of hiring Red Adair.

"In other words, you need to demonstrate you're willing to do the ultimate to correct this situation. You should not try to explain it, defend it, or take halfway steps toward a solution. You need to figuratively hire Red Adair."

"Okay," Gates said, "I get what you're saying. We need to come up with a comprehensive plan that will address this whole situation. What do you think, Bob?"

"It sure makes sense to me. We've already been discussing some steps we need to take. Sounds like we need to expand on that and then make a public announcement. That way everyone will be aware we're hiring Mr. Adair."

Over the next few days, the chief developed, with his staff, a ten-point plan to address the crisis. Then he held a press conference to announce the plan. One of the components was the appointment of an independent commission to examine the facts and make appropriate recommendations. Retired Judge Manuel Arguellas was announced as chairing that commission.

The plan went over like a lead balloon with the politicians. The mayor wanted to form his own investigative commission. Eventually, that's what occurred, with a small compromise: Judge Arguellas would join the mayor's commission, which would be led by Warren Christopher, a west-side liberal Democrat and staunch supporter of the mayor. They didn't show any serious interest in the ten-point plan. Apparently they weren't really interested in problem solving. I believe they were more interested in using the King incident to develop their grand scheme, seeing this as their opportunity to get rid of Gates and finally change the charter to allow politicization of the LAPD.

The other components of the chief's plan were implemented. One of them was a speakers' bureau. Its mission was to respond to public concern over the King incident. Officers who volunteered and possessed public speaking skills would be prepared for this important job. They would not only be educated in the relevant facts, but they would also be prepared philosophically. Area commanding officers were directed to generate opportunities for them to appear at service clubs, neighborhood organizations, governmental agencies, police officer meetings, and any other community groups that were interested.

I was given the responsibility of delivering the "closing" at the training session for volunteer officers. I put a lot of thought into my preparation. My top priority was to bathe the whole process in integrity. They had to be honest. They had to be candid. They needed to believe sincerely in our values. They must also be ready and willing to listen. I suspected the most valuable part of such an effort would be the feedback we would receive from the people of the city. I asked that the group be renamed the "listeners' bureau."

The training session was scheduled quickly. I appeared at the last hour to wrap things up and was favorably impressed with the quality of the officers who had volunteered. We had the cream of the crop and a good mix of ethnicity and gender.

I made sure they understood their mission. I explained the Red Adair principle. They seemed to realize they were part of the department's effort to do the best we could in meeting the problem head-on. Then came the most important part as far as I was concerned. I had to model truthfulness. I was anxious about this part of my presentation.

There's so much I don't know about the King incident, I thought. *I've seen the video, as they have. I don't like what I saw. It seems obvious there were too many blows. Yet I haven't talked to even one of the involved officers because it's not permitted to interfere with an official Internal Affairs investigation.*

How can I be candid about my feelings without prejudging the officers? How can I address the basic issues without either coming across as unfairly biased or as concealing my opinions?

I decided to demonstrate what I felt they should do by telling them about my tension. I explained the problem I was having. I guessed they would have the same tension and said they should admit it. Then I hit the two major criticisms we were taking as an organization.

"Our department is accused of being brutal and racist. Do we have brutal cops? Do we have racist officers? Absolutely. Let's be honest. We have an organization of more than eleven thousand employees, including civilians. And as Jack Webb once said playing Sergeant Friday, 'Our problem is we have to recruit from the human race.' He was right. We're not Robocops, we're human beings, with all the baggage that goes with that. We all have the potential of being brutal and bigoted. But that's not the issue. The issue is, what is our goal, and what are we doing about getting to it?

"Our goal is to achieve the ideal in both of these issues. No racism. No brutality. Will we ever get there? Probably not, as long as we recruit human beings. But we've got to have an ideal. If we're not reaching for a higher goal, we'll never make progress. We must have a position of zero tolerance to racism and brutality.

"When I joined the LAPD in the early '50s, white officers and black officers did not work together. Have we made progress on that practice? Yes, we have. I see much less racism now than I did then. Have we arrived on that score? Absolutely not. How do we make more progress? By being honest. By adopting zero tolerance and backing that up with practices that reinforce our commitment. Racism is both immoral and stupid.

"That's the position of the department. We admit we have racism, but we don't tolerate it. And our goal is to eliminate it. We haven't arrived, but we're reaching."

I could see in their eyes that they were identifying with me. I sensed most of them wanted the ideal.

Next I addressed brutality. I related a perspective an old-timer had given me. There are two sides to what is commonly called "officer survival," he said. To many cops, that label refers to courses and tactical training that help them survive the knives and bullets on the streets. He described the other aspect as more sinister, more threatening, and more effective at destroying an officer's career.

The greatest threat to a cop, he said, is his own nature. The unique experiences of the job can push a person past the limits of self-control. The real test is confronting your own humanness and surviving at least the minimum years to qualify for a pension.

We had a standard called the LAPD partner principle. It works like this: In a tactical situation, a confrontation where we're facing dangerous criminals or a hazardous situation, my first commitment is to cover my partner. I'm trained to look after his or her welfare in our approach to danger. The reverse, of course, is also true. My partner is covering me. The theory is that one will naturally and instinctively practice survival. But if partners are looking out for one another, it becomes double coverage.

This principle is no more important than in the so-called other side of officer survival. Rarely do all officers in a given situation get pushed over the edge. The ones who have control have an obligation to look out for their partners' interests, to not allow them to be "taken out" by their own humanity.

The officers present could relate to the dangers of their own emotions. I could tell by the five-year hash marks on their sleeves—most of them wore at least two. These were veterans. They had all been in pursuits and seen some "dipstick" racing in front of their cars, blowing red lights, glancing off the cars of innocent bystanders. They had felt the fear, the adrenaline, the anger. They had made their share of death notifications, experiencing the grief and tragedy that results from flaunting the law. And they knew the frustration of injustice had a way of building up.

They realized we needed each other, had an obligation to each other. Police officers understand that people who have never carried a badge can't identify with us. They never experience the unusual pressures of the job, the hurt for the victims, the rage of a cornered felon, and the terror of a gun battle. Most people believe in movie tactics. They ask questions like "Why didn't you guys shoot to wound?" or "A karate kick would have stopped the whole donnybrook, wouldn't it?" These vets didn't have to be convinced that the use of force needs a lot of control and that we're in the best position to make sure that happens.

After a session of questions and answers, the class was dismissed. I hung around. A lot of them were hurting. Most stood by, listening. Some expressed their frustration, shame, anger, and depression. They felt they were all being judged by the video that was still being rerun almost daily. I listened. I tried to encourage. I watched them eventually leave, walking to their cars. They didn't need motivation. They knew we had our work cut out for us, but they wanted to help. They were committed.

A few days later, I walked into room 619. The chief's secretary handed me the May issue of *Los Angeles Magazine*. "Have you seen this, Bob?" she asked. "Looks like they're going after you, too."

She had it opened to a page titled "Insider." The first article, "The Dan Quayle Principle Strikes Again," was circled. There I read:

"Liberals eager to give police chief Daryl Gates the heave-ho may first want to check out who's in line to fill his standard issues. The LAPD's current number-two man is 26-year-vet [sic] assistant chief Robert L. Vernon—and he holds some, well, controversial religious beliefs indeed. A longtime member of the board of directors of the 10,000 member Grace Community Church in Sun Valley, Vernon also stars in *The True Masculine Role,* a six-part series of audio tapes produced by the church, in which he condemns homosexuality, depicts cops as 'ministers of God,' instructs churchgoers that 'the woman is to be submissive to the man' and adjures men to 'recognize the concept of disciplining followers, whether it be your son, employees or anyone under your control—your wife.' Vernon also cites biblical scholarship to tell parents that if a child is rebellious 'you must break them. If it takes beatings, you give them beatings.'"

"Yeah, that's what I believe all right," I said. The secretary could see by the look on my face as I rolled my eyes that I was being facetious. "They had to do some pretty thorough research to come up with this. I recorded that series over 10 years ago—maybe 15. Sounds as though they've taken some things out of context and changed some key words to radically change my meaning."

"Well, you know how good they are at that. We've seen that before, haven't we?"

"But each time, I'm still shocked. I guess I shouldn't be. That's just the way some of them operate."

"Bob, the people who know you won't believe this trash, and the ones who don't know you don't matter."

"I know what you're saying, but it does bother me that quite a few people are going to believe I'm a weirdo."

Later, when I listened to the tapes, I confirmed the magazine had been grossly dishonest in every detail. For example, the so-called statement about "beating a rebel" was my use of a real-life illustration, where a misguided father had spoken those words. In the tape, I *condemned* the father for that attitude and practice. I did present the biblical teaching of appropriately using controlled chastisement as an act of love, but that's a far cry from child beating.

I was surprised, however, by the lack of response to the article—at least for a while, I didn't get any letters or phone calls. Apparently not many people read the magazine.

Then on Tuesday, May 7, a local paper picked up the story. My hometown

Pasadena Star News featured the story on the front page of its "Local News" section. The headline read, "14-Year-Old Tapes Spark Controversy."

The story revealed the groups that were apparently behind this attack against me. The paper described "Los Angeles women's, civil rights and gay and lesbian groups" as being concerned about the tapes. Joe Hicks, a spokesman for the ACLU, was quoted as saying, "It indicates setting a moral tone in the Police Department that is certainly unhealthy." The story stated, "The activist groups, some of which already had called for the resignation of Vernon and LAPD Chief Daryl Gates, said they want to know if Vernon still holds those beliefs." The story went on to quote Hicks, "If he doesn't believe that, he should come forward and that would be the end of it." In other words, he wanted me to change my religious beliefs.

The article continued, "Dave Smith, spokesman for the Los Angeles Community Services Center, said gay and lesbian activists were urging the ouster of Gates and Vernon before the beating of Rodney King. . . . 'We know of these tapes. He [Vernon] has made several remarks that were derogatory to the gay and lesbian community. We want him out because he's an admitted, unapologetic homophobe.'"

Significantly, neither of those first stories made any allegation of wrongful action on my part. No acts of misconduct were even implied. Apparently, thought control was their motive.

I chose not to lend any dignity to those inaccurate and biased stories by responding with an interview, but I did release a prepared statement calling attention to their illegal actions. The *Star News* published a portion of that statement: "Discrimination against anyone because of their religious beliefs is against the law and deprives [individuals] of their civil rights." The attacks stopped temporarily while my opponents regrouped and considered my comment.

The next day, on May 8, the new "independent commission" under the direction of Warren Christopher held a public meeting to receive testimony from concerned citizens. Michael Zinzun, a self-proclaimed black community activist, was quoted by the *Times* as proclaiming there, "We are thinking of taking this to the streets. And we ain't talking about marching." According to the *Times*, he was wildly applauded. His prophecy was to be fulfilled a year later. (Interestingly, he was part of the crowd at Parker Center when the guard shack was burned, the windows were knocked out of police headquarters, and the riot spread downtown.)

The attacks against me seemed to be placed on hold for a few weeks. Then, on May 22, the battle heated up once more. Police commission appointee Michael Yamaki appeared before a city council committee for confirmation. When councilman Zev Yaroslavsky took the floor, he referred to the article in the *Los Angeles Magazine,* calling attention to the statements describing my alleged beliefs. He then said, "It's one thing to have an opinion. It's another thing to have an opinion when you're in charge of virtually every promotion." He asked Yamaki if he would investigate this matter if confirmed. Yamaki said he would.

Once again, no instances of misconduct were cited. The only articulated matter of concern was my beliefs. In addition, the truth was that I was *not* in charge of that portion of the department responsible for hiring and promotions. Even the deputy chief over our Personnel and Training Bureau had very limited influence in that area. The city council and police commission—including Yaroslavsky—were well aware that the L.A. Civil Service Commission has a separate staff that governs LAPD's hiring and promotions.

I responded with shock. I told the media I would seek legal counsel. I explained that calling for an investigation of anyone's religious beliefs was prohibited by law. I emphasized that I would not object to an investigation of my on-the-job performance if specific allegations of misconduct were ever presented.

That must have grabbed Yaroslavsky's attention. After the weekend, he sent a carefully worded letter to the police commission. The letter, dated June 3, 1991, reads as follows:

"As you are aware, questions have arisen recently about whether the views of Assistant Police Chief Robert L. Vernon may be improperly shaping the operations and policies of the Los Angeles Police Department. During his confirmation hearing Commissioner Yamaki indicated a willingness to conduct an investigation of this matter. I am writing today to confirm my interest in such a review.

"Chief Vernon is, of course, entitled to his personal religious and political views. I vigorously defend his right to his views. However, when one's views interfere with one's ability to perform official duties fairly and without bias, it is no longer a personal matter, but a matter of public policy.

"Allegations concerning promotion, hiring and treatment of gays and lesbians, and, most recently, the consultation of religious elders on issues of police policy, deserve to be reviewed. If the allegations have merit, then they should be addressed and the problems corrected. If they are without merit, then they should be laid to rest at once. It is critical that this issue be dealt with thoroughly and expeditiously.

"Thank you in advance for your attention to this matter."

At first glance, it sounded good. He wanted to defend my rights to my beliefs. But upon reading it carefully, I found that nothing had changed. He was still troubled by my beliefs. He referred to vague, anonymous, nonspecific allegations about the treatment of gays and lesbians—in my opinion, to "cover his tracks" on his initial call for an investigation based solely on my beliefs. I learned later that he refused to meet with the investigator from the chief's office who was sent to track down any specific charges. I was absolutely shocked that he would refuse to cooperate with an investigation *he had ordered and then announced by a press release.* Apparently he was more interested in having the false accusations broadcast than in getting to the bottom of the rumors.

Being a councilman for more than ten years, he had to have known very well that hiring and promotions within the police department are based on civil-service exams; that those exams are administered by the personnel department of the city, which is under the control of the city council; and that any assistance of the police department requested by the personnel department in those processes was under the control of a different chief officer, not me.

The real intent of the campaign against me was revealed in the way the letter was handled. It was attached to a news release and distributed to the media. It's city policy to not comment about personnel investigations until they're completed. Usually there's a commitment to due process and fairness—especially when no specific act of misconduct is present.

The efforts to perform character assassination were well under way. As reported in the *Times* on June 4, the mayor had joined the call for an investigation of my beliefs. "The Police Commission and the City Council, I understand, are taking a look at that [my beliefs]," he said. "It is quite appropriate that they do so." Still no specific charges were made, just a general assumption that my religious views must be improperly influencing my work.

I was devastated. Newspapers and the electronic media picked up the story. The perverted and warped versions of my sincere, mainline Christian beliefs were being used to make me look like an idiot. Furthermore, the unsubstantiated insinuations were beginning to take on a life of their own. Many people believed there must be some truth to them or the charges would not have been made.

I felt helpless. *How can I disprove something that's not charged?* I thought. *If only they can be tacked down to say, 'On this day, Vernon committed this act against this person or city policy.' Then I can fight it. Then I can confront the lies with the truth. But as long as they keep making general charges with no specifics, I'm dead in the water.*

I needed to get my side of the story out, so I chose to grant a TV interview. I had experience with many reporters, and Linda Douglas of the local NBC affiliate was a reporter who had established some credibility with me. She interviewed me on June 3. I corrected some of the false information, and then I hit the real issue head-on.

"Linda," I said, "it seems to be, frankly, outrageous that because a person believes this, we ought to go on a witch-hunt to see if it affects his work." I pointed out how they had decided to start an investigation based on my beliefs; that there were no specific allegations that could be looked into; that they "had a motive and were now on a fishing expedition, looking for a crime." I announced that I had contacted the U.S. Attorney's office to take action to protect my rights.

Chief Gates wisely assigned the investigation to his chief of staff. It would have been inappropriate to assign it to IAD since there were no specific complaints of misconduct. I later learned that his chief of staff was told to make a thorough investigation to see if anyone could come up with an actual accusation. If a specific complaint had been found, a full-blown IAD investigation would have resulted.

The next morning, Esther and I prepared to fly to Sun Valley, Idaho, for the annual joint meeting of the National Executive Institute of the FBI and the Major Cities Chiefs' Association. As we packed our bags early that morning, we listened to the CBS affiliate in Los Angeles, KNX Newsradio. They ran a story about the investigation of me ordered by the police commission. Again there were some inaccuracies, so I called the news director and asked if he were interested in hearing my side of the story. He said he was.

Tom Sermons, the special assignment editor, recorded the interview over the phone. "Tom," I said, "this is a hatchet job. They have announced to the world that they've started an investigation of me based on rumors and generalizations. First they requested an investigation because they were bothered about my religious beliefs. Those beliefs, by the way, were distorted by the media. When I challenged the legality of investigating me on that basis, Zev Yaroslavsky added that he had anonymous complaints about the hiring and promotions of gays and lesbians. Tom, I do not have authority over the personnel practices of the city."

"Wait a minute," he said. "You're saying that you're not over hiring and promotions?"

"Right. Personnel and Training Bureau is under the direction of another chief officer in the department. And even he has limited input. His organization just assists the personnel department of the city. They do the testing and selecting."

"You don't have anything to do with promotions?"

"Yes, I do, Tom, but very little. I sit as one member of a four-person board that conducts the interview portion of the promotional exams for the top two ranks—commander and deputy chief. That portion of the process is only half of the overall score, the other half being the written exam, which the personnel department prepares and administers. I have nothing to do with the other civil service tests, and not a thing to do with hiring."

"Well, I don't get it. Don't they know that?"

"Of course they know that. But what makes me very troubled about this is the repetitive malicious labels and charges done in such a manner that I can't refute them. It's like saying, 'Tom Sermons is a thief; Tom Sermons is a thief' and never saying that on this specific day you stole this particular item. I'm helpless, Tom. I can't defend against nonspecific rumors."

I hung up the phone, and Esther and I dashed off to LAX to catch our flight. We later heard from several friends that the story was presented with balance and fairness. Arriving in Idaho, we rented a car and took the long way to Sun Valley, driving through Stanley and past Red Fish Lake. We needed time to talk and reflect.

Over the years, I learned to cope with many of the pressures of being a public figure. But one thing I never learned to deal with is false accusations—especially when they're published nationwide. Until I experienced it, I never really understood the heartache of seeing your reputation broken. I can now more fully understand the words of Solomon recorded in the book of Proverbs: "A good name is to be more desired than great riches; favor is better than silver and gold."

It is a terribly wicked thing to maliciously damage a person's reputation. In many ways, when the false information is proclaimed, the bell cannot be unrung. It's hard to put into words the depth of helpless feelings I experienced. During the days before we left, we had heard from people across the nation who had caught news of the slander.

Every place we went, it seemed people were looking at me differently. Even some neighbors and friends seemed to be wondering about us. We both anguished over the sense of loss. Our character, the very essence of our being, was robbed from us. We turned to our only hope—our relationship with each other and with God. We reminded one another of His faithfulness to us in the past. We didn't like what was happening, but we took it to Him in prayer and asked Him to defend us.

That night we checked into our room at Sun Valley. They had us housed in a beautiful condo next to the golf course. It's a beautiful setting with a babbling brook. The owners of the condo we rented had done an exceptional job of decorating. The library contained books that gave mute testimony to well-read, thinking people.

We prepared for bed. As is our custom, we read from a devotional booklet called "Our Daily Bread." The reading was on the subject of facing life's difficulties. It was timely, to say the least. The suggested Scripture was from the first epistle of Peter. The last verse read as follows: "Therefore, let those also who suffer according to the will of God entrust their souls to a faithful Creator in doing what is right."

I turned out the light. Justice in L.A., for Rodney King or for the city's police (including me), was open to serious question, but God is bigger than any problems. Still, as I drifted off to sleep, I couldn't help thinking about the tremendous change that had taken place in recent years in how people thought my faith affected (or should affect) my work as a cop. That change says a lot about our society.

7

WHEN FAITH
WAS AN ASSET

My committed Christian faith had not always been seen as a negative in my work. On the contrary, during most of my early career it was considered a plus. I had always been "up front" about it. I didn't push it on people, but if someone asked, I would respond.

One of my strong convictions is to comply with the ancient proverb "A brother offended is harder to win than a walled city." I believe that means I shouldn't push my belief system on others. On the other hand, when one's relationship with the Lord is important, as mine is to me, there's a desire to share a good thing. That tension demands wisdom to strike the correct balance.

I once explained how I try to maintain that balance in an interview with a *Los Angeles Times* reporter. The interview followed some of the recent twisted accounts of what I believe. I'm sure the reporter was curious how I achieved such high rank if I was so strange. He was trying to find out if I was as eccentric as some of the media accounts implied.

"Do you bring your faith to work with you?" he asked. "In other words, does your religion have any influence on your decisions here at work? Is your on-the-job performance affected by your faith?"

"Yes," I answered, "I hope my faith is evident in my behavior and decisions here at work."

My answer shocked him. He was visibly taken aback by what he surmised was an admission of guilt. He made sure his recorder was working and positioned his pen at his note pad. He couldn't conceal his excitement as he prepared to take down my confession.

"Yes, Chief," he said. "Could you give me some examples of how you have allowed your faith to affect your work?"

"Well, I hope I have a reputation for telling the truth. I hope I'm known to keep my word. I trust I've established a pattern of working well past the required commitment. I've tried to pursue excellence in all I do. My desire is to have my troops feel I have demonstrated my support for them.

"That's how I hope my faith has intersected with my work. I hope people have observed that I'm a sincere, diligent, compassionate servant. I hope they've seen actions that cause them to believe that."

I could see the disappointment in his eyes. That wasn't what he had hoped to hear.

"Okay, Chief," he tried again. "I understand. What I was wondering is if you talk about your religion at work. Do you talk about the gospel when you perceive people have a need for it?"

"The city of Los Angeles pays me to be a police administrator, not a preacher. When I'm on duty, I try to be the best police executive I can possibly be. I think that's demonstrating my faith. If I were to preach on duty, I would be breaking faith with my employer. I think I would be abusing my authority to do so. I hope my life 'preaches.' I assume you're aware that I've been asked to perform chaplain functions. For example, I've conducted funerals upon direction of the chief, and I've married a few officers who are not affiliated with a church."

Once again, I could see he was disappointed. "Chief, does God ever speak to you?" he tried.

"Yes, He does."

This time he was sure he was going to get a response that would suit his mission. "Oh, He does," he said. "When and how often does this happen?"

"Practically every day."

"Well, I mean, how and where does this happen? Could you please explain?"

"Of course. I believe God speaks to me when I get my orders, or direction, from Daryl Gates. I believe I experience the leading of the Lord when the police commission declares policy or the city council enacts an ordinance."

"What are you saying? That you believe—"

"Bill," I said, "my belief about God's leading in my life is not really dramatic or mystical. I accept the biblical admonition to submit to authority. I believe that principle implies that God will usually lead me through a chain of command. In other words, He often uses human instruments to give me guidance.

"Of course, there's one important caveat. If the authority over me asked me to violate a specific command from God, I would be compelled to follow God's direction rather than man's."

"What do you mean, 'a specific command from God'?"

"I mean a specific command, like one of the Ten Commandments. For example, if Chief Gates asked me to lie to the media about an investigation, I would have to refuse. By the way, he has never asked me to violate one of those basic principles."

"So what you're saying is that you've never experienced an actual conversation with God?"

"I have never had God appear to me in the morning when I'm shaving and give me my orders for the day—if that's what you're asking. I'm not saying He's incapable of doing that. He can do anything He wants to. But that has never happened to me. It's my belief that generally speaking, God uses very conventional ways to speak to us. Our bosses. Circumstances. Abilities and interests. And, of course, what I believe to be His inspired Word, the Bible."

Disappointment was written all over his face. He was hoping he would hear some dramatic revelation. My answers were too ordinary. They didn't fit the mold of a mystic or a fanatic. The interview ended abruptly.

Some time later, I learned from our press relations officer that the paper was planning another article about my religious beliefs. The word was that it wasn't going to be complimentary. The reporter who interviewed me was writing the story.

The story was to run on a Tuesday. Naturally, I could hardly wait to see the Tuesday edition. The day came, but there was no story. I had our press relations officer call the reporter; he looked puzzled when he returned to my office.

"There isn't going to be another story," he said. "He told me to give you a message—said you would know what it means. I know this sounds strange, but he said to tell you he got a message from God through Tom Johnson."

I had written an earlier letter to Tom Johnson, the publisher of the *Times*, complaining about what I thought was unfair reporting. Now I thought, *That reporter got my point.*

This practical approach to integrating my faith on the job worked well—when I lived it. Naturally, I made my share of mistakes. But my goal was to establish a reputation as a hard-working, committed professional. That's the most credible way of demonstrating your faith. I'm grateful that I worked with some of the best cops in the business to help me pursue that goal, and I had some great bosses, too. Recognition and good opportunities followed. I was promoted up the chain of command quickly.

Getting your "railroad tracks"—the double bars of a captain—is one of the most significant promotions. They indicate heavy responsibility. You're a CO, the commanding officer of a division. That means you're the "Old Man" of somewhere between 250 and 300 officers (if it's a patrol division).

I was promoted to captain in 1969, at 36 years of age. My first command was a large traffic division with more than 300 personnel. We specialized in investigating accidents. In addition to the uniformed officers, I had a contingent of detectives to follow up on hit-and-runs and other serious cases such as manslaughter.

It was a dream come true. I loved every part of it. The buck stopped at my desk for most decisions. I was also given a take-home plain police car. The rationale is that a captain has 24-hours-a-day, 7-days-a-week responsibility. He's expected to "roll in" and handle all the tough decisions. But I even enjoyed that. If you like leadership, there's nothing quite as challenging and fulfilling as commanding a police division.

After eight months in that first command assignment, I was just beginning to understand the job. My boss, Commander Tom Janes, was a great mentor. He gave me all the guidance and accountability I needed but didn't meddle. Then came a change in assignment that shows how my religious convictions were viewed as an asset at that time.

Chief of Police Ed Davis called me to his office to give me the new job in person. "Bob," he said, "as you know, we've had some trouble in Venice. At this time, that station needs our attention. The community has not been happy with us. There are certain parts of the area where a black and white can't go without getting pelted with rocks and bottles. Our officers have responded in kind. One prisoner got his eye knocked out in our jail there. Things were pretty hairy until I sent in Lembke [Al Lembke, a top-notch cop]. Now I'm giving Lembke his star. He's being promoted to commander. I want you to command Venice."

Venice had been in the news in recent months. A captain had been transferred and disciplined—many officers, too. I couldn't remember for sure, but it seemed a few were fired. Trouble City.

The boss continued, "Lembke has done his job well. He's only been there a few months. But I knew that was going to happen when I sent him there. He had a mission to accomplish quickly. He did it. He was the heavy. That's just what I wanted. It's just what Venice needed—someone to tighten the screws.

"Now I want you to go in there and be the 'good guy.' I don't want you to turn around anything Lembke has done. It's still needed. But your mission is to keep morale going up. Lembke has set the ship on the right course. You keep it going. You be positive. You probably won't have to cut off any more heads. That's been done for you. This is a great opportunity."

I was nervous but excited. To command a station was a big assignment, and this was a tough one. Davis watched my reaction for a few moments, and then he concluded, "Well, Bob, you start next Monday. I hope you take this as a compliment, because it is. I know you'll do a great job. There's a lot of bitterness and mistrust in Venice. You're a good Christian boy. Go out there and heal that community. Be a champion to those cops out there, too. Most of them are good."

We talked about some of the specifics of his expectations, and I was dismissed. I was high, starting a new, exciting adventure.

This was the early 1970s, when the flower child phenomenon was still in full swing. And Venice Beach was their favorite hangout in the Los Angeles area.

Venice was a microcosm of the city. We had a marina, the airport (LAX), an industrial area, a couple of federally subsidized housing projects, an upper-middle-class district called Westchester, and Oakwood, a black neighborhood. The population of slightly over 150,000 was very diverse. That created the potential for conflict. For example, just as the Jewish community of mainly retirees in Venice proper was going to sleep, the hippies from the canal area were getting out their bongo drums to begin the celebration. The police were caught in the middle.

During the summer, almost every weekend brought a "love-in." Fledgling rock bands set up their instruments on the end of the flood-control pipe on the beach near Rose Street. It wasn't unusual to see more than twenty thousand fans join the tribal rituals. With drug and alcohol use widespread, violence often erupted. I decided we needed to set a tone to reduce violence.

After one particularly deadly event, we planned a comprehensive strategy to get the message out. The next summer holiday promised a bigger-than-usual crowd. We were prepared. Early in the day, I had undercover officers mingle with the crowd. Their mission was to buy dope. When they did, they signaled their cover partner, who was watching with binoculars from the top of the Rose Hotel. When they gave the signal—perhaps removing their baseball caps—whomever they were facing was the pusher.

Arrest teams in swimsuits were directed by the observer using a grid system. As soon as they made contact with the pusher, they surrounded him and walked him out. There was so much noise and jostling in the crowd that no one seemed aware of what was happening. That's the way we wanted it: Remove as many drug sources as early as possible, and do it quietly and unnoticed.

By noon we had a bus nearly full of drug dealers. The bus was parked out of sight, behind the hotel. Then, just before the bus pulled away, some in the crowd figured out what we'd been doing. A small group of them ran to the edge of the main body of the throng and convinced nearly a hundred to follow them to the bus. Before we could get it out of there, they had the bus surrounded and were demanding we release the prisoners.

I was on the roof of the hotel, monitoring events. We had planned for this type of contingency. More than two hundred Metro riot troops were one block away, hidden in the RTD bus garage. Additionally, we had nearly one hundred regular officers stationed at discreet locations around the event. My aides offered me the alternatives, but I didn't like any of them. Violence was near—maybe big time. An immediate decision was necessary. I shot up a quick prayer for wisdom.

"Arv," I said to my adjutant after a few moments, "let's go down and talk to them."

"Talk to them? Skipper, that's a mob, and it's growing."

"That's why we need to move now. Put Metro on standby."

"I've already done that, Sir." We were getting aboard the elevator. "You sure you want to do this, Skipper?"

"Arv, hold on to that radio. If this doesn't work, have Metro save our bacon."

You couldn't get more Nordic than Arvid Keidser. His blond hair was covered by a riot helmet. His face was more ruddy than usual—it was over 90 degrees. We had on the standard LAPD navy blue wool uniform. I could feel the sweat trickling down my backbone, some of it caused by the heat, some by fear. We opened the door and walked toward the crowd surrounding the bus. It was getting ugly. *Maybe Arv was right,* I thought.

Someone saw us approaching. The word quickly spread, and a chorus of catcalls began. A short, skinny, redheaded young man noticed the bars on my collar. "Hey, it's the head pig," he said to the mob. "The head pig is here. Are you the head pig?"

"Yeah, I'm the head pig. I want to talk with you."

"Did you hear that? The head pig wants to oink."

The air was tense. It could go either way now. I tried to appear calm, hoping I was concealing my real feelings. I knew my next words were important.

"We're here to help you enjoy the music and the day," I said to the crowd.

Curses and shouts of rage made me stop. I had to try once more. "May I tell you why we're here?"

More curses and yelling, but not as loud as before. A few of them apparently liked my asking their permission to talk. The redhead asked the group, "Shall we let him oink?" A few said yes. More curses, but far fewer. It seemed the tide was turning.

"At the last concert," I said, "many people were injured. Several were stabbed. One young man lost his life. I don't think you want that to happen today. I don't. That's why we're here."

I went on to explain our strategy. Some were buying in, others were not. I was about to lose control of the situation when a teenage girl stepped forward. She handed me a potato and said, "I love you." I was taken aback. So was the crowd. Everything got quiet except for the concert and people in the distance.

"I don't understand," I answered. "What's the potato for?"

"It's all I have to give," she said. "It was meant to be my food for today. I want you to have it."

She turned to the crowd and said, "He has a few hundred riot cops in the bus garage. He could have called them down on us, but he didn't. He came down and talked to us. I love him for that."

She was a flower child, probably a runaway or a throwaway. But she saved the day. Someone said, "All right, Sister. You're cool," and the crowd started breaking up. Not everyone was happy about it, but the momentum was gone.

The bus drove away. I was standing there staring at the potato in my hand. When I looked up, the girl was gone.

Healing in Venice did not come about easily. Talking didn't always work. Confrontations persisted. We had to persevere in the healing process.

Our overall strategy to improve the quality of life for the people was simple. It was based on the assumption that most people in any community want to be able to walk the streets without being accosted. They want to be secure in their homes. In short, most people don't want crime to go unchecked in their neighborhood. Most police officers see their mission in similar terms.

Based on those simple assumptions, the strategy was also simple. The people of a community and the police should develop a *partnership* since they have the same goal. That's what I wanted to help advance. A variety of methods would be used; many activities were already in place.

Lieutenant John Cleghorn had been assigned to Venice a few months before my arrival. His job was assistant commanding officer and community relations officer. I didn't select John, but whoever did could not have made a better choice. John is one of those rare human beings who loves people and shows it easily. They, in turn, respond to his sincerity and gracious spirit.

Working together, we formed a council representing all elements of the community, not just the police groupies. Businesses, service clubs, other community agencies, some of our antagonists, and just plain folks formed the cross section. We met regularly with them, usually at breakfast. We brought the issues they wanted to discuss to the table. We broke bread together. We communicated.

Each of the primary patrol car teams in the area was doing the same. At the neighborhood level, they also had monthly meetings and impromptu "coffee klatches."

Communication began to bring about understanding, but not on every issue, and not in every neighborhood. There was still antagonism on both sides in the Oakwood district. The focal point was a government-funded group called the Community Activity Aides (CAAs). They stated their mission as being a "buffer" between the police and the community. The executive director was a talented young black man named Vermont McKinney.

McKinney was concerned about some police practices. Some of my officers, in turn, saw him as a threat. He hired neighborhood young people to follow the police and observe them in their contacts with the public. An understandable adversarial relationship had developed.

Since McKinney was on our Community Advisory Council, I thought we could tackle the problem head-on. I set up an appointment to talk with him on his turf. Some of my men were skeptical about the benefits of such a meeting, and they insisted I take some of them as security. I agreed to that but mandated they keep a low profile.

The day for the meeting arrived, and after perfunctory greetings were exchanged, I noticed a poster on his office wall. It depicted an arm thrust from a crowd and grasping an assault rifle. I can't recall the exact words under the picture, but they said something like "When oppression becomes too great, off the pig."

We discussed several issues. McKinney complained about my officers' always having their hands on their guns when they approached anyone in the neighborhood. "Your officers seem like they're just waiting to shoot someone. They look angry. Why can't they treat us with dignity?"

"Maybe they're scared," I answered.

"Scared? Why should they be running scared?"

"For one thing, Vermont, the word about that poster has spread around. It made me cautious about coming here." I pointed to the poster on the wall.

"Oh, that. That's just rhetoric. The young people here are frustrated. I need to establish credibility with them."

"It may just be rhetoric with you, but we're threatened by it. It tells us some of you may be thinking about killing cops."

He thought about that for a minute. I made myself keep silent and let it sink in.

"Captain," he finally said, "do you honestly think there's a connection between your officers' aggressive behavior and that poster?"

"Yes, I do, Vermont. I don't want to oversimplify the problems we have to work out, but I think we may have a starting point. You take down the poster, and I'll tell my officers to be more careful in how they approach people in their contacts. Agreed?"

"Agreed. I'll take it down. But we'll be watching you cops."

It was a small start, but it was a start. We kept working with the community, and by the time I left Venice, CAAs were actually walking foot patrols with officers in a supportive role. The officers began to realize there were many people who could be trusted as partners in Oakwood.

Before I got my first star and moved on in 1972, we were using team policing, the precursor to what is now commonly called community-based policing. I was pursuing a master's degree and had come across the concept while researching various contemporary policing strategies. As far as I could determine, team policing was tried for the first time in Aberdeen, Scotland. The emphasis in this approach is on service. Officers in a given district work as a team rather than employing the typical bureaucratic, specialized model. Community members are mobilized as partners in problem solving. Authority and accountability are decentralized. Results are measured in terms of crime and fear levels rather than in numbers of arrests.

Venice was the first area in the city to employ this type of policing. The partnership was working, and working well. Chief Davis took our model and mandated that the whole department adopt it.

Everything I did there was based on Judeo-Christian principles, and they were successful. Taking my faith to work in that practical way was not only tolerated but considered desirable. The community, the top brass, and even the politicians were pleased. It was okay—more than okay—to be a Christian and hold a top job in the LAPD.

To give you an idea of how much progress we made in Oakwood, I was invited to speak at a testimonial dinner for Vermont McKinney. He later got a job with the federal government as a professional mediator, but we've stayed in contact. I consider Vermont McKinney a friend to this day. He attended my retirement dinner to wish me well.

Society was changing rapidly, however, and before long I would find myself dragged into the middle of a raging controversy.

8

GAY RIGHTS:
AN EXAMPLE OF
CHANGING VALUES

Beginning in the 1970s, as society's standards of acceptable behavior changed dramatically, I found myself embroiled in two controversial issues. One was the question of whether homosexuals should be hired as police, and the other was the question of how and how much the LAPD should be involved in intelligence gathering (discussed in chap. 9). My experience in these areas shows how far society was moving away from values that had helped to hold it together in the past.

I was appointed deputy chief in mid-1973, and my first assignment was to head the Personnel and Training Bureau. That bureau, among other things, assists the city's personnel department in the processing of police applicants. And at that time, homosexuality as a factor considered in hiring became an issue. I was dragged into the debate.

Until then, homosexuality had been a bar to employment as a police officer. But in July 1974, a motion was introduced in the city council which specified that a candidate for city employment should not be discriminated against because of sexual orientation. In November 1974, the Civil Service Commission and the city attorney's office asked Chief Davis to provide his opinion on whether the LAPD's policy should be changed.

The chief directed that my office prepare the response. His direction came to me from my boss, Assistant Chief Dale Speck. In the written direction, dated November

25, 1974, I was given specific instructions about what the paper should include. I, in turn, assigned the project to a sergeant on my staff.

He completed the task and presented his first draft. The document was written like a college term paper, with quotations from various experts and documents. Footnotes established the sources of the most significant data and opinions.

The research paper argued the position that homosexuals should still not be employed as police. The professional consensus of that time supported the city policy. For example, until 1973 the American Psychiatric Association (APA) had classified homosexuality as a mental disorder. In December of that year, its board of trustees changed the classification to that of a "sexual orientation disturbance."

That decision caused such a furor within the APA that a referendum was held by the membership. In April 1974, the decision of the trustees was upheld by a slim margin; 42 percent of those members voting did not agree with the change. Many who did vote for the change did not mean to imply that homosexuality is normal, but they felt they should not be labeling a group of distressed individuals as "mentally ill." Their hope was that the change would make homosexuals feel more free to seek psychiatric care.

In another paragraph of the LAPD's paper, Dr. E. Mansell Pattison was quoted. In his article published in *Psychiatry*, he stated: "Yet the flush of liberal enthusiasm to defend and glorify homosexuality may not be scientifically defensible or socially acceptable. Social suffering should not be confused with personal suffering. The elimination of social persecution will not eliminate the personal confusion, anguish, and fruitless search for love which may be the by-products of maldevelopment."

Furthermore, certain acts regularly practiced by homosexuals were felony crimes in the state of California. (As political agendas began to emerge on this issue, however, the acts were decriminalized.)

The point I want to emphasize about that document is that it was the result of careful research, a compilation of the professional wisdom of that time. It was never intended to be, nor was it, a statement of my personal opinion (although I did then and do now agree with most of its contents).

I have opinions and convictions on a wide range of issues, just like everyone else. As I said in the last chapter, however, one of my firm convictions is that I don't have the right to impose my opinions or morality on others. It would be in direct conflict with my value system to use my position in that manner.

The paper was accepted by Chief Davis as accurately reflecting contemporary professional insight on the subject. It was approved as the position of the department. He used it in supporting his recommendation not to change the hiring standards for the LAPD.

In his November 25 note, Assistant Chief Speck had also indicated the paper would be valuable to distribute within the department. Accordingly, I sent copies to all division commanding officers. They were to use it in answering questions about the department's position on this issue. The paper was sent out with a cover memo from me explaining why they were receiving a copy; the memo was printed on my desk note pad, with my name and logo.

A few weeks after that, the paper, together with my memo, emerged in a newspaper catering to the homosexual community. It came to be known as the Vernon position paper, and excerpts from it were identified as statements from me. The fact is, however, that the statements were not made by me but by experts or publications footnoted in the paper. For example, the most-quoted statement attributed to me was this: "Any person who willingly engages repeatedly in homosexual activity is an emotionally sick person and definitely constitutes an unacceptable risk when qualifying as a police officer." But that statement was actually made, as a footnote in the document clearly indicates, by an LAPD staff psychologist.

Because of that shoddy journalism, from that moment on, some homosexuals viewed me as an archenemy. They labeled me an "unrepentant homophobic."

The response of the homosexual community to that story raises another issue as well. Some have written letters or made public pronouncements that people with my beliefs should not hold positions of public trust. Apparently they believe that those in government service must pass a test of political correctness or else have no opinions or values.

The Constitution, however, prohibits any religious or "political correctness" test for public office. I'm as entitled to my opinions and values as the next person. That leaves the second option. But does anyone go to work without some beliefs? Human beings are not capable of erasing those portions of their brain that contain their belief systems. Even an atheist has a strong belief system based mostly upon—*the horror of it all*—faith.

Nevertheless, the homosexual coalition has used my religious beliefs on this issue to brand me as unfit to hold the public trust. This first surfaced during the competition for the office of chief of police in 1978. The gay rights people did all they could to keep me from being appointed. In fact, their efforts may have been the primary reason I was not selected from the list of three finalists. All the local media described me as a born-again Christian and a lay minister. The June 5, 1978, issue of *New West* labeled me "a born-again Christian with a rumored antipathy to 'perverts.'"

Daryl Gates, Charles Reese, and myself were presented to the police commission as the finalists with the highest scores. After extensive interviews, they narrowed the choice to Gates and myself. For more than two weeks they seemed unable to make a decision. I later found out that two commissioners favored Gates, two were leaning toward me, and one was undecided. It was during this time that I was asked many questions by the media about my position on homosexuality.

Wayne Satz, a reporter for one of the network TV stations in L.A., requested an interview on this subject. Contrary to the advice of some friends, I granted the interview. Satz said that my beliefs on the issue were of great concern to many in the community. I requested a 30-minute discussion with him prior to going on camera, and he agreed.

In that time, I was completely open about my faith and its impact on my behavior. I explained that part of my belief system prohibited me from forcing my understanding of morality on others. He told me he appreciated my candor and said he would try to fairly communicate my beliefs. That night, when I viewed his edited story on TV, I was pleasantly surprised: He had captured the essence of my position. In the end, however, Daryl Gates was given the job.

Just before the selection process for chief of police began again 14 years later, in 1992, I was grilled by one of the police commissioners on this subject. The commissioner asked me about the 1974 position paper. I explained the background of the document. The commissioner understood the significance of the time frame and the purpose of the research.

"But do you now believe homosexuality is immoral—that it's sinful behavior?" he asked.

"Yes, I do," I said, but I also reiterated my conviction that I couldn't impose my beliefs on others. Then I added, "Perhaps more important to you is my firm conviction that I must not use my beliefs to improperly make on-the-job decisions."

The commissioner looked puzzled. "What do you mean by that? Do you now believe we should hire homosexuals as police officers?"

I wanted to be completely honest. I couldn't be deceptive in any way, yet I also didn't want to raise an unnecessary "red flag."

"Commissioner," I said, "my personal preference would be to not knowingly hire homosexuals. It's my opinion that the statements of the experts in the research paper are still valid. Read it sometime. The credibility of the sources and conclusions is compelling. But that doesn't mean I can't implement present city policy on this issue.

"There are many city policies I don't agree with but that I conform to every day. For example, I would prefer not to hire applicants who are not at least five feet seven inches tall. As you know, the present standard is now five feet even. I believe that's too short to do the job of policing in this city. But that's not my choice to make. My job does not include hiring and promotions, but if it did, I would adhere to the standards set by the Civil Service Commission or else get out."

"In other words, if you were in charge of hiring, you would not exclude people because of their sexual preference?"

"No, I would not. Neither would I exclude people who are under five feet seven inches in height. Both of those practices would be against my better judgment and preference. But those decisions are not mine to make. I see my role as providing insight and judgment to the decision-making body. Then, once I've done that, I must abide by their decision as long as their decision doesn't make me violate one of my principles."

The body language of the commissioner indicated some confusion still existed. The next question confirmed my suspicion.

"Would you explain what you mean when you say 'violate one of your principles'?"

"Well, if the Civil Service Commission said to me that they wanted me to commit a homosexual act to prove, by example, that I was tolerant of that behavior, I would refuse to do so."

"I would certainly hope they would never make such a request."

"That's what I mean. Being involved in a system that has policies you don't agree with is one thing. Having those policies force you to get involved in or personally endorse something you believe is morally wrong is another matter.

"For example, I have officers working for me who are involved in adulterous relationships. I believe adultery is immoral and sinful. I believe it's also dysfunctional to a supportive, stable life-style. But when it comes to evaluating their on-duty performance, I don't take their off-duty behavior into account. I don't have the right, as a public administrator, to force my personal beliefs of morality on them. But I also don't believe that means I have to give up my civil rights. I still have the right to hold fast to my personal beliefs and to discuss them in my house of worship, freely and without fear of reprisal or loss of job."

The commissioner looked somewhat relieved in replying, "I must say I feel better about your thinking on these subjects. I'm glad we talked."

"Commissioner, I'm grateful you took the time to listen. All of this is a red herring. I have nothing to do with hiring. The real agenda is to raise a cloud over my reputation. I'm not happy about that. I would not resist an inquiry into any specific charge of wrongdoing or misconduct, because I've done nothing wrong. What's frustrating is seeing these sweeping rumors repeated in the media."

The commissioner walked out of my office. I sat alone and reflected. It seemed to me to be a remarkable paradox. People who don't want to be discriminated against because of their moral beliefs or behavior were attacking me for mine. Individuals who champion personal privacy were now calling for investigations that violated my privacy. The defenders of due process demanded action that violated that principle in my case. I was suspected of doing something wrong just because I have beliefs they don't like on certain high-profile issues.

Something is desperately wrong in Los Angeles and elsewhere. The attacks against me in this area make that painfully clear. And the assault on the LAPD's intelligence-gathering capability drives the point home even more forcefully.

9

THE ATTACK ON
LAPD INTELLIGENCE

Simply put, the primary purpose of police intelligence work is to prevent crimes before they can happen. Who would say that's not a worthwhile goal? Yet the LAPD's efforts in this field became the second controversial issue in which I got caught up in the early 1980s. It was another area where public values had changed greatly over the years—for the worse, in my view. In the process of standing up for what I believed to be right, I added to my "undesirability" in current Los Angeles politics.

In August 1982, I was assigned to direct the Office of Special Services (OSS). It's that part of the LAPD that included the Organized Crime Intelligence Division (OCID), Narcotics Division, Administrative Vice Division, and the palace guard—Internal Affairs. One of its most controversial programs was the Public Disorder Intelligence Division (PDID).

PDID had its roots many years ago in the valid concern about dangerous revolutionary groups. At one time it had operatives within many of those groups. Terrorists like the Weather Underground were monitored, and many acts of violence were prevented through the division's effectiveness. In June 1982, for example, a senior detective in PDID signed a sworn declaration in which he listed more than 50 serious crimes of violence and terrorism prevented by the division. Included were contract killings, bombings, and kidnappings.

As far back as the 1930s, the people of L.A. recognized the need to allow the police to gather and store as much intelligence information as possible. The prevailing logic was that information itself was neither good nor evil. Gathering it was, therefore, benign. If the information revealed illegal conduct or plans, law enforcement should be aware of it. It followed, then, that the only people who needed to worry about the police gathering information were criminals or conspirators.

After the so-called McCarthy era, however, people grew concerned about the potential misuse of intelligence information. In the mid-1970s, the police commission and Chief Ed Davis recognized the need to place limitations on the department's intelligence-gathering operation. But even then, the focus was on retention (what information was kept in our files) and dissemination (who was allowed to see the files). There still wasn't much worry about the simple collection of information.

In a police commission PDID audit report dated October 28, 1978, this perspective is clear. Then-Commissioner Marianne Pfaelzer, now a U.S. district court judge, stated:

> We looked at the problem of *retention* and we did not address ourselves to the problems of *gathering*. . . . [I]t's a very difficult job to approach, but it's one that I may be suggesting and I probably will be suggesting that there be some sort of discussion about this. Just how that will be carried on I really don't know. But I do see a problem or a distinction between gathering and retention. (emphasis added)

In 1976, the commission adopted guidelines addressing the issues of retention and dissemination. Many files were ordered destroyed (which was done). The commission was trying to strike a constitutional balance between an individual's right to privacy and free expression while simultaneously recognizing the broader societal need for protection.

By the late 1970s, however, certain groups were determined to hamper the department's ability to gather information, and their first effort came in the form of a lawsuit against the city alleging abuses of privacy. In 1978, the PDID was accused of violating the civil rights of several individuals and organizations by "illegal spying." The ACLU joined in the suit, which became known as the CAPA (Coalition Against Police Abuse) suit.

The CAPA attorneys worked hard from the start, requesting all kinds of documents from us. The city attorney assigned to the case part-time as the department's defense counsel wasn't nearly as effective, and before I took over the division, thousands of documents that should never have been released were handed over.

Some of those documents allowed the groups we were monitoring to learn the identities of most of our undercover agents (UCs). That forced us to bring in all but those who had the proper kind of "deep cover," whose covers had not been blown. One UC, Genny Lester, was held against her will and interrogated by the group she had infiltrated before we could get her out—she needed psychiatric help as a result.

Later, we learned how those dangerous groups probably got the list that exposed the UCs. One of our operatives, a member of the Communist Party, told us that on her way home from a meeting of one of the revolutionary groups, "something had gone wrong with one of the men's cars that night, and he asked me to take him home. On the way home . . . I made some statement about, 'I can't understand how CAPA got the list,' and he laughed and said that the list was deliberately given to CAPA by the ACLU."

Soon after assuming command, I was also told by a supervising detective in PDID named Jake that the CAPA suit was only the tip of the iceberg in a plan to ruin the department's intelligence-gathering capability. "Chief," Jake said, "in my opinion, this city is in jeopardy of becoming another victim of corruption. There's a group of politicians and big money power brokers who want to seize control."

I had known of Jake for several years. He had a good reputation; he was reliable. Despite the heavy stress of working intelligence, he had not lost his balance.

"What's their next goal?" I asked. "Assuming they can either eliminate or cripple our intelligence operation, what comes next?"

"They will have to take over the leadership of this police department. Under the present circumstances, and with the current personalities involved, they couldn't pull it off. They will either need to change the charter or get some guy in the job of chief that they can control. You know what I mean—a puppet."

I learned that young, inexperienced UCs (we recruited them at the academy so they weren't already known as cops) reported on everybody and everything of interest at meetings of groups they were observing. More-experienced officers then gleaned the information we had reason to keep in our files, and only that data was retained. The source reports would have been trashed at that point—including the names of people who were at meetings but doing nothing wrong—except that the law (the Public Records Retention Act) and the courts (after the CAPA suit was filed) required us to keep them! So the raw reports had been stored away, unorganized and unused, in a vault. But many of those source reports were among the materials obtained by the CAPA attorneys and formed the basis of their claims of invasion of privacy.

Once we started putting the proper effort into preparing to explain these things in court, I felt the situation was smoothing out. I believed that if we got all the relevant facts to the people of L.A., we would have their support.

Then it happened. Murphy's Law was alive and well. On November 2, 1982, Joel Sappell, a reporter for the *Los Angeles Times,* contacted police commissioner Reva Tooley. A confidential source had indicated that PDID files had been removed from the police facility, Sappell said, and were being stored in a vault in the office of Eugene Ingram of the L.A. City School Security Section. Unfortunately, no one in the LAPD was informed until a fruitless search of the vault had already taken place— the day *after* the possibility of such a search had been discussed with Ingram. In fact, because of Tooley's delay, IAD wasn't able to start an investigation until some 55 hours after she had heard of the allegation. I guess we'll never know if any documents were there.

IAD started its investigation, and the officers soon concluded they were not getting complete cooperation from all involved. In discussions with the district attorney's office, they decided that bringing the matter to a grand jury might smoke out any reluctant witnesses. The grand jury set its first date for January 4, 1983.

Then the other shoe dropped. Also in November 1982, Captain John Cleghorn, who was the new commander of PDID, informed me that one of his subordinates, Lieutenant Gus Drulias, was "feeling hinkey" about a PDID detective named Jay Paul.

"What's his hink about, John?" I asked.

"Paul says the previous administration allowed him to do some of his work at home. In this kind of work, that makes us nervous. We want to pull in the leash on him."

Cleghorn looked as nervous as he said he was. I suspected he was bouncing this off me because he wondered if Paul had some kind of direct mission from above. I hit the issue head-on.

"John, you and Gus take whatever action you deem appropriate. When I was briefed about my job here by Gates, he just told me to keep this operation legal, within policy, and professional. There were no limitations or 'off limits.' If Gus wants to reel in a detective, go for it. I have complete confidence in you guys. I know you'll use good judgment. I'm glad you told me about this. I can't understand why an intelligence cop would have home assignments. Keep me informed."

A few weeks later, on the morning of January 4, 1983, Cleghorn brought me the bad news. With a pale face he said, "Jay Paul has brought in some documents. He has had them off site. Some of them are newspaper articles. Some of them could be intelligence documents. This may be connected to that allegation IAD is investigating about someone removing intelligence files."

"Get IAD on the phone. I want them in on this immediately."

"I've already called them, Boss. They're on the way up now."

As we headed out of my office and up the stairs to PDID, I realized the significance of what was happening. Gus Drulias had begun to tighten the screws of control. Detective Paul was being looked at under a microscope by IAD, and now the grand jury would be involved as well. Today was its first day of hearings. Perhaps Paul realized he was about to be discovered doing something out of policy, or maybe the previous leadership had allowed him to do certain things that he now realized would not be tolerated. I didn't know which was the case, but I didn't like either possibility.

From that moment on, events escalated rapidly. The chief was informed, the DA's office joined with IAD, and search warrants were served on Detective Paul's residence and another building. Boxes of material were seized. Most of it was public material like newspaper articles, but some of the documents had private information about politicians, judges, and other high-profile personalities.

To call the discovery of those files a bombshell would be a major understatement. It was, indeed, troubling that such PDID documents were in the private possession of a detective. But the information had been collected in a time when the public's attitude about such things was very different, and the files would have been destroyed long before if the law and the courts hadn't required us to hold on to them.

The media handled the story like sharks in a feeding frenzy. Daily stories told of spies, intrigue, agents provocateur, and all sorts of other supposed police abuses. It seemed no one was safe from the "snoopers." Over the next few weeks, many politicians joined in the accusations as well.

Chief Gates realized the significance of the IAD investigation and directed that it focus on the entire PDID operation, not just the activities of Detective Jay Paul. Then he prepared a confidential letter to the captain of IAD ordering him to pursue responsibility for any misconduct or violations of the law or policy as far up the chain of command as necessary. His directions left no room for misunderstanding on this issue.

Understandably, the police commission flooded us with requests for more information. City council committees scheduled hearings. We had little time to do anything but respond.

Then, on January 17, 1983, a shocking event took place during one of the council hearings on the matter. Ira Reiner, the city attorney at that time, joined the crowd of hecklers. He condemned the officers and operations of PDID—the very clients he was defending in the CAPA lawsuit! He seemed more interested in being politically correct than in adhering to the almost sacred attorney-client relationship.

The client officers immediately obtained temporary legal counsel and sought to have Reiner removed from the case. He and the entire city attorney's office were removed on March 1. The city then had to hire private counsel for all the officers who were defendants in the suit, including myself and Chief Gates. Reiner's blunder resulted in great unnecessary expense to the city. He was later reprimanded by the state bar for his breach of ethics. I was learning about the workings of politics and how ambition can affect a person's judgment.

All this was happening as the CAPA lawsuit was moving ahead and Councilman Zev Yaroslavsky was proposing a freedom of information ordinance that could harm our legitimate intelligence operations. On top of all that, the Olympics were coming to Los Angeles in a year and a half, and we did not want a Munich-type terrorist act occurring here.

Solid intelligence is the best weapon against terrorism. Once terrorists get a plan moving toward implementation, they can be practically impossible to stop. But good information can forestall the whole operation before it gets off the ground. We never needed such data more desperately. With events coming together as they were, however, we could lose our capability altogether or have it so crippled as to make it ineffective.

As overall Olympic security planning went forward smoothly under Commander Bill Rathburn, I was particularly interested, as the head of OSS, in our antiterrorist strategy and plans. I became a member of the Interagency Antiterrorist Task Force. This group comprised mainly personnel from the LAPD, the FBI, and the L.A. County Sheriff's Department. The sharing of antiterrorist intelligence was at the heart of this effort.

Our work in this area was directly affected by the raging debate over the proposed city freedom of information ordinance. The other intelligence groups were hesitant to provide information to us, fearing that if the ordinance were passed, we could be required to disclose their confidential and highly sensitive material. We could not afford to be cut out of the combined efforts against very probable terrorist activity.

It just didn't make sense that the city's leadership was seriously thinking of exposing important intelligence files at a time like that. But, on the other hand, what better time could there be to try to push through something labeled "intelligence reform"? We were right in the middle of a so-called spy scandal. For those opposed to the LAPD's intelligence operations, it was the moment of opportunity.

Chief Gates assigned me to lead the department's representation at the city council hearings. On May 9, 1983, I appeared before the Police, Fire, and Public Safety Committee of the council. It was my opinion that, as proposed, the ordinance would devastate not only our intelligence operations, but practically all other police operations as well.

I began my testimony by telling the committee that this issue was one of the most important they would ever consider. I reminded them of the upcoming Olympics and our responsibility to protect the athletes and other visitors, as well as of the lasting damage that would be done to the city's reputation if a terrorist attack occurred. "It would be immoral," I said, "to unnecessarily expose our people to the violence of terrorism."

That got their attention. What I had said was true, and everyone there knew it.

Normally, committee meetings are held in small conference rooms. But there was a lot of interest in this issue, and more room was needed, so this meeting was held in the main city council chamber. It was packed. Its magnificent marble columns, tile floor, and ornate architecture would make it practically impossible to build today. Carved into the granite above one of the main City Hall entrances is this biblical truth: "Righteousness exalteth a nation."

I continued my testimony. The TV cameras were rolling. Reporters from various media were feverishly taking notes.

"Whether we like it or not," I said, "terrorism is a reality in our world today, and we must continue to be diligent in order to protect our citizens from these cowardly acts. During the past three years, the LAPD bomb squad has responded to approximately 2,000 suspected bombs. Over 150 bombs have actually been disarmed. . . in this same period, this city has experienced 95 bombings. On 4 separate occasions, bomb squad members have disarmed a terrorist's bomb moments before it was due to explode.

"'Complete security of identity is one of the underground's most important advantages in guerrilla warfare. In ideal circumstances, no one would know the identity of any member of a combat unit except other members.'

"This excerpt from a New World Liberation Front publication explains why the revolutionary campaign to cripple local police intelligence is now in full swing."

I glanced up from my notes to make eye contact with the members of the committee. Yaroslavsky looked furious. I continued to implore them to use caution, to act like statesmen rather than politicians. We were in danger of throwing out the baby with the bath water.

I felt uneasy. I wanted to present a convincing argument, but I realized it would probably cost me politically. Nevertheless, I had to tell it as I saw it, so I continued.

"I see a cover-up. I do not fully understand why, but this committee and the local media have been repeatedly told that the federal freedom of information acts have not presented any serious problems to federal law enforcement agencies. This simply is not true. . . . I must publicly set the record straight. Judge Webster, director of the FBI, reported that over 200 important FBI investigations have been compromised because of the federal Freedom of Information Act. The Drug

Enforcement Administration reports that over 14 percent of their investigations have had to be aborted because of these acts."

I gave other illustrations of the problems with federal regulations. Then I addressed the financial costs. My final argument targeted those pushing for such an ordinance.

"Finally, I am concerned about a hidden agenda. Who is behind the move locally, in Los Angeles, to enact a freedom of information ordinance? The *Los Angeles Times* quoted Councilman Zev Yaroslavsky as giving credit to Linda Valentino of the ACLU and Michael Balter. In that March 27, 1983, issue, the *Times* stated that Balter calls himself a Marxist and a socialist. It further quoted him as saying, and I quote: 'Revolution may be necessary to change the U.S. social system. Whether such a revolution would be violent would depend on political circumstances.' I hope this committee and the full council will listen to the responsible citizens of this city and not to Marxists and socialists who would even consider the use of violence in achieving their objectives."

If Yaroslavsky was furious before, now he was livid. As the meeting broke up, council members and I were swarmed by the media. There were strong feelings on both sides. It's difficult to advocate a position you believe in strongly and not be perceived as making your remarks personal.

Councilman Yaroslavsky approached me as I was about to leave. I could see he was angry. "Bob," he said, "what you just did was dishonest and vicious. You called me a communist—a revolutionary. I will never forget this. You will live to regret this day."

"Councilman," I responded, "I did not call you a communist or a revolutionary. I merely pointed out what the people you worked with on this issue called themselves."

He wasn't appeased. "I will never forget this," he said again.

"Councilman, I tried to tell you that the course you were on was wrong. The ordinance, as you submitted it, would have had a devastating impact on law enforcement and the welfare of the city in general."

He appeared too angry for reason as he stormed away. Somehow he overlooked the fact that the one he called "the continuous force that has kept this issue on the public agenda" (Balter) had described himself as a Marxist. But I clearly understood his meaning: There would be a payback time.

The ordinance went before the full council on May 24, 1983. Then-Sergeant Dan

Koenig was my staff expert on the issue. He's one of those guys who has common-sense savvy. Whether he's taking down a barricaded robbery suspect with four hostages or doing business with politicians, he's got the necessary street smarts.

"Let the blue-suiters make the case before the council for you, Chief," he advised. "You've made your pitch. But you're perceived as carrying the department torch because it's your job. Bring over some uniformed watch commanders and let them tell their story. Have them give it to them straight on how the ordinance will hamper their job."

We did it. Dan lined up several harness bulls to give their opinions. They backed every position with a real cop story. The vote was taken. The council locked up seven to seven. Yaroslavsky failed to get the necessary eight votes. He wasn't about to give up, however.

During the next few weeks, the action continued in the hallways and back rooms of City Hall. Some changes were made to the ordinance. But in my opinion, it was still dangerous to the security of the city.

Late in June, Yaroslavsky apparently thought he had enough votes to win. He took the ordinance back to committee on July 5, 1983. I again appeared on behalf of the department. The debate was fierce, but the way was cleared to set the matter before the full council the next day. The *Times* ran the headline: "Police-Council Showdown Set for Today." The story read in part:

> At stake at the meeting, and in related activities outside the chambers, were decisions that are likely to affect police-City Council relations for the next two years. If the Department loses, its hostile attitude toward liberals who have much influence in city government could continue. If Yaroslavsky loses, he said, the defeat "will be just the beginning" of more fighting.

Reporting on the events that occurred the day before, the story continued:
> Seated across a table in the chambers were the adversaries. On one side were Yaroslavsky and committee member Joy Picus, who favor the act, along with Chairman Peggy Stevenson, who is trying to work out a compromise. On the other was Assistant Chief Robert Vernon, on the

front line of the department's fierce assault against any measure that would allow people access to its files.

Outwardly, Vernon looked like the recruiting poster version of a Los Angeles police officer—calm, unemotional, seldom smiling, even-voiced, always in command. But as the meeting went on, he fought his case with the intensity of any other high stakes City Hall lobbyist, offering to negotiate but refusing to concede a point. Finally, an angry Yaroslavsky said, "I'm not dealing with you because I can't deal with you."

When the full council debated the ordinance, things were just as stormy. Before the day was over, I wrote an amendment to the law that resolved most of our fears. It narrowed the application of the ordinance to the intelligence division, and it made it easier for us to prove that releasing certain information would have harmful effects. But even though the amendment was accepted as part of the measure adopted by the council, the foot was in the door. And while we had won a partial victory for public safety, I had angered some powerful players in the city's political game. I realized that, but I didn't understand the depth of their animosity. Many years later, I would feel the full impact.

———————————————

At the time of all the action on the freedom of information ordinance, much was also occurring with PDID. The division had been disbanded and replaced with the Anti-Terrorist Division (ATD). Also, on April 5, 1983, the premier L.A. law firm of Gibson, Dunn, and Crutcher was hired to replace City Attorney Ira Reiner in defending the city and its officers in the CAPA case. Tom Holliday and Nancy McClelland from the firm were assigned to the case. They immediately began to represent the city's interests aggressively.

The ACLU lawyers started to learn some lessons, as they were now confronting a well-supported litigation team. They not only faced legal challenges, but they also encountered increased financial costs. Demands were made for the ACLU to pay for the "dailies"—the transcripts of each day's court proceedings produced by the court reporters—which can get expensive.

The first big victory for the LAPD came in December 1983. After two days of executive sessions with Holliday and McClelland, the city council voted 11 to 0 to go to trial. The lawyers had presented the most vulnerable portions of the department's case. After hearing this candid report, one of the council members, an attorney, expressed his amazement. He said that if those were indeed our case's weakest areas, there was no doubt that the city should proceed to trial. He felt we could win.

Mayor Bradley was out of town when that decision was made. Upon his return, things turned 180 degrees in City Hall. The word was that the ACLU was in financial trouble. It couldn't afford to lose the case or continue facing Gibson, Dunn, and Crutcher. A settlement had to be worked out. Some people in L.A. politics sincerely believe that the ACLU is an important force in keeping political balance in our community. They didn't want it to become ineffective or financially ruined.

Shortly after Bradley's return, our attorneys told us their direction had been changed by the council. They were to pursue settlement discussions. We were floored. What made the council change from its firm resolve to fight the suit, we wondered. I asked the attorneys if any further facts had emerged that changed the prospects for victory. The answer was no.

Late in January 1984, we got the word that a settlement had been worked out. The CAPA group and their attorneys would get nearly $2 million of the taxpayers' money. But that wasn't the full extent of the settlement. The ACLU-guided plaintiffs won the power to negotiate the new guidelines for the ATD. Those guidelines were translated into an order issued on January 23 that specified the parameters within which the officers of the division must operate. For example, the guidelines stipulate what meetings officers can attend, what groups and individuals they can investigate, and what information can be reported, retained in files, and later disseminated.

I have talked to many intelligence officers since that order came down. Some of them say the new guidelines are so unwisely restrictive that the division can no longer do its job effectively and should just be shut down. Others say we must continue to do the best we can regardless. Either way, the ability of the LAPD to gather good intelligence was severely damaged, and this was happening only months before the Olympics were to begin.

Despite the handicap of its new guidelines, I believe the ATD played a major role in making sure no terrorist acts took place during the Games. Certain terrorist suspects were identified. Some were deported because they were in the country illegally. Some were arrested for violating the law. But some remained in L.A. as the day for the opening ceremonies approached.

During one of our regular briefings about the status of the terrorist threats, ATD officers told me there was nothing we could do to remove the remaining suspects. They weren't wanted for past violations, and we couldn't prove they were presently breaking the law. I thought the one thing we could do would be to make sure they knew we were watching them; maybe that would keep them in check. So I told the officers of the terrorist task force to "door knock" them—just go to their residences and tell them we would be around to ensure they committed no acts of terrorism or violence. This was done, though we'll never know just how effective the tactic was.

What undoubtedly *was* effective was the monumental effort of many committed law enforcement officers. Near the end of the Games, I ran into one of our counterterrorist surveillance units at the academy. A weary-looking cop captured the commitment in a brief statement: "Chief, next time we do this, I want a shower installed in the back seat of our car. We're living out of it, you know, and my partner is starting to smell like a goat."

Unfortunately, with a crippled police intelligence capability, the city could not survive so well in every situation. The riots of 1992 were a tragic case in point. More recently, just two weeks after the new police chief was placed in office, another crisis arose over police intelligence. This time the OCID was closed—locked down tight. The excuse: ten-year-old rumors retold by a former police officer who left the force in the early 1980s under questionable circumstances.

Then the whole story came out. Ramona Ripston, local head of the ACLU, had been working with that officer since October 1991 to get his book containing the rumors published. Ripston is married to controversial federal appeals court judge Stephen Reinhart, a former Bradley appointee to the police commission. One of Reinhart's former law clerks, Mark Fabiani, was deputy mayor under Bradley at the time. According to some, he was the power behind the throne. The opportunity was great, and the timing was magnificent.

Hampering the LAPD's effectiveness in this area, however, was only half of the game plan of those who wanted to take over the department.

10

GETTING RID OF
THE OLD LEADERSHIP

If the PDID detective I talked to upon first taking over OSS was right, the enemies of the LAPD had a second goal: to replace the current leadership in the department with people more amenable to their goals. Once the Olympics were over, I asked myself, *Would moves toward that goal now be taken? Would attempts be made to ensure that the next chief would not come from the current leadership team?* Just a few months later, a clear answer emerged.

On December 14, 1984, the city's Civil Service Commission took action to drastically reduce the importance of seniority with the city as a factor in selecting the next chief of police. In the past, in the points system used for choosing a chief, one-quarter point was given per year of service in a qualifying position with the city. That was now reduced to one-tenth of a point per year, to a possible maximum of one whole point. There was also talk of eliminating any objective test and shifting to an interview as the sole examination of candidates.

What inspired the commission to make that change? In my opinion, there were two major reasons. First, prior to the Olympics, Chief Gates had announced that he would retire when they were over. (He subsequently changed his mind and didn't retire until the summer of 1992.) So they wanted the new rules in place in time to govern the choice of his successor. And second, just weeks before the commission's decision, the so-called Garcia Report was leaked to the press.

Dan Garcia, a close Bradley ally and chairman of the city planning commission, had prepared a confidential report assessing management responsibility for the alleged spying abuses by PDID. The report said PDID's errors occurred because of "the attitudes of senior staff officers at the highest levels of the department." Blame was laid on past and present assistant chiefs, including Daryl Gates. Although I wasn't mentioned by name, the newspaper and TV stories also identified me as one of those responsible—never mind that the suit alleging such abuses was filed in the 1970s and I wasn't assigned as director of OSS until August 1982.

The media figured it out. They commented that I had been considered a leading candidate to replace Gates. Their analysis was that this report would not help my chances. Another candidate for the position, Assistant Chief Marvin Iannone, was also criticized. He had been director of OSS just prior to me. The *Times* quoted him as saying, "There is a conspiracy theory circulated wherein there are people who would do anything to prevent this department from producing the next Chief of Police [from within its ranks]. This theory states that they want someone whom they can control."

My reaction was recorded in the December 23, 1984, issue of the *Los Angeles Herald Examiner:* "I'm not a politician, and I don't want to be. I just want to direct my full energies toward rendering professional police service to the citizens of this city. Frankly, that is being made difficult by these continuing false and unfair smears. The real scandal here is the shamefully relentless attempts to politicize a professional police organization. One need only look at Chicago's history to see that the stakes are high in seizing political control of a big city police department. The first step in the process is to discredit and discourage present leadership."

Now those words ring in my ears as being prophetic. But I more or less expected attacks from without. What I never expected was skullduggery from within. My purpose in telling the story that follows is not to say "Poor me" but to show the tactics used by those who wanted to ensure no one from the existing LAPD leadership would succeed Gates in the chief's office. Nevertheless, what happened was surprising and deeply disappointing to me and Esther.

One morning in January 1989, I was out walking our dogs around the neighborhood. We had two Siberian huskies at the time (Vashti and Boaz, who has since died), and they needed companionship and regular exercise. As we walked, we came upon a neighbor named John Crowley.

Although we're not close, I consider John a good friend. He had been a Pasadena city director for a number of years and had also served as mayor. In my opinion, he's one of the primary reasons Pasadena has experienced a renaissance in recent years. He has a fine family, too, and we've developed good friendships with two of his sons.

The dogs and I were approaching John's house when his car pulled into the driveway. John stopped just inside the sidewalk, got out of the car, and picked up a newspaper as we exchanged greetings. I asked him how things were going in the city. Although I live in Pasadena, my responsibilities in L.A. kept my allegiance and attention there. I didn't follow local events closely. John reminded me Pasadena was about to have an election. I was embarrassed to show my ignorance; I didn't even know who was running for what office.

John commented about recent events in L.A. and said he thought I had a difficult job. Then he asked, "Haven't I heard or read that your city has also had some experience with Michael Zinzun?"

"Yes, Michael has made himself known," I replied.

"Did you know he's running for city director here?"

I had to admit that was news to me.

"What can you tell me about him?" John asked. "Is there anything we should be aware of that can be discussed?"

I paused. John could see I was hesitant to reply.

"Look, Bob," he said, "I don't want you to say anything if you don't think you should."

I faced a dilemma. I did know some interesting things about Michael Zinzun, such as the fact that he had been a Black Panther, but I couldn't remember how I got the information. Was it through public sources like the newspaper, or was it connected with my role on the police department? If it was the latter, I had a professional code of ethics to uphold regarding confidentiality.

"John, I don't think we should talk about it now," I finally answered. "I'll give the matter some thought. If I feel we should discuss it further, I'll contact you."

John Crowley is a smart and honorable man. "Bob," he said, "I want to again say that I'm not asking you to discuss something you don't think you should. If there's any doubt in your mind, just forget it. Okay?"

And that's the way we left it.

Several days went by. I didn't think much about the conversation, but I did have some knowledge about Michael Zinzun. He had taken highly controversial positions on public matters. Since he was seeking public office, I thought those views should be known. Yet I couldn't sort out in my mind how I had learned what I knew about him.

Something at work triggered an idea about a way to solve my dilemma. We had a leased Lexis/Nexus dedicated terminal. This terminal provided access to a public data base of news stories. I had used it in the past to gather information for speeches I had given for the department. All you have to do is give the system the parameters for the search, and thousands of news stories are surveyed. For example, on one occasion I had asked for stories about capital punishment printed in a given time period. The system provided me 20 or 30 stories on the subject.

The Lexis/Nexus data base can also conduct a name search for a given time period. My problem was solved. I could use the computer to search newspaper stories on Zinzun. That way I could be a responsible citizen in Pasadena without drawing on police information. Perhaps I was being overcautious. Most people would have just discussed what they knew. But I had established a reputation of being a committed Christian, and I didn't want to jeopardize that reputation in any way.

Each leased Lexis/Nexus terminal costs money, so the department has only one. Since the ATD uses it the most, it's housed in their outer office. I asked the staff there for a printout of news stories on Zinzun, making it clear that *I absolutely did not want any police files searched.* I also directed the staff to seek appropriate approval for this request through their chain of command. The captain was not available at the time, and I was then the director of operations, out of their chain.

A few days later, the printout was delivered to my office. It contained more than 50 news stories about Zinzun—all material that had been printed in the public media. I took the articles home with me, intending to read them and then summarize the significant facts for John Crowley. That never occurred, however, because other priorities kept me from reading the stories. Finally, I told Esther to let John read the stories himself. I could see no problem in sharing news stories with a neighbor. There was nothing on them to connect them to the LAPD; they were clearly marked with the Lexis/Nexus logo.

On January 15, Assistant Chief Dave Dotson came into my office. He was the chief who supervised ATD, and he asked about the Lexis/Nexus printout. I was candid about my request and the purpose for it. He said he saw some problems with the request and asked me to return the documents I had received. Of course I agreed to do so.

Later in the day, out in the field, I received a call on my car phone from Dotson. He said he now wanted the documents immediately, so I drove home, got them, and took them to him. I asked him what the rush was all about. The *Times* had been tipped, he said, that I had requested and received an intelligence run from confidential police files about Zinzun. *Obviously, someone was trying to damage my reputation by spreading a lie. I was troubled that anyone—especially within the department—would stoop to this kind of character assassination.*

Dotson went on to say that Chief Gates wanted to see the documents. I accompanied him into the chief's office. Gates examined the documents and asked me to explain my reason for getting the newspaper stories. I explained. He then called the *Times* and, in my presence, talked to Bill Overend, the reporter researching the story. Gates explained that Overend's source was not telling the truth. He described what had actually occurred. He offered the reporter the opportunity to come across the street and view the documents himself.

Overend refused. He said he understood what a Lexis/Nexus terminal was all about because they had several in the *Times*'s office. Gates emphasized several times that no police files or computers were involved.

Overend asked if Gates thought that what had occurred was okay. Gates told him he thought my motives were good, that I was trying to balance my civic responsibilities in the city where I lived with my ethics as a police officer. He said that in his opinion my judgment was poor, and for that he had "chewed me out." The fact that a newspaper reporter had the impression that I had inappropriately requested and received information from confidential files was "proof" of my bad judgment, and I should have anticipated an inaccurate perception.

In spite of Gates's attempt to set the record straight, the *Times* published the lie. The following morning, the headline read: "Gates Reprimands Aide for Using *LAPD Files* for Political Research" (emphasis added). Clearly, the story led the public to believe I had inappropriately used confidential police files.

Perhaps the most blatant evidence that the *Times* was purposely trying to damage my reputation was a paragraph in the story that referred to my Christianity. It read in part: "A devout Christian and a lay minister in a fundamentalist church, Vernon in 1987 was accused by some in the Police Department of giving promotional preference to fellow Christians. He strongly denied those allegations." What the article didn't say was that an extensive IAD investigation had conclusively established those allegations to be absolutely untrue. The *Times* mentioned only the proven-false accusations, deliberately creating a misimpression.

On February 20, I wrote a letter to the publisher of the *Times*, Tom Johnson. I had met Johnson and was impressed with his character. Mutual friends confirmed my opinion and encouraged me to write directly to him. In the letter, I explained what had happened, as well as my motives. I asked that the *Times* correct its error.

On March 8, the *Times* published a "For the Record" correction. It read: "A headline in the Metro section of Feb. 16 read: 'Gates Reprimands Aide for Using LAPD Files for Political Research.' As noted in the story, the 'files' were not actual police files, but were newspaper articles and other publicly available documents stored in a commonly used computer data base. The material was retrieved for Assistant Chief Robert L. Vernon via a computer at police headquarters."

Perhaps it was a good attempt to correct the record, but they still gave the wrong impression. No LAPD computer was used. A leased terminal at our office was used to access, by phone lines, a computer available to the public. I reimbursed the city for the costs of the run. Chief officers have the privilege of using certain resources as long as they pay for them. For example, we pay for the private calls we make on our city car phones. The rationale is that our long hours at work do not allow us to tend to personal business necessities. In return for our uncompensated overtime, certain privileges are granted.

On the way home the night of March 8, when I had the opportunity to think, I became discouraged. The whole situation seemed ironic. In my zeal to adhere to my professional code of ethics and not make inappropriate use of police information, I had taken action that had been used by someone to sully my reputation with a vicious, calculated lie. That lie had been repeatedly proclaimed by the media to the public. Many people who had read the headlines would never read the "For the Record." To them, Chief Robert Vernon was a person who abused his position and power. I had a hard time dealing with that. I wanted to explain, to make everyone understand that the action I had taken was an attempt to do the right thing.

I also was curious about who had fabricated the leak to the *Times* and what the motive was. Later, in retrospect, i realized that what happened to me was just a part of the overall scheme to get rid of the Gates administration of the LAPD, to replace the department's professional leadership with people more susceptible to political control.

Michael Zinzun filed a suit against me and the city. He alleged that I had defamed him and caused him to lose the Pasadena election. He had been successful in at least two previous lawsuits, one against the Pasadena police and then the CAPA suit, where he was described by the *Times* as "playing a central role."

The suit against me came to trial just a few weeks after the Rodney King incident. The timing could not have been worse. As the trial began on April 16, 1991, the *Pasadena Star News* reported, "The videotaped beating of Rodney King by Los Angeles Police Officers became a prominent theme Monday in Pasadena Activist Michael Zinzun's lawsuit against LAPD Assistant Chief Robert Vernon."

The evidence presented in the trial seemed to clearly support my position. The sergeant from ATD testified under oath, "The Chief [Vernon] said, 'I want to make it perfectly clear that I want nothing from the files.' I took that to mean no intelligence information. . . . It was like he was asking for a copy of last week's *Wall Street Journal*." John Crowley testified he saw no classified materials, just newspaper stories. If anyone was culpable, it was the *Times*. Their story did give the impression that there was a file on Zinzun in the Anti-Terrorist Division of the LAPD. Based on the facts, I expected the jury to decide in my favor.

On May 10, however, the jury ruled in Zinzun's favor and awarded him more than $3 million in damages. Mary House, the deputy city attorney representing me, said to the press, "The jury's decision may, in part, reflect the diminished public confidence in the police as a result of the March 3rd beating of King."

I received the news of the verdict while flying to Boise, Idaho, where I was to present a seminar. The news hit me hard. The lie was now supported by court action. The newspaper stories would start all over again. I was very depressed.

Presenting my seminar the next day was extremely difficult. I had to step back from emotions, which are subjective and often unreliable, and stand on something solid. I needed encouragement from facts I knew to be true. I had committed my life to God's care. That didn't give me license to do stupid or wrong things and then expect God to bail me out, but in this situation, I had proceeded in good faith.

I know who God is—the ruler of the universe. He knows all things and doesn't make mistakes. Those facts gave me strength. I'm sure it wasn't one of my better presentations as a teacher, but I survived the day and left early that night to get home to Esther. She was taking it pretty hard as well. We needed each other.

Nearly two months later, Judge Berg, who had presided over the Zinzun lawsuit trial, took rare action. On July 2, he overturned the jury's verdict. The *Times*'s story read, "Judge Berg says there was no evidence to indicate Assistant Chief Robert Vernon's conduct defamed the black activist or caused him emotional harm."

I had been praying earnestly that the judge would do the right thing, even if that meant something other than complete exoneration for me. And I think it was more than coincidence that when responding to the objection of the plaintiff's attorney about his decision, the judge said, "I am interested in doing the right thing in this case."

The media had covered the story many times since the incident occurred in 1989. The spurious accusations against me had been repeated in every way possible. But when the court vindicated me, the stories were brief and disappeared from the news altogether after a day or so. Since that time, however, when I've been in the news, the accusations are often repeated: "Chief Vernon, who in 1989 was accused of using confidential police files for personal reasons. . . ." The beat goes on.

I never found out with absolute assurance who had given the false story to the press. Much later, a close associate of one of my competitors for the chief's job (and a man close to the mayor's office) told me that the competitor had done it. I'll probably never know for sure. What I do know is that the Zinzun incident was part of the ongoing effort to rid the LAPD of its professional leadership team and throw it wide open to political control.

11

THE CHRISTOPHER
COMMISSION

The so-called Christopher Commission gave the opponents of Chief Gates and his administration their greatest opportunity ever to push for his ouster. On June 14, 1991, I was summoned to provide testimony before the commission. It was charged by Mayor Bradley "with the responsibility of conducting a full and fair examination of the structure and operation of the LAPD" in the wake of the Rodney King incident.

The hearings were held in the Security Pacific Bank building at 5th and Hope. I arrived several minutes before my scheduled time of 9:00 A.M. Dodging the media, I slipped into an elevator and rode it to the fourteenth floor. The young lawyer from the commission staff who led me to the hearing room explained this was an executive session and that they wanted me to be candid and open. To me, "executive session" always means the testimony is confidential and will not be released to the public.

Arriving in the hearing room, I was a bit surprised it wasn't larger. The ten-member commission sat around a medium-sized conference table, and someone directed me to sit at one end. The general counsel, John Spiegel, stood at the opposite end behind a small podium. There was just enough room for a few members of the staff to sit behind the commissioners.

The chairman, Warren Christopher, put me at ease. He explained that the morning's session was devoted to the leadership of the LAPD. Then he offered me the opportunity to make an opening statement. I discussed briefly how I viewed my role within the department.

Spiegel next began to ask questions. He asked how I would implement community-based policing. I responded by rehearsing how I *did* implement the concepts when I was captain in the Venice area. I also gave my analysis of why the department had to pull back somewhat from the ideal model due to severe personnel shortages.

Spiegel then asked about the culture of the department in regard to racism and excessive force. I admitted that both of those existed within the department. I said that because we had to recruit from the human race, our recruits reflected what's happening in the general population. I voiced my opinion that the move to drive any vestige of religion from government had gone too far, and that that was a large part of the problem.

"I think there's been an overreaction on the part of some," I said, "where they're . . . afraid to even talk about morality—everyone's afraid to talk about whether something's right or wrong. I don't think that's the way to go. . . . I talk about things as being wrong or right. I don't think that is being religious. I think we can agree on some basic morality. I think it's wrong to use excessive force, and I think we ought to say that. . . . It's wrong morally to judge someone on the basis of the color of their skin. It's just plain wrong. . . .

"I think we are reaping a little bit of the whirlwind here. . . . This commission needs to go back and say, 'Let's start talking in terms of right and wrong again.' Let's not be afraid of that. I'm not talking about religion now. I'm just talking about some basic morality. . . . And there are certain basics we could agree on. Racism is wrong. It's not only wrong, it's stupid. Excessive force is wrong. . . . It's morally wrong. And there's a consensus on that in this city."

More questions were asked about excessive force. I explained that although the use of force is repugnant, it's sometimes mandatory. I stated: "Force is always gonna be necessary in police work. It's just a reality. The only question is, is it going to be reasonable? . . . It's tough to sit in that position of chief of police, and here you have someone who has committed a crime, and you've asked your officers to apprehend them, and in apprehending them they get resistance. It's tough to get that line down [the judgment between reasonable versus excessive force] in the right place—to know whether the officer has gone too far or not."

As I look back on my testimony, I realize I could have been more articulate. But the message I was trying to impart was simple. A police department takes human beings from society at large, trains them, equips them, and expects them to perform professionally at all times. That's becoming more difficult when society has lost a moral consensus. In fact, instilling principles to guide officers and supporting the training they've received is almost impossible.

That's because our culture has been saturated with the acid of relativism, which eats away at absolutes. It attacks the clear boundaries of accepted behavior. It says things may be right or wrong. Taken to the extreme, it says racism and excessive force may be all right sometimes. That's what I was trying to communicate to the commission—that all the institutions of our society need to support the idea of a moral consensus.

Even Will and Ariel Durant, self-proclaimed agnostics, acknowledge this mandate. In their book *Lessons from History,* they discuss moral codes and their necessity and then state: "A little knowledge of history stresses the variability of moral codes, and concludes that they are negligible because they differ in time and place, and sometimes contradict each other. A larger knowledge stresses the universality of moral codes, and concludes to their necessity."

This important concept was not mentioned in the commission's final report.

I also emphasized the necessity of looking at the whole picture with regard to violence. As the commissioners asked me about police violence, I urged them to not focus their attention too narrowly.

"We're looking here at one side of the equation. I think the commission needs to make a statement about the other side also. I think that this commission ought to deal with the public violence side of the equation also to see that attention is paid over here to reducing the violence, period, so that police don't have to use violence. . . . For goodness sakes, look at the police side of the equation like you are—I encourage you to do that. But I also encourage you to look at the other side of the equation."

Once again, on reflection, I could have said it better. What I was trying to communicate is that there seems to be a climate in our culture that excuses violence or resistance directed toward the police. As a result, law violators are more apt to try to evade the police, to fight them, than in years past. Many people in our society believe "that just comes with the territory." Confronted with this, the police must use force or walk away from their responsibilities. When they use force, being human, they can cross the line of reasonableness. This whole climate of violence needs to be addressed, not just police use of force.

The commission's report didn't address this issue, either.

I also called the commission's attention to our training problem in the LAPD. Our hiring schedule was (and is) controlled completely by the politicians and the city administrative officer. The mayor and the city council control the budget, as they should. Our problem was that these leaders allowed the department to gradually drop in numbers from about 7,400 to a low of about 6,800. Then the drug and gang problems got out of control, and rather than having a five-year plan for the growth of the department, these leaders mandated our hiring to go from zero growth to *adding several hundred in one year.* To make political points with the people, they actually began seeing who could add the most officers to our authorized strength. The result was that in the recent years of heavy hiring, we hired too many too quickly.

When I joined the department and graduated from the academy, I was assigned to work with an 8-year veteran. I soon learned that it took several years of experience to become an effective officer. When we shifted into a heavy hiring mode, that wise practice all but disappeared. Today it's not unusual to have a rookie working with a training officer who has all of 18 months' experience. The sharper recruits often find themselves working a 1-person car—on their own—near the end of their probationary period. This is another reason we're not adequately passing on the principles of police professionalism.

The commission failed to adequately address this problem, too. In my opinion, the commissioners did not want to address the real root causes of L.A.'s problems, the larger problems of crime, violence, and a lack of moral consensus in our society. Rather, they wanted to narrowly focus on the police and brand the officers as brutal, even though force is used in only 1 percent of all arrests made and few complaints are lodged against officers. For example, a total of 267 excessive force and improper tactics complaints were adjudicated in 1990, when 309,660 arrests were made—less than 1 complaint in every 1,000 arrests.

Perhaps the most surprising line of questions addressed my relationship with my church. The media had reported that I sought counsel regarding the issue of abortion and the department's role in policing public demonstrations on that issue.

Spiegel asked, "Could you tell us the situations where you do feel it's appropriate for you, as assistant chief, to consult the leadership of your church, and where you would follow that guidance versus maybe the secularization approach that you mentioned?"

"Yes, I'm very happy to answer that question," I said. "I believe that seeking counsel is a badge of honor. I'm not ashamed of it. I have a basic principle, and the people who work in my office get, I guess, tired of me saying it. I quote from an ancient proverb that says, 'There's wisdom in many counselors.' . . .

"That's a moral issue [abortion] that's dividing this country. On that kind of issue, I think I need counsel. . . . I wish that some three-star officer like me in Selma, Alabama, had gone and got some moral counseling and ethical counsel on whether it was right to keep blacks on the back of the bus and not allow them to get an education. I wish they had . . . some counsel instead of blindly following a law that was immoral."

I then carefully explained the implications of receiving counsel.

"Let's assume that . . . they [the elders of my church] convinced me that what city policy is asking *me* to do is against *my* moral, ethical beliefs. . . . What I would do is go to that authority over me, . . . and I would say, 'You know, what you're asking me to do, in my opinion, is immoral, and let me tell you why.' And I'd lay it out. If they'd say, 'Well, fine, we heard you, but we're still ordering you to do it,' I would resign my position. I want to make it real clear. I would not disobey or subvert. . . . If I can't get under the authority of this city, I'll leave."

My testimony before the commission consumed the entire hour, plus a little overtime. I tried to slip out of the building quietly but couldn't. At least 15 TV cameras and reporters were set up in the lobby. I refused to discuss my testimony before the commission. They asked me about seeking counsel on moral issues, and I gave them the same answers I gave the commission. For a change, most of the stories were reasonably accurate.

The commission's report was released on July 9, 1991. It was critical of the LAPD and presented a host of recommendations. Most of them were actually sound. Over the next few months, the department would respond favorably to well over 80 percent of them. For example, in recent years, because of affirmative action and other concerns, it had become difficult to fire young officers during their probationary period. Many training officers had given up trying because of the administrative hoops they had to jump through. But the commission's second recommendation to improve field training states: "The Department should encourage and facilitate FTO (Field Training Officer) efforts to terminate unsatisfactory probationers, including those exhibiting an inability to interact appropriately with the public" (p. 135). That will help the department to screen out unqualified officer candidates.

Some of the other recommendations would be rejected for good reason, however. For example, on page 148 of the commission's report, the suggestion is made that summaries of *not sustained complaints* against officers, as well as of sustained complaints, should be kept in their personnel files. "These complaints, or computer summaries, should be available to, and carefully considered by, interview boards and those making discretionary paygrade advancement decisions. . . . As with promotions, histories of 'sustained' and 'not sustained' complaints should be available to managerial officers for use in making desirable assignments."

Not sustained complaints are cases in which allegations were made, but the investigation neither proved nor disproved them. To consider such unproved charges in promotional or assignment decisions would go against the basic American belief in due process. Besides, it's well known that some criminal groups have filed false complaints against officers who are particularly effective in order to damage their careers.

In the end, the civilian police commission would support the department's position on some of the rejections. Others would be modified to make them realistic and practical. From my perspective, however, the commission's conclusions were a greater problem than most of the specific recommendations.

For example, the commission used the mobile digital transmitter (MDT) messages to arrive at the conclusion that racism was rampant within the LAPD. They quoted some messages that were indeed outrageous and racist. What they didn't say was that of the thousands of MDT messages they reviewed, less than two-tenths of 1 percent had anything in them that could be considered racist, sexist, or condoning of excessive force. My point is not to say that even one racist message should be condoned. The tolerance level should be zero. I'm just saying that the commission made dishonest use of the data to build a case for a pervasive problem.

The report generated much interest. I believe it will be used well by many police departments to develop excellence and professionalism. But the underlying problems were ignored. Police must still cope with increasingly violent behavior by a growing criminal army. They must still face a virtual civilization crisis with insufficient resources and support. They are scrutinized, criticized, and second-guessed as they attempt an impossible task.

The next day, July 10, I experienced my biggest disappointment relative to the Christopher Commission when it published the executive-session testimony of Chief Gates, myself, and the two other assistant chiefs. I wasn't worried about my testimony being released, even though I thought the commission broke its word to do so. But those things happen in the political world. What hurt me deeply was the testimony of Jesse Brewer.

I thought he was my friend. I had known him for many years and enjoyed working with him. He had reported to me in his role as deputy chief. I had recommended that he be promoted to assistant chief, to be one of my peers, and I was delighted when Chief Gates did so. After the announcement of his promotion, Esther and I honored him at our annual Christmas party in our home. I thought we had good communication and mutual respect.

The Christopher Commission report all but recommended the removal of Chief Gates. Jesse Brewer's testimony did the same to me. Here is an excerpt:

Brewer: "I'm going to be very critical of one of the assistant chiefs here, and that's Robert Vernon."

Spiegel: "Why don't you tell us your views on Robert Vernon."

Brewer: "I think Robert Vernon is back in the '50s. I think Robert Vernon is a very, very conservative person. I think he is devious. I think he has his own agenda. I think he promotes people that he thinks or have similar beliefs."

Spiegel: "Do you mean religious beliefs?"

Brewer: "Religious beliefs."

Holliday: "There's a term for them in the department, Chief. You can tell us that this is . . ."

Brewer: "He's the head of the God Squad, as we refer to it. The way to get ahead, it's commonly known that the way you get ahead as far as Vernon is concerned is to become aligned either with his church or to profess that you are born again."

Spiegel: "A born again . . .?"

Brewer: "Christian. Yes."

Spiegel: "Christian fundamentalist."

The commissioners then asked Brewer about specific officers (although their names were deleted in the documents released), inquiring if they were Christian. It gives the appearance that they were searching for a subversive group. They apparently thought it was appropriate to formally identify and label police officials on the basis of their religious beliefs. I was shocked.

Commissioner Richard Mosk may have felt uncomfortable about the substance of the testimony regarding religion. At the conclusion of Brewer's testimony, the following exchange was recorded:

Mosk: "Last question. Since we discussed what you referred to as the God Squad, the religion and so forth, have you detected any religious intolerance within the department or any circle within the department, that is of any particular religions or either in hiring or discipline or community or otherwise?"

Brewer: "I'm afraid I can't say I can put my finger on any indication that that exists."

Near the end of his testimony, Brewer was asked his opinion on the willingness or capability of Chief Gates and his assistants to carry out the recommendations of the commission.

Brewer replied: "I think the biggest, I would say Chief Vernon should not be in the Office of Operations. . . . In fact, he probably should be gone, in my opinion, because I feel he might be an obstacle."

"Deeply hurt" doesn't begin to adequately communicate my reaction to Jesse Brewer's testimony. In all our years of working together, breaking bread together, and enduring struggles together, he had never given a hint of these feelings. My thoughts went back to our last luncheon, ironically just a few hours before the Rodney King tape was given to me. The purpose of the luncheon was to receive candid feedback from a friend. He had said nothing of this—not even a clue.

I still have trouble understanding what happened to my friendship with Jesse Brewer. Was I mistaken all those years? Was he faking friendship, all the while suspecting my character and motives, or had something happened to cause him to change his relationship to me? Had I done or said something to produce his distrust and lack of respect?

Weeks later, Mayor Bradley appointed Brewer to the police commission. I met with him privately after one of the meetings and told him how disappointed I was over his testimony. I tried to let him know how much I had been hurt that he had never said those things to me face to face—that I thought we were friends. He apologized, stating he didn't want to hurt me, that he didn't know his testimony would be released. He missed the whole point.

Reflecting on his appearance before the commission, I noticed something peculiar. In the opening paragraph of his testimony, General Counsel Spiegel referred to a meeting of preparation. Unlike the other witnesses, Jesse Brewer met with a staff lawyer the day before his testimony. Then, throughout his testimony, he was asked leading questions, as if to remind him to cover certain issues.

Another fact makes me curious. The whole issue of the "God Squad," including the name—which I take as a religious slur—was a rehash of earlier rumors.

On July 12, 1987, the *Times* ran an article with the headline: "Piety in LAPD's Ranks Raises Concern, 'Born-Again' Christians Occupy Key Positions." The story discussed the perception that a "born-again Christian 'hierarchy' within the force" existed. Members of the police union said some believed that to get ahead, one needed to be identified as a "born again."

Mr. R. Samuel Paz, chairman of the police commission's Hispanic Advisory Council, sent a letter to the commission at that time, asking that an investigation be conducted to determine if the allegations in the article were true or false. An investigation was done and found the allegations to be without validity.

A disgruntled officer made essentially the same allegations. Apparently he wanted to be promoted to higher rank. According to his complaint, he discussed his ambition and frustration in achieving it with at least one other officer, and that officer told him that the way to get ahead was to affiliate with my church or beliefs. I'm not questioning whether that conversation took place. Whether it did or not, the alleged statement of the other officer is just not true. Promotions in the LAPD are based on civil service tests prepared and administered by the city's personnel department. I couldn't "rig" them even if I wanted to.

I don't doubt, however, that some officers in the department honestly believed the rumors. An event early in my career gives me some understanding of that type of perception.

I was walking out of Highland Park Police Station one day with some study material from our small library. One of my fellow officers passed me in the parking lot.

"Hey, Vernon, are you studying for sergeant?" the man asked.

I was a little embarrassed, almost like being caught doing something wrong. "Yeah, John. I thought I would give it at least one try," I answered.

"Well, let me give you some advice. If you want to get anywhere in this department, get the ring on."

"Get the ring on? What do you mean?"

"You know, join the Masons. Get in a lodge. All the brass are Masons. Chief Murdock is high up in the lodge. He's about to be chief potentate of the Shriners. You want to get ahead, join up and wear the ring."

He was sincere. I could see it in his eyes. I wondered if he was right. I should have known better, but I did wonder.

Well, I didn't join. I had other priorities. Besides, I wanted to believe that merit and hard work had something to do with promotions, not affiliation or politics. I took the sergeant's exam and scored near the top of the list on all portions. I was promoted rapidly. Later, I ran into my friend and told him he was wrong.

Based on that experience, however, I wouldn't be surprised if some people in the LAPD assumed I pushed people ahead who believed as I do. They were wrong. I had no control over the civil service process, and those in city government knew that. I did make many personnel decisions regarding *assignments*, and my 38-year record will show that I made those decisions based on performance and merit.

My betrayal by someone I thought to be a friend was another blow in a series of disappointments and character assassination. After my confrontations with the enemies of police intelligence in 1983, my public image began to suffer. I had been unfairly condemned as responsible for spying abuse. Then came the rumors of religious preference in 1987. Although the investigation had exonerated me, the cloud remained.

The fabricated leak to the media on the Zinzun matter and the subsequent lawsuit came next. Then followed the *Los Angeles Magazine* article on "The Dan Quayle Principle" and the investigation requested by Yaroslavsky. For the last several years I was a regular in the media, but definitely not in a good light. To many people, Bob Vernon appeared to be a radical religious fanatic. I had been painted as someone who improperly used his position to advance his personal agenda, someone who tried to force his beliefs and morality on others and who subverted public policy.

I've followed the media's humiliation of many public figures. I thought I understood the feeling some of them have had when falsely accused. I did not. Words can't express the frustration, anger, sadness, hurt, and depression. When you value your reputation, as most people do, it's devastating to have it sullied. It also hurts to see those whom you love grieving for you. On many nights, I came home to find Esther in tears because she had just seen the six o'clock news and was troubled to the point of being sick. My oldest grandson asked me why the TV and newspapers said certain things about me.

I had heard about the connection between anger and depression, and now I experienced both emotions. I was angry about the lies, and that led to depression. Before, I had difficulty understanding depression. Rarely had I knowingly been afflicted with it. Now I understand. I had difficulty sleeping. The future looked bleak. At times, I was immersed in a feeling of gloom. Even my appetite was affected. I wanted to withdraw at the time I most needed support and encouragement.

Neighbors and people at our church have been very supportive. Many have written letters and notes of encouragement, voicing their frustration at the unfair attacks. Most of their support is a result of having the wisdom to see through the false accusations. The troubling fact is that some of them remain supportive yet either believe or at least question the truthfulness of some of the charges. How much of that condition exists, only God knows.

The grief has been most profound, however, due to reasons that may not be obvious. I've made a deliberate decision to publicly identify with Jesus Christ. On my off-duty time, I have declared my belief in Him as the Son of God and my Savior. I have taken opportunities to speak at churches, Christian conferences, prayer breakfasts, and similar meetings. As far as my position with the police department is concerned, I've tried to honor God by pursuing excellence in my work.

A principle appears many times in the Bible regarding this issue: "Whatever you do, do your work heartily, as for the Lord rather than for men" (Colossians 3:23). The many references to this principle and the context clearly indicate this should be the way true believers best give evidence to their faith. I have attempted to live out this principle.

Many people have asked me, "Do you express your faith at work?" My response is always, "I hope so. I hope that my commitment, diligence, compassion, and integrity give silent but powerful witness to my faith. But if you're asking whether I preach to arrestees and fellow officers, the answer is rarely. And when I do, it's always off duty. I believe the city of Los Angeles hired me to be a police officer, not a preacher."

I have taken extreme measures to appropriately discharge the public trust. When I rose in the ranks to the point where I was receiving calls and correspondence from the Christian community, which is a legitimate part of Los Angeles, I hired a private secretary and purchased personal stationary. I have been very careful to not give a perception of bringing religious proselytizing or preference to on-the-job activities or decisions. Yet that was the very thing I was accused of doing.

The deep hurt I experienced was that those false accusations and rumors were bringing shame to the God I try to honor and serve. My identification with Him now brought His name into all the allegations. My biggest fear—of bringing discredit to the name of Jesus—had come true.

I pray daily about this whole experience. My humanity wants to be delivered from it. I want the truth to be told. I want the deception exposed and the wrongs righted. So far, however, God's answers have been: "No," "Wait on the Lord," and "My grace is sufficient for you." Frankly, I haven't welcomed those answers. At first, I became angry when God did not answer our prayers the way we wanted, when we wanted. I wanted some action, and I wanted it now. It didn't make sense to me. Why was God allowing this to happen? Why wouldn't He step in and rescue us?

In the context of L.A. politics, however, I realized that the attacks on my integrity were a part of the larger campaign to rid the LAPD of its professional leadership, and especially of anyone in the top echelon seen as an ally of Daryl Gates. Those attacks would continue unabated.

12

BRINGING SUIT
AGAINST THE CITY

Being a cop for more than 37 years, I have investigated many people. I've surveilled them, collected information on them, and interrogated them. I've never looked on those investigations as being threatening in themselves. My attitude has been that an innocent person should not be afraid of being examined. Now that I've been under the microscope myself, however, I have a different perspective. It hasn't been fun.

I still feel that innocent people shouldn't fear the uncovering of the truth. But I understand better some other implications of an investigation. In my case, City Councilman Zev Yaroslavsky went to the media in the summer of 1991, in the midst of the Christopher Commission hearings, to announce the investigation of me. He deliberately broke ethical standards. He broadcast anonymous and unsubstantiated rumors as allegations. Being investigated is one thing. Having the allegations and the investigation announced to the world is something else.

To me, what was happening was now clear. I was being "taken out" because I was not politically correct. My traditional Christian beliefs were no longer tolerated by certain power brokers. I began to realize that my faith—as well as my allegiance to Chief Gates—was going to cost me my job.

The June 15, 1991, edition of the *Times* carried a story that summed up my thoughts. The headline read: "Vernon Sees His Police Ambitions Fading." The article quoted me correctly as saying: "My reputation is going down the tube. Without divine intervention, I am all through as far as my career." The story rehearsed the events of the preceding weeks and the initiation of the investigation.

Ramona Ripston, executive director of the ACLU, was also quoted. She justified the investigation, saying, "I don't necessarily say that where there is smoke there is fire. But I would say that where there is smoke, you always investigate to find out whether or not there is fire."

I wonder if she would use that same reasoning if she were being investigated by the FBI on some unsubstantiated charge that she was a dangerous revolutionary? I think not.

The story did include an encouraging statement from a retired LAPD commander, Larry Kramer, who went on to become the police chief in Colorado Springs, Colorado. He said: "There was never any confusion as to whether or not Bob Vernon was a born-again Christian. I think it is just such an integral part of who he is, and what he is all about. Many times his personal beliefs would intertwine, like a tapestry, with his professional beliefs. . . . But I don't recall any instance where his judgment was clouded because of his religious convictions."

My career was fading. That caused me disappointment and, of course, uncertainty about the future. But an even bigger fear entered my mind. Was my experience an indication of the beginning of the end for religious freedom in America? I sensed there had been a gradual but powerful surge toward intolerance by the media and political elite. Many of those molders of policy and public opinion have very narrow minds toward thoughts that don't match theirs.

Just today, for example, as I was working on this book, my wife called my attention to a nationwide talk show on TV. The subject was homosexuality, and the hostess was getting opinions from members of the audience. A woman stood to speak and began by saying, "I am a Christian, and the Bible says—"

The hostess immediately interrupted with "We don't want to hear about the Bible" and went on to another person.

In a second example, the U.S. Supreme Court recently ruled that high school graduation ceremonies may not include an invocation. This rule applies even if every graduating student wants to have the commencement solemnized by a prayer. Intolerance abounds.

On June 19, 1991, a local Christian radio talk-show host, John Stewart, organized a rally at police headquarters. Several hundred people attended to demonstrate their concern about the investigation. The *Times* reported the following day that Stewart "called on the Police Commission, the City Council, Mayor Tom Bradley and others to halt the investigation into Vernon, which he called 'an inquisition' and 'religious McCarthyism.'"

The story went on to quote Stewart: "What seems to be on trial here is religion in general, Christianity in particular. The inquisitors want you to keep your religion inside your church or inside your synagogue, and it must not influence your life, especially if you are in public service."

Mary Jordan, a retired teacher attending the rally, was quoted as saying: "Christians are becoming an endangered species in political life. I really think our days are numbered. We have to support people in leadership who stand on principle."

As I reflected on the investigation and what various people said that day, I came to a stark realization. This was a serious situation—not just for me, but for freedom. I began to see this growing intolerance as a first step toward what happened in totalitarian countries like Stalin's USSR. Perhaps it was a small step, but it was significant nonetheless.

As I took my turn at the rally microphone, I warned the audience not to let our nation take that first step. "We can't allow that to happen in America. It must not happen in America. It shall not happen in America. What America is all about is racial and religious tolerance, not exclusion. And that is what I see here today. This is not just a rally for Christian freedom, this is a rally for religious freedom, and for that I am very grateful."

The rally was a great encouragement to me. I wasn't alone. Many saw through the veil of deception and manipulation. Many were concerned about this blatant frontal attack on religion.

Tim Rutten, a columnist for the *Times,* wrote an editorial on June 14, 1991, about the issue that was surprisingly supportive. In it he agreed with Chief Gates's categorizing of the investigation as a witch-hunt. He wrote:

"He's right [Gates]. So are those who say that Vernon's views are being quoted selectively and out of context. None of the council members, police commissioners or civil libertarians to whom I spoke this week has listened to the tapes. One had read the interview."

Later in his editorial, he summarized the heart of the issue: "In point of fact, this disturbing affair involves a confrontation between two serious groups of people acting on behalf of legitimate--indeed, indispensable—rights. On the one hand are those who rightly insist that the police department must not discriminate against anyone. On the other are those who just as correctly insist that no agency of government may hold a man or woman accountable for his or her religious beliefs.

"In such a confrontation, the guarantor of civility is due process. And by its standards, Vernon is getting a raw deal. This inquiry did not begin because of something Vernon did, but because of something he said. On that basis and on the word of anonymous accusers, who cannot be seen or confronted and who offer no specific evidence, the police chief has been asked to investigate whether his assistant's private religious convictions have, in some wholly unspecified way, influenced the conduct of his duties.

"That is not an investigation; that is a fishing expedition."

The whole situation really started to come into focus. I had to look at it from a broader perspective. To this point, I had been concerned only about myself. I didn't like what was happening to me. But this was bigger than me. I was involved, like it or not, in a struggle that would set a precedent. I had to begin looking at this conflict as a matter of principle.

This was a strategic move against religious freedom, a crucial strike that will have nationwide impact. A victory in Los Angeles almost assures a trend that eventually sweeps the nation. If this action was allowed to go unchallenged, it would be repeated in city after city. Christians would ultimately be forced out of public life unless this violation of basic rights was stopped dead in its tracks. I began to realize that if I did nothing, other people of sincere religious convictions would also be victimized.

Until then, I really had not considered taking civil action. I had talked to the U.S. Attorney, hoping her office would move swiftly to stop the abuse of my civil rights. Although she admitted there may indeed be some violations, she told me to consult a private attorney.

I've always viewed being involved in a civil lawsuit as repugnant. There's something about it I just don't like. Perhaps it's because I believe so many people abuse the system. I also have had friends who have sued, and their experience has not been good. Civil litigation is expensive, too, and I'm not wealthy. Furthermore, civil litigation usually takes years. During the lengthy process, the emotional drain is heavy. I've heard it said that nobody really wins in a lawsuit except the attorneys. I didn't want to sue.

Then I read a tongue-in-cheek letter to the editor of the *Times* signed by James MacQuarrie of Monrovia:

"Yes, by all means, let's investigate Vernon's religious beliefs, and use them as a weapon against him. We must purge Los Angeles of this too-prevalent belief in the existence of God.

"After we remove the last vestiges of Christianity from City government, we can set to work on the greater task of purging our citizens of it. I recommend a law requiring all Christians to wear large yellow crosses on their clothing, so we can see them from a safe distance, lest their pernicious doctrines of love and forgiveness and salvation disrupt our prized independence and self-realization. Then after we round them up and put them safely away, we can take a look at the Jews among us."

Reading that letter sobered me. This was not small potatoes. The thought hit me that if I let the investigation go on unchallenged, I would be guilty of standing by while a major erosion of rights took place. I began thinking about doing more than just answering questions from the media. I started talking to friends about the issue. Esther and I prayed for guidance.

People and events caused us to think further about legal action. One such event was an encounter with Ken Poure, a close friend since college days in the early 1950s. He's one of the godliest men I know and has more common sense than most, too.

Later that summer, Esther and I were on vacation. We stopped off the highway to have lunch at a McDonald's in Fresno, California. I had just pulled out my wallet to pay for our meal when I heard Ken's familiar voice in the next line over. My head snapped around. He saw and recognized me at about the same time. We sat down to eat together, and I explained what we were going through.

"Well," he said, "what are you going to do, just take it? I think you should go on the offensive. You don't believe in anything weird. Most of the people in America would not think your beliefs are strange at all."

To make sure I didn't miss his point, he added, "You're not some type of wimp. God knows you can handle it or He wouldn't have allowed you to go through this. Things are going according to plan. But in my opinion, you've got to take the attack. Don't apologize for your beliefs. Your beliefs are right. Get in their face. Reveal them for how weird they are."

It's always encouraging for me to be around Ken, and that day was no exception. As I look back on it, the odds of our meeting in that restaurant were remote. My resolve to take some action was being formed.

A little later, a mutual friend introduced me to David Casterline. David, a partner with Tim Agajanian in a Los Angeles law firm, was interested in my case. He had been reading the papers and didn't like what he saw happening; he thought my civil rights were being violated. I began meeting with him to discuss my situation. He also conducted relevant legal research. But I was still hesitant to file a suit.

I consulted a personal friend of many years who is also an attorney. He urged me to move slowly and deliberately. He also reviewed the facts of the situation and discussed them with some of his associates.

In the early fall, things began to come together. My friend and David Casterline were brought together. My friend also introduced me to William Bentley Ball, a foremost barrister on the issue of the U.S. Constitution and religious rights. A consensus began to develop from their combined wisdom: My case demanded civil litigation.

Mr. Ball was later to write:

"[Your] case is direct and simple: Government may not invade the religious conscience of its citizens. People have constitutional rights to freedom of religious belief and association. They may consult their minister, priest or rabbi without reporting to government agencies. Under our Constitution, religious tests for public office are forbidden. Acts and allegations of actual misconduct may be investigated, but religious beliefs are protected against censure and even from disclosure.

"The city's investigation violates these sacred principles. City officials deliberately went to the media to cast aspersions on [you], and to publicize their attack. They stated openly that their investigation was intended to determine whether Chief Vernon's conduct, unquestionably legal, was motivated by his religion-based values.

"The object of the investigation is not Chief Vernon's actions but his thoughts."

That was chilling. *Thought control.* If their action was allowed to go unchecked, where would it stop? In my case, because of my religious beliefs and my decision to talk about them—off duty—I was under suspicion. Some powerful people in city government and in the ACLU were stereotyping me as a born-again Christian. Using an unconstitutional "undifferentiated fear," without any evidence of wrongdoing, they "just knew" I must be violating antidiscrimination laws or department policies because of my religion. To make it even more absurd, their interpretation of my religious beliefs, either by design or by ignorance, was based on gross distortions of those beliefs.

The decision to investigate my religion sends a loud warning to public employees of other faiths as well: Be wary. Don't show your faith in public or you, too, may be the object of prejudice, ridicule, groundless investigation, and discrimination.

Esther has a deep sense of justice. She doesn't get rattled about many things, but injustice "bugs" her. She is vexed when she sees an injustice occur against anyone. Another thing about Esther: In my opinion, she's the ultimate lady. Most of our acquaintances describe her as having class. But her whole demeanor can change when she feels I am endangered. And when you put those things together, Esther can be aggressive. Her perception that I was being unjustly attacked made her ready to fight.

On September 23, we attended a private dinner honoring retired Police Commissioner Sam Williams. The party was hosted by Commission Chairman Stanley Sheinbaum and his wife at their home in Bel Air. Sam Williams had always seemed fair to me, and I wanted to acknowledge his years of service, even though I knew it would be awkward for Esther and me. Many of the people who were hurting us would be there.

The social hour came to an abrupt close when an unusual squall began pelting the guests with large drops of rain. We all moved quickly into the spacious house. The tables were set throughout the large living and dining areas. The Sheinbaums are art collectors, and paintings and sculpture adorned practically every wall and appropriate area. Knowing some people in the room would be uncomfortable sitting near us, Esther and I rushed to an empty table in a corner. That way, people could choose or reject our company as they wished. Councilman Joel Wachs, Councilwoman Joy Picus and her husband, and another couple joined us.

Mayor Tom Bradley and the honoree were at the head table with the Sheinbaums, along with Chief Gates and his wife. The conversation there promised to be interesting—normally Gates and Bradley didn't speak to each other.

We had just started on the main course when one of the waiters asked if the people at our table could make room for a late-arriving couple. We began moving in closer when Esther elbowed me in the ribs and darted her eyes toward the entry hall. The late arrivals were Mr. and Mrs. Zev Yaroslavsky.

As they were led to our table, I thought I saw a look of "Oh, no!" on his face. All of us welcomed them. They were in the middle of sitting down when a bolt of lightning flashed across the sky with a loud clap of thunder. Zev was startled along with the rest of us—maybe even more so, because he was looking right out the window.

"Did you see that?" he almost shouted. "A bolt of lightning!"

Esther couldn't resist the opportunity. "Of course," she answered. "God has a sense of humor. With as much friction as there is between you and my husband, no wonder there's lightning."

That broke the ice and ushered in a time of light-hearted exchange. Actually, we enjoyed the evening.

We continued to consult with our friends about what we should do. The investigation of my faith continued. I formally asked Commissioner Brewer for a copy of the document ordering Chief Gates to conduct the investigation. He first replied that he wasn't sure one existed. Then he said he would have to consult his fellow commissioners. I thought I had a right to see the specifics of charges against me under the California Police Officers Bill of Rights.

I also consulted the board of elders at my church. I wanted to be sure I wouldn't take any action contrary to Scripture. Some Christians believe we are not to challenge people when we're wronged but to "turn the other cheek" instead.

My situation seemed covered by another principle in the Bible, however. When the apostle Paul was treated unfairly—indeed, unlawfully—by the Roman government, he demanded his rights as a citizen. My situation seemed similar. I wasn't considering civil action in order to "get even" with those who had done wrong. My reasons were threefold. First, a basic American freedom had been violated. Second, if unchecked, this violation of religious liberty would probably spread. Finally, the government needed to speak out on this issue. A precedent would be set one way or the other. If I took no action, an evil, un-American precedent would be set. But taking civil action would force the issue and maybe stop this form of evil.

I explained my position to the elder board, and they saw no reason why I should not proceed.

The investigation continued into late October. The witch-hunt had been going on for five months and was wearing on us. We finally decided to go forward with a civil suit. It was filed in the U.S. district court on November 4, 1991.

The headline the next day declared, "Vernon Files Suit to Block Investigation. Calls City's Religion Inquiry 'Witch-Hunt.'" Commissioner Sheinbaum was quoted as saying, "We knew this was coming."

On November 22, 1991, the City News Service reported that the city attorney's office would not represent the city or the individual defendants. Deputy City Attorney Linda Lefkowitz was quoted as saying, "We felt ethically constrained not to handle this case." Now the city would have to hire an outside firm.

Meanwhile, the bombardment continued. Sheinbaum appeared on the Geraldo Rivera show "Now It Can Be Told" that aired on December 10. In its usual style, the show sensationalized my personal beliefs. Sheinbaum cooperated with them fully, saying, "He [Vernon] will never tell us he didn't hire X or Y because she's a woman or he's gay. He will never say that. So we don't have a smoking gun, in that sense. All we can do is keep the pressure up."

Without any due process or finding of guilt on my part, this member of the national board of the ACLU pronounced his religious bigotry. He continued, "He should get out. He shouldn't be turning to people in other organizations for decisions about what to do in this organization. He's got a responsibility to the public. His church isn't paying his salary, the public is."

Ironically, the very next day, December 11, the *Times* reported, "Inquiry Clears

Vernon of Religious Favoritism on the Job." The *Daily News* reported, "An LAPD investigation has been closed after finding no evidence that Assistant Chief Robert L. Vernon let his religious views affect police operations, according to court papers filed Tuesday."

Those papers were filed by attorneys for the city in reaction to my request for a preliminary injunction to stop the investigation. The *Times* reported that the judge had refused my injunction, saying that since the investigation was now over, the matter had become moot. According to the *Times*, he "cited a sworn statement released last week by Chief Daryl F. Gates, in which Gates said an LAPD investigation of Vernon, requested by the Police Commission, had turned up no evidence of wrongdoing."

The stories about the investigation's clearing me from all wrongdoing ran one day. But in the future, other stories would rehash the rumors and stereotyping. Few if any would refer to the fact that a six-month inquiry had found no truth in the wild accusations.

As we proceeded toward trial, I began to look forward to putting the rumormongers on the witness stand for cross-examination. I wanted those who had made general allegations to be pinned down to specifics.

On February 25, 1992, we had our next appearance in court. The defense had filed motions for summary judgment. In other words, they asked the judge to throw the case out before it ever went to trial. One of my attorneys, William Bentley Ball, had flown out from Pennsylvania to represent me. When the hearing began, the following exchange took place between him and the judge.

> Judge: "Who speaks for the plaintiff?"
> Ball: "I will, Your Honor."
> Judge: "I am going to ask you first to tell me, in response to the comments that I made, what injury you claim under the exercise clause other than the fact that an investigation was started?"
> Ball: "Your Honor, here a demand was made that this man's religion be investigated, his religious beliefs and associations. Now here we are at the most basic fact of this case. I completely disagree. And here is where we have a major collision of fact as to what this demand was all

about. When you read the Lomax declaration—"

Judge: "Mr. Ball, respectfully, and I am going to say this to you right at the outset. I am not here for a dissertation."

Ball: "I don't intend to give you one, Your Honor."

Judge: "You respond to my comment. What injury do you allege? That's the question. If you don't intend to answer my inquiry, then I don't want to hear from you."

Ball: "That this had a very chilling effect on his religious profession."

Judge: "Thank you very much. You may be seated."

Ball appeared stunned. I was shocked. In my many years of experience with various courts and judges, I have never seen an attorney cut off so rudely. Ball sat down. He had thoroughly prepared to present briefly the basic issues of our case, and the judge would not allow him to do so. He wanted to present the fact that an investigation had been ordered because of my religious beliefs, an investigation that was conducted amid damaging press releases by the city without any specific charges being made.

The judge made more statements about the case and allowed the defendants' attorneys to comment liberally about their position.

Then another issue was addressed. The judge asked Mr. Ball to specify what the defendants had done "that offended the First Amendment."

Ball: "Here is a part of this mandate which directs attention to his personal beliefs."

Judge: "But, only insofar as his personal beliefs may or may not have interfered with his role as an Assistant Police Chief. Isn't that the import of the letter?"

Ball: "No, I don't think so, Your Honor. I think as Mr. Sheinbaum said in his deposition, he didn't see how you could focus on those beliefs in relation to their impact on conduct without knowing what those beliefs are. It seems to me this entire investigation was rooted in concerns over the plaintiff's religious beliefs."

Judge: "That may be your conclusion. You may be the only one in the courtroom who thinks that. All right, thank you."

Ball: "May I add this merely—"

Judge: "No, you may not."

Once again, I couldn't believe what I had witnessed. The judge was not allowing fair representation. Mr. Ball has a national reputation on the subject before the court, yet he was not being allowed to speak.

But rudeness to Ball was not the most shocking action by the court. The judge had ignored the central issue in the case—namely, whether government may mandate an investigation of a citizen's religious beliefs and associations.

Thus, the judge pared away the most important portion of our case, but he didn't grant the summary judgment. We were not happy with our treatment. Our main complaint about the attack on my free exercise of religion was gone. We couldn't understand why the judge had taken that action. But we had a court date of March 10 on the rest of our case. A jury would hear the facts. I would finally be able to confront the witnesses.

13

CHOOSING
A NEW CHIEF

We were moving toward a jury trial, but in the meanwhile, much had happened. The process for the selection of the new chief of police had begun in late 1991. For the first time since 1938, there would be no objective test in the examination process. As many of us had feared, another step was taken in politicizing the LAPD.

During the reform of the late 1930s, a fair and effective promotional system had been set in place. To prevent excessive political influence, an objective test became a key part of that civil service process.

When I competed for the chief's job in 1978, all the candidates were subjected to a nine-hour written exam. Half of the day, we wrote essays on relevant issues. The other half, we responded to an "in basket" exercise. The entire process was monitored by proctors. We weren't allowed to bring in any materials to assist us. Later, our responses were typed, and coded numbers replaced our names. That way, when the experts graded our papers, they had no idea whose tests they were scoring.

This time there would be no objective examination graded "in the blind." Those doing the choosing would have ample opportunity to include or eliminate a specific person. I didn't like it. Neither did many of my peers. I felt at the time that I would not be selected, but I submitted my application anyway. I would give it my best shot. (Former LAPD detective Mike Rothmiller wrote in a recent book of a meeting on March 19, 1992, with Stanley Sheinbaum and others, in which Sheinbaum assured him the next chief would come from *outside* the department.)

Another pivotal event had occurred in the fall of 1991. California Governor Pete Wilson had vetoed a so-called homosexual rights bill. Certain spokespeople from homosexual political action groups claimed that he had promised to support such a bill and had now betrayed them. In any event, mass protests began to occur in the streets of L.A. almost every night. I gave directions to our officers to follow the long-standing LAPD policy regarding civil disobedience and law breaking.

That policy is to professionally and impartially enforce the law. Those who choose to violate the law are arrested. For example, if people parade without a permit, trespass, or "sit in," they are arrested. If they go limp, they are forced to cooperate with the arresting officer by the use of "come along" holds (commonly referred to as pain compliance). This policy has been applied with consistency for many years, whatever the cause of the protesters.

In the recent past, I had taken a lot of criticism over the department's enforcement action against Operation Rescue. On March 25, 1989, our officers had made more than 700 arrests in conjunction with a "rescue." Over the next 2 years, we would arrest many other pro-life demonstrators. I agree with Operation Rescue's goal of saving the lives of unborn babies, but I disagree with some of the organization's methods. After much thought, prayer, and counsel when the first L.A. rescues were announced, however, I decided I could enforce the law regarding their actions with objectivity and consistency.

City Councilman Michael Woo didn't give me credit for such objectivity. At the time of that first confrontation in March 1989, he publicly attacked my integrity. The *Times* reported he questioned my ability to fairly and impartially enforce the law in conjunction with the abortion debate.

In response, I wrote Woo a letter expressing my indignation. I assured him that although I had personal opinions on issues like abortion, my long record with the LAPD proved I was willing and able to enforce the law fairly and without bias.

"It is outrageous," I wrote, "to publicly suggest that in the future I may not continue to honor that proven professional commitment. Such statements are not only unfair but demonstrate religious bigotry. Would it be right to suggest that

Assistant Chief Jesse Brewer [a black man] would not fairly provide police leadership at a demonstration against racial bias just because he is an outspoken critic of that bias? Of course not. That would be equally outrageous."

I asked him to correct the news report if he had been misquoted. If he had been quoted correctly, however, I requested an apology for wrongfully bringing shame to my name and reputation.

Woo ignored my letter completely.

The abortion issue has divided the nation, and the controversy about the role of law enforcement at the sometimes-violent demonstrations has been very public. Among those of us who want to prevent the murder of babies, there are many opinions about the best tactics. I believe strongly that we should stay within the law. I believe the 700 who were arrested in March 1989 would have saved more babies if they had participated in lawful sidewalk counseling. That many people, scheduled over the whole year, could have covered the involved abortion clinic every day. But I have sincere Christian friends who strongly disagree with me. Many of them have voiced intense criticism of the arrest posture of the LAPD.

My main argument for not treating pro-life demonstrators with special arrest procedures is *consistency*. I have told them that the LAPD has a consistent record in dealing with demonstrators who use the tactic of passive resistance. Integrity mandates that all those who use civil disobedience to make their statement get the same treatment.

When the illegal homosexual demonstrations began in the fall of 1991, I again reminded everyone in the department of our policy and the importance of consistency. Some at the executive level argued otherwise, however. They said the homosexuals were "understandably upset" and that we should be tolerant and allow them to vent some of their frustration and anger.

I knew I was already viewed as antihomosexual. I wanted to make sure every step I took was professional and did not even appear to be due to my personal beliefs. I brought up the subject at Chief Gates's next staff meeting. The Thursday morning meetings included all bureau commanding officers. That means all those attending had at least one star on their collars.

The chief went through his agenda. Then he started the around-the-table ritual, giving each of us an opportunity to introduce a subject. When it was my turn, I brought up my concern about the first night of homosexual protests. Demonstrators had taken over a few intersections, jumped on some cars, and paraded down certain streets, causing traffic jams.

In response, some in the room played down the problems. They argued that the demonstrators needed to let off steam and that it would soon be over. I compared that lenient approach with the very different approach we had taken toward Operation Rescue, and I again emphasized the need for consistency.

I probably made a mistake bringing up the pro-life issue as a point of comparison. No doubt some in the room turned off everything else I said, chalking up my comments to "Vernon's religious agenda." They missed the whole point.

As for the chief, he was either preoccupied or didn't realize the seriousness of what I felt was our neglect. His orders were general: Field commanders should use good judgment and continue to comply with our policies. My whole point was that they were *not* following our established policies.

Several days went by. The demonstrations did not stop—they got worse. One night, demonstrators marched through the airport, practically closing it down for nearly 45 minutes. Many people missed their flights. In addition to parading without a permit, several other violations of the law occurred. Demonstrators jumped on car hoods. Windows were broken. LAPD officers actually led the illegal parade. The disruption was far more significant than blocking the doorway to an abortion clinic.

Captain Pat McKinley, CO of Metro Division, later told me he was ashamed to get out of his vehicle as he sat there in his uniform. He had been directed to stand down by the field commander, and he didn't want the victims of crimes to see him involved in what he thought was neglect of duty.

At the next Thursday morning staff meeting, on October 10, 1991, I didn't have to bring up the subject again. Maurice Moore, who had been promoted to commander, brought it up instead. He had been at one of the demonstrations where the homosexuals had blocked streets and intersections. He described in detail some of the blatant violations of the law and the understandably irate victims. He also described the tough but fair position the California Highway Patrol officers had taken at the same incident. (Apparently, when the homosexuals tried to get on the freeway, they stopped them cold on the on-ramp.) Moore said our officers were asking why we were allowing the lawlessness.

Chief Gates was upset. He apparently hadn't realized just how far some of the bureaus had gone in their tolerance of lawlessness. He asked for more details. I reviewed the airport fiasco. He accepted the responsibility for allowing a false impression to be formed during the previous staff meeting. Then he laid down the law, making it clear that the inconsistency would stop immediately. He directed that not one more illegal parade or demonstration would be tolerated.

"We have always been consistent in our approach to so-called 'civil disobedient' law breakers," he said. "We are not about to change that policy. I want it clearly understood that law breakers will be arrested."

After a few moments of silence, one of the under chiefs said, "Chief, the homosexual community is very upset about the governor's veto. If we force a confrontation, it's likely things will get violent."

Gates appeared to be disgusted and struggled to keep his composure. "Look," he said, "I don't want violence. I want everybody in this room to take the responsibility to keep order in this city, hopefully without violence. But we cannot allow a group—any group—to have special consideration. I want you to communicate with the leadership and do all the things you have been trained to do to prevent violence. But we shall keep order in this city. Is that understood?"

We all got the message.

The monthly meeting with my deputy chiefs was the next day, October 11. The subject again came up. Most of those at the meeting had also been present the day before, and they wanted to further define their marching orders. One deputy chief argued vigorously to not change the way things were going. He stated that if Chief Gates's orders to not allow any illegal parades were followed, the blood of homosexuals and police alike would flow in the streets.

After a lengthy discussion, I directed my deputy chiefs to meet with the various homosexual groups and leaders to give them advance notice of our return to regular policy. They were to let them know, firmly but courteously, that we would not allow the violations of previous nights to continue.

The illegal demonstrations came to a stop almost immediately, though some of the homosexual activists were furious. Several appeared at the next police commission hearing, and one took out his anger on me. He accused me, before the TV cameras, of wanting to see violence committed against homosexuals. He testified that a high-ranking LAPD officer had told him that I had said I wanted to see "their blood flow in the streets." I recalled how a deputy chief had argued to continue our permissiveness using that same phrase, and I wondered if that was a coincidence.

Clearly, the past cohesiveness of the department's leadership team was breaking down. It wasn't good for the men and women in the patrol cars. Everyone was talking about it. At a retirement dinner for one of our officers, the master of ceremonies, well known for his use of humor, said, "Chief Gates was going to be here to present the service certificate, but he has been delayed. Seems he had to roll on a 'Staff officer involved, back stabbing,' on the sixth floor of Parker Center."

The press was also aware of what was going on. The *Times* ran a story on February 26, 1992, over which the headline read, "Infighting for Chief's Job Grows Fierce." The reporters gave several illustrations of what was happening, including a reference to my belief that there was an orchestrated campaign to ruin my future by publicly painting me as a religious fanatic. They also reported the opinions of clinical psychologist Samuel Culbert, a UCLA professor of management. He was quoted as saying, "I see an institution that has been ravaged being further destroyed by internal combustion."

The article explained that he perceived that in some respects, the LAPD resembled the Kremlin in its last days—the old power structure breaking down, and "the entire system lacking trust."

Culbert concluded, "You might say it is understandable, but it will take ten years to repair. All the antagonists aren't going to go away."

I survived the first cut in the selection process for the new chief. I wasn't too surprised to be in the list of 12 semifinalists, but I didn't expect to make it as a finalist. That's because my attorney had announced he would take action to remove Commissioners Sheinbaum and Brewer from the final selection process since they had both made public statements against me. That could throw the selection to the Board of Referred Powers or some other authority, making it difficult for Sheinbaum and his allies to control the final choice. They couldn't let that happen.

On Friday, February 28, 1992, I was formally notified that I had been eliminated from consideration. To be perfectly honest, even though I was expecting it, I was

21–YEAR-OLD BOB VERNON AT HIS POLICE ACADEMY GRADUATION.

VERNON RECEIVES THE BADGE OF ASSISTANT CHIEF FROM CHIEF DARYL GATES IN 1979.

↓ VERNON,
DEPUTY CHIEF RATHBURN
(NOW DALLAS CHIEF OF
POLICE), CHIEF GATES, AND
COUNCILMAN ZEV
YAROSLAVSKY AT THE L.A.
COLISEUM DURING AN
OPERATION HAMMER ROLL
CALL.

← EVEN AS
A SENIOR STAFF OFFICER,
VERNON REGULARLY SPENT TIME
ON PATROL TO STAY IN TOUCH
WITH THE NEEDS OF FIELD
OFFICERS. HERE, HE'S PICTURED
WITH OFFICER O'NEIL CARTER,
WHO TOLD VERNON, "YOU CAN
BE MY PARTNER ANYTIME."

↓ VERNON
WITH CHIEF GATES, DEPUTY
CHIEF RATHBURN, AND
MAYOR BRADLEY AT
OPERATION HAMMER
COMMAND POST IN 1990.
(BOTTOM)

↓ VERNON
ADDRESSES A COMMUNITY
SUPPORT GROUP AT LOCAL
POLICE STATION.

PRESIDENT BUSH→

MEETS WITH OPERATION
HAMMER ANTI-GANG TASK-
FORCE—VERNON, CHIEF GATES,
AND DEPUTY CHIEF RATHBURN.

VERNON↓

AND THEN-PARTNER NICK
NAJERA WITH A CONFISCATED
MARIJUANA PLANT.

ROY VERNON, ↑
BOB'S DAD AND HIMSELF A 20-
YEAR MEMBER OF THE LAPD, IN
THE CENTER OF A MONTAGE OF
FAMILY PHOTOS.

VERNON ↘

AND HIS WIFE, ESTHER,
AT A RECENT BANQUET.

VERNON ↑

SPEAKS AT CHIEF GATES'S
SUPPORT RALLY ON
MARCH 24, 1991.

A YOUNG BOB ↗

PINS HIS BADGE ON HIS
SON AS DAUGHTER PAM
AND WIFE ESTHER LOOK
ON.

THE COMPLETE ↑
VERNON FAMILY TOGETHER IN 1992.

disappointed.

That night, Esther and I drove out to the high desert northeast of L.A. I had a breakfast speaking engagement in Victorville the following morning. We didn't talk much the first hour of the drive. The finality of what was happening was sinking in. I was being rejected from further leadership in the city. My career was drawing to a close.

Esther is one of the reasons I've been able to keep my balance in a stressful job for so long. She's a skilled counselor. Over the years, she has helped me put into words my reasons for tension, anger, fear, frustration, and other harmful emotions. She has recognized the importance of allowing me to talk about my feelings, sensing when I'm not yet ready to speak and when I am.

That night was one of those times when I needed to talk. I was doing a lot of thinking as I drove. At the right time, Esther started our conversation.

"You're really disappointed, aren't you?"

"Yeah, I am. I knew this was going to happen. But—I don't know—it's still disappointing."

"I could see it coming, too. But I know what you mean. It's discouraging to have it actually happen. I know how much you've loved the department."

"That's just it. I love police work, I love the LAPD, and it looks like it's all over. I've known for the last few years it would end soon, but I guess I didn't want to think about it."

"Bob, with what's happening in L.A., I think it's probably best that you leave. I don't think you can work in those conditions. We've been praying that God would continue to lead our lives—that He would let us know when your work there is finished. He's been faithful in the past. I think He's leading us now."

"Intellectually, I know you're right. But from my human point of view, I'm disappointed. I wanted to be chief in order to try some strategies and programs that I think would be good for the people of L.A. Now those dreams won't be realized.

"The team-policing system that worked so well for me at Venice would work wonders today. A true partnership with the various communities is possible. My idea of re-engineering the city into cul-de-sac neighborhoods was proved effective in Newton Area [see chap. 21 for details]. It would work elsewhere in the city. Decentralizing more authority and accountability through a new organizational structure is another plan that I won't be able to put into effect. It hurts to see those dreams die."

We just sat there for a few minutes. Then the conversation continued.

"Bob, for most of your life, your whole identity has been intertwined with your position on the LAPD. How are you going to handle that?"

"You've hit on a major issue. I'm used to certain attitudes and acknowledgment because of my position. That's all going to stop. Soon I won't be Chief Vernon anymore, I'll just be Bob Vernon. That will demand a big adjustment."

"One thing on that score in your favor: God has given you a ministry in addition to your job. Your seminars and men's conferences will probably continue and may even expand. One thing I know—He won't let you down. He has led us all our lives. Remember all the incredible things He's done for us. I don't think that's about to stop now."

We continued our conversation the rest of the trip. It was good. I was encouraged.

That evening, we had dinner with the Christian businessmen who had invited me to come and speak. One of them owned the restaurant where the meeting, a civic prayer breakfast, was to take place. During dinner, we discussed the news. They expressed their concern for us, but they also gave us great hope. They were convinced of God's sovereignty and His ability to guide us through circumstances— even disappointments.

The following morning, we drove to the restaurant, which was packed out. Many elected officials and community leaders were there. Richard Williams, the sheriff of the county, sat next to us. When it came time for me to speak, I commented on my recent disappointment.

The papers the following morning carried the Associated Press wire story: "Speaking to a gathering of the Christian Businessmen's Association in Victorville Saturday, Vernon, a Pasadena resident, said he was considering whether to remain in law enforcement. 'I'm a little bit disappointed, to be honest with you. You know, 38 years moving in this direction, and it's shut off,' Vernon said. 'But I have to tell you, I'm going to leave a very grateful man. God brought me into this work, and it appears he's taking me out.'"

I discussed my perspective on recent events in L.A. But most importantly, I was able to say with conviction that my personal relationship with God, through Jesus

Christ, was strong enough to carry me through the adversity.

The adversity wasn't over, however. More was to follow—soon.

———————————————————

The following Monday, the press wanted to hear from me. I appeared at a press conference at my attorney's office, where I delivered a statement to a battery of reporters and TV cameras.

"To this point, my attributes of being a 'progressive traditionalist' have moved me rapidly up through the ranks. I haven't changed."

I gave several examples of leading progressive change in my various assignments: team policing, the forerunner of community-based policing; Jeopardy, the gang-prevention program; SAFE footbeats and bicycle patrols; TRAP, the program to target repeating predators; and "Operation Safe Summer," the program to offer free first-run movies in areas of the city that had no theaters. Then I addressed the "traditionalist" label.

"I do remain a traditionalist regarding basic American values. That combination of attributes has been an asset until now.

"The interview board that selected the finalists has been described as being representative of the people of Los Angeles. That being the case, the people of Los Angeles have changed in their expectations as to the values they desire their leadership to possess. Apparently, I am no longer 'politically correct.' I submit to the mandate from the people and accept their decision. I am grateful for the opportunities they have given me in the past and pledge my continued commitment to serve them with integrity and diligence until the day I retire."

Then I responded to questions. The following day the *Times* reported that "Vernon also said his reputation has been 'sullied' by accusations that he has improperly infused his fundamentalist religious views into police work, and that may have influenced the panel that rated the finalists.

"'I'm not angry, I am disappointed—big time,' Vernon said."

Then on March 11, 1992, we got another setback. I received a call from my attorney, David Casterline. "Bob," he said, "I've got some bad news. The judge just threw out our case. He granted full summary judgment to the city."

"Well," I responded, "I can't say I'm really surprised. It seemed to me from the start that Judge Wilson didn't like this case. He has been tough on us from the beginning. But I'm sure disappointed."

By throwing out my case before it could go to trial, Judge Wilson essentially said I had failed to demonstrate that a departmental investigation violated my religious freedom. He wrote that I had "not alleged, let alone offered any evidence, showing that the investigation interfered with a tenet or belief that is central to [the] religious doctrine of Christian fundamentalism."

This was depressing news. Even though I expected it, I felt queasy in my stomach. It seemed as though everything was crashing in on me. The leaders of my beloved city had turned on me. I was investigated for my religious beliefs as if they were subversive and un-American. The same beliefs that had earned me trust and respect in the past were now the cause of suspicion and rejection. And now came the last straw—the federal government, as represented by the U.S. district court, condoned this religious bigotry. I hit one of the lowest emotional points of my life.

I don't fully understand the process of civil litigation. My case seemed so clear and straightforward. An investigation had been ordered based on some statements I had made about my beliefs while off duty. It was assumed that because of my beliefs, I would not follow city policy. I had publicly objected, stating the investigation was illegal. A few days later, anonymous, nonspecific charges were added, probably after the error was realized. No specific charges had ever been proved. How could such a witch-hunt be in accordance with the First Amendment?

Judge Wilson, in his original 42-page decision, remarked that the investigation's consequences—"in particular, the conclusive determination that plaintiff was in fact not guilty of on-duty wrongdoing, and the putting to rest of allegations and rumors to the contrary"—were part of the reason for his conclusions. He also stated, "It may well be that in hindsight, it can be said that there was no basis to the allegations made against plaintiff."

In my interviews with TV reporters, I referred to those particular comments by the judge. A few days later, he issued a revised opinion from which both of those supportive statements were mysteriously omitted.

Naturally, I felt some disappointment. But I also felt an even deeper concern about the broader implications of this decision. If allowed to stand, it would encourage the religious persecution of others. Many people had been watching this series of events unfold. One could see a sinister message in the results so far: "If you have any religious beliefs, keep them secret. Don't talk about them, even in your church or synagogue. If someone in power disagrees with your beliefs, he can use them to hold you up to public ridicule. He can assume that your beliefs will cause you to act improperly."

During the previous few months, I had noticed a change in the behavior of some LAPD employees. It seemed that they were purposely distancing themselves from me. They avoided conversations with me.

I remember the time a sergeant approached me in the underground parking area as I was preparing to leave for the day. "Chief, may I speak with you for a moment?" he asked.

"Sure," I replied. "I'm not in any hurry."

He grimaced and paused, apparently having a hard time finding the right words. "Well, Sir, I'm sure you noticed it the other day—when we were talking outside your office. When I saw a commander and a deputy chief approaching, I cut the conversation short. After I left, I really felt badly about that. I mean—I guess I'm in fear about my future. I've seen what they have done to you, and—"

I broke in. "Look, I understand. I know you have quite a few years ahead of you before you can—"

Now he broke in. "But that's not a valid reason to do what I did. I displayed a lack of courage and true friendship. I'm sorry. I'm ashamed of myself. I won't do that again."

Our conversation continued as I tried to offer him hope for the future. I'm sure my body language revealed my true feelings. If he became known as a committed Christian or as sympathetic toward me, his future was probably not very good with the city of Los Angeles.

The results of the judge's decision were immediate. Zev Yaroslavsky, basking in his victory, introduced a motion for a new city ordinance that would ban all indications of religion from public property and government functions. The true meaning of Christmas would be eliminated from public entities. No nativity scene, no wise men, no star over Bethlehem.

My mind went back a few months to a luncheon I had attended at the University of Southern California. The university had sponsored a seminar that had involved several officers from the Soviet police system. They called themselves the militia. I was introduced, through an interpreter, to their highest-ranking official.

After an exchange of normal "shop talk," he grew agitated. His volume increased, and he became animated. His hands moved across his chest, pointing in opposite directions. Then he pointed at me and seemed to be asking a question.

I assumed I must have said something to offend him and asked the interpreter what I had done wrong. He assured me I had said nothing offensive. Then he interpreted the official's statements.

"When he gestured with his hands, he was saying that our two countries are passing one another. They are going in the direction we came from, and we are going in the direction they came from. When he pointed at you, he was asking, 'Why are you going in that direction? Why are you moving more toward socialism? Why are you trying to remove God from your culture? Don't you know we have tried that system and it does not work?' He doesn't understand why we are going in the direction of failure."

Those were good questions. I had been asking them myself.

14

THE PLAN THAT
WASN'T CARRIED OUT

In the months following the Rodney King incident, I could see that the potential for a riot was increasing. Understandably, there was much concern about the episode. Unfortunately, some opportunists were exploiting that legitimate concern. Some were even suggesting "taking it to the streets." Both criminal prosecution and internal disciplinary action against the involved officers were in progress. At every step of these dual-track proceedings, media coverage was heavy, so the whole issue remained in the forefront of news and commentary.

News stories, special programs, and talk shows explored all the ramifications of the incident. As the public debate continued, feelings intensified, and some polarization began to occur. Conflicting opinions were expressed regarding the incident itself, race relations, root causes of societal ills, and the function of the LAPD.

Key facts about the incident were also debated. The California Highway Patrol accused King of evading arrest and driving at speeds over 90 miles per hour. Others maintained the type of car King was driving could not achieve that speed. Police officers talked of the police commission policy prohibiting upper body control holds; they argued that such holds would have eliminated the need to use their batons. The Christopher Commission concluded that the LAPD had serious racial problems, citing computer messages sent from car to car as their main evidence. But police officials were quick to point out that less than two-tenths of 1 percent of the thousands of messages scrutinized had inappropriate comments of any kind.

As these positions were argued in the public forum, emotions attached to them deepened. I could sense the tension building. At my staff meetings, beginning shortly after the King incident, I started to discuss the likelihood of riots.

Several incidents had occurred that fanned the flames of racial tension. Conflicts between Korean merchants and black customers had resulted in tragedy and anxiety on both sides. A 13-year-old black girl had been shot and killed by a Korean grocer in a dispute over suspected shoplifting. A Korean grocery store was firebombed. Strong tension also existed between some blacks and Hispanics. For example, an entire Hispanic family had been wiped out when their home was firebombed by blacks. The Hispanic family became a target after they objected to drug trafficking around their unit in a housing project. Two well-known black athletes had been stopped, in separate incidents, by the police. The celebrities were convinced the only reason for their temporary detentions was their race.

Thus, the Rodney King incident was the climax of a number of incidents that fueled the fires of unrest. It also provided ammunition to those who regularly exploit conflict, strife, and rivalry.

A few months later, in the summer of 1991, an incident occurred in New York that caused extreme tension between the Jewish and black communities there. A vehicle chauffeuring a rabbi struck a black child. Public disturbances followed.

I arranged, through the top command of the NYPD, to send one of our officers to observe the situation as it developed. Deputy Chief Matthew Hunt carried out this mission from August 27 to 30, 1991. I sent him because he was the CO of Operations South Bureau, that portion of the city most likely to suffer the major brunt of a riot.

During our regular Office of Operations staff meeting on September 13, Hunt's findings were presented. His most significant conclusion was that the "field commander had failed to allocate sufficient personnel resources *quickly enough* to control the problem" (emphasis added). The thrust of the discussion that followed was that we should learn from their mistake and not make the same one here.

This insight supported the basic strategy mentioned again and again in the LAPD Tactical Manual. In its introduction, for example, the principle is stated this way: "Must quickly reestablish order." In the very beginning of chapter D, dealing with riot control, a section on strategy says in part, "Utilize a field task force of sufficient strength and apply necessary force at the proper time and place to *rapidly gain control*" (emphasis added). It goes on to say, "Present a dominant appearance."

The tactical manual was developed after the Watts riots of 1965. It contains detailed, comprehensive plans to guide supervisors and top management in what the department refers to as unusual occurrences (UOs). Chapter D covers everything from overall riot strategy to detailed squad formations and operations. In my opinion, it's one of the best documents addressing contingency planning available. Many police departments that have UO plans have utilized the LAPD's manual extensively in their own planning processes.

To understand what went wrong with the initial police response to the riots, critics need to realize the significance of the tactical manual. People who are not aware of its contents have asked why the LAPD didn't have a unique plan for the riots. After all, they argue, the department prepared a unique plan for the security of the 1984 Olympics. So why wasn't there a unique plan for the King verdict aftermath? That's a fair question that deserves an answer.

The LAPD does prepare unique plans for certain events. That type of preparation is appropriate when a police agency knows in advance the specific details of what, where, and when events will take place. In the case of the Olympics, we had detailed information about what would happen. As a result, Bill Rathburn and his staff planned diligently for more than five years to develop the department's response. It was a superb, massive, detailed plan.

On the other hand, the department had little or no specific information about what would occur in the aftermath of the jury verdict. Earlier, our important PDID had been disbanded and replaced with ATD. Its restrictive guidelines prevent it from providing the kind of intelligence needed to make meaningful, detailed planning possible.

Many officers have told me the department suffered from a lack of intelligence information that, in their opinion, contributed to the LAPD's slow and inadequate response. A *Times* article by LAPD Detective Lou Koven, published on November 4, 1992, stated: "Hampered for months and second–guessed at every corner by politicians and community leaders, normal police operations were handcuffed. For example, after being lambasted by Councilmen Michael Woo and Zev Yaroslavsky for more than a year for conducting routine police intelligence, street police officers and those assigned to intelligence were too shell-shocked to do their job. As a result, normal intelligence-gathering—talking to 'people on the street' and monitoring known criminals and troublemakers—came to a virtual halt."

Koven also reported,"When the breakdown in intelligence was going to be exposed in the Webster report as a contributing factor to the riots, the report's authors ordered it removed because it would tend to support Gates."

The department's once-effective intelligence operation was crippled and unable to provide the kind of information that would have made more-detailed planning possible. In my opinion, the city council was responsible for that damaging blunder, having knuckled under to the demands of Zev Yaroslavsky and Mayor Bradley.

I further believe the ACLU was behind that strategic crippling of the LAPD's intelligence-gathering capability. Its involvement in the CAPA lawsuit, the shutdown of the PDID, and its strong influence in forming the new intelligence guidelines all helped to almost completely eliminate our infiltration of dangerous groups. Paul Hoffman, an ACLU attorney, represented plaintiffs in those important actions. To understand the motives of the ACLU with certainty would require mind-reading ability. It seems logical to me, however, that only those who are involved in criminal or subversive enterprises—or who would protect the freedom of criminals above the rights of the public—fear the presence of the police.

When a police agency does not have specific details of an upcoming event, contingency planning is the only remaining option. The more-than-200-page LAPD Tactical Manual is just that—a thorough contingency plan. Chapter D, mentioned earlier, has all the specifics of how to respond to a riot except for where and when. But its comprehensive plans were not the only planning that took place prior to the riots. Much more preparation followed.

A common criticism of the department's response to the riots is that confusion and ineffectiveness obviously reigned at the field command post (CP). That should not have been the case, and I'll explain why.

A CP is an organization of specially trained officers designed to facilitate the rapid mobilization and deployment of arriving officers. The tactical manual identifies the various components of a CP, defines the duties of the necessary positions, and outlines its operation. Individuals are trained in advance to participate as members of the CP.

On January 8, 1992, I issued a training order to all bureau COs under my command to ensure that each bureau (quadrant) of the city had staff trained in the various positions necessary at a CP. For example, a logistics officer is supposed to ensure that essential equipment is available and deployed; a personnel officer organizes arriving officers into squads and platoons; an intelligence officer gathers information from all available sources, including vice undercover cops who are converted to field scouts; and an operations officer prepares specific tactical plans and submits them to the field commander. Other positions may also be staffed depending on the requirements of the UO. Our standing operating procedure was to train three or more individuals for each CP position to make sure at least one was always available for immediate duty.

The training was held at the Naval and Marine Corps training center on February 4 and 5 and was provided by the Tactical Planning Section of our Operations Headquarters Bureau. Representatives from all four of our geographical bureaus participated.

Once I was sure each bureau had a trained CP cadre, I took the next step. I announced we would have a simulated UO in which an unnamed bureau would be tested. My intent was to have each bureau CO double-check the readiness of his cadre. No one likes to look bad.

On March 16, 1992, I sent an order to Operations Central Bureau explaining that their cadre had been selected for testing. The exercise was held at the Dodger Stadium parking lot on March 19. The department's field command post fleet was used to give the participants a feeling of realism and experience with the various hardware and systems available. The exercise was deemed successful. Some deficiencies were identified, but that's part of the reason for such tests. Overall, at the conclusion of the exercise, the personnel appeared to be trained and ready for an actual event.

Next, I called an unusual meeting for April 10, 1992. Normally I communicate to the 18 area COs through their chains of command. In other words, I meet with the deputy chiefs, who, in turn, pass on the information to them. I felt such an urgency to be prepared for the possibility of a riot, however, that I ordered all the area COs or their representatives (in the case of excused absence) to attend. I wanted to communicate directly with them; I didn't want any misunderstanding or filtering to occur. This matter was too important to allow any possibility of poor communication.

Before the meeting, I discussed my agenda with Chief Gates. "Boss," I said, "I'm calling an unusual meeting of all our area COs. My feeling is that a riot after the King verdict is very likely. It's my opinion we'll have some disturbances regardless of how the verdict goes."

"Bob, I'm afraid you may be right," Gates agreed. "I'm aware of the preparations that have already been made, but I guess we can't do too much to ensure readiness. Just let me caution you to give a word of warning to our COs. Make sure they understand I don't want to put the LAPD in the position of predicting a riot. I don't want us to be accused of issuing a self-fulfilling prophecy. You know how the media can put a negative spin on a good thing."

"Chief, I agree completely and will do just that. I want to be sure each of them gets the word straight from the horse's mouth. As you know, there are some problems with communicating through the chain of command these days. I will definitely make them aware of your concern."

As the meeting day approached, I vacillated between having written handouts or communicating solely by the spoken word. The department had developed several leaks of written materials to the media, and riot contingency plans could be used negatively as Chief Gates feared. On the other hand, I wanted to be sure that communication was comprehensive and presented in such a manner that no one could later say he didn't understand his marching orders. In recent months, some deputy chiefs had tended to not follow the direction of myself or Chief Gates. Possibly they viewed us as lame ducks. I didn't want any doubt in the record about the directions this time. Finally, I decided to pass out a copy of the outline I used as I ordered preparations for a possible riot.

I didn't like what I perceived was happening to the top leadership of the department. There had always been intense competition for promotion, but in the past it had not caused disloyalty and insubordination. For the first time, I was seeing signs of that unhealthy condition. The body language of some chief officers at staff meetings became downright hostile. During the last few months, I had been forced to take the initial steps of disciplinary action against two executive-level officers. (Their cases were still pending when I retired.)

The meeting was held on April 10 in Parker Center. I explained the chief's concern about not issuing a self-fulfilling prophecy. Then I delivered the comprehensive directions, accompanied by several handouts. The outline that was distributed included sections on training, equipment, vehicles, deployment, intelligence, a response plan, liaison with other agencies, and station security plans.

I ordered the COs to review the tactical manual and their own area plans. Specifically, they were directed to do the following: (1) provide refresher training in civil disorder procedures; (2) revitalize their mobilization rosters to ensure that each officer was assigned either the "A" (daytime) or "B" (night) 12-hour watch in the event of a riot (a normal watch is 8 hours); (3) update call-up and notification plans, which involves verifying that current phone and pager numbers are correct for each officer, and that contingency plans are in place in the event of communication system breakdowns; (4) develop appropriate ratios of officers to vehicles, depending on the size of a division's fleet and the number of officers available; (5) develop platoon-size response to looters, since most officers are not normally deployed in a platoon-size configuration (30 to 60 officers); (6) develop and train personnel in field jail operations to support mass arrests; (7) ensure all detectives had required uniforms; (8) ensure proper logistics for all personnel (including helmets, face shields, chemical agents, batons, and protective vests); and (9) identify potential targets of rioters (e.g., a list of all gun stores was distributed to each CO).

Additionally, Metro Division, the department's specialist in responding to UOs, was given several specific missions. I had already met with Lieutenant Mike Hillman, the acting CO of the division, to make sure his direction was clear. In addition to ordering specific preparations for his division, I asked him to make his people available to train other branches of the department.

Hillman had arranged for several days of off-site training for his riot specialists. The instruction was comprehensive and very specific for riot control and urban combat. He was also able to obtain valuable equipment, such as special ammunition and heavy-duty body armor, that was not readily available through regular city requisition. Mike Hillman, more than any other CO, could not have been more responsive to the need for riot preparation. He not only carried out his orders, but he seized the initiative and did much more. His division was uniquely ready for any contingency.

During the April 10 meeting, I focused particular attention on the split force concept that's essential during a riot. The importance of this approach was obvious in our mistakes during the 1965 riots and in other riots throughout the nation. Normally, police officers work as a unit. When they make arrests, they immediately transport the arrestees to a station and book them in.

As I explained to the COs, however, "During the riots of 1965, we found that moving into an area and making arrests utilizing normal procedures did not work. We would rush upon some looters and arrest as many as we could. The remainder would flee. We would then gather up those we had arrested and transport them to the station. As soon as we left, the area would again be overrun with looters. We learned through experience that once an area has been secured, it must be held.

"Based upon that principle, we developed the concept of sectoring that is explained in detail in your tac manual. A platoon should be assigned to an involved area and left there. When they make arrests, they're to summon a field jail unit to pick up the arrestees. That way, we're able to retain the security of areas that are pacified.

"The other part of the so-called split force responds to emergency calls. Of course, that force will be much smaller, since we will only dispatch units to dire emergencies during a riot."

Then, to make sure I had their attention, I told them, "I will direct Operations Headquarters Bureau, Tactical Planning Section, to conduct a follow-up audit of at least one area in each bureau to ensure these directions are followed." A follow-up audit is a hands-on inspection at the police station, examining documents (e.g., verifying the accuracy of phone numbers on call-up rosters) and asking questions of involved personnel. Auditing one area in each bureau, without announcing which areas would be chosen, was intended to ensure all would be in compliance.

On April 14, I sent a written order to Operations Headquarters Bureau with the specifics that I wanted covered by their inspection. I directed that this audit be completed by April 24—before my retirement date. Part of the instructions mandated a document reporting the findings of the inspection. Then, just to make sure all the bases were covered, I sent the following memo to all COs on April 20:

The potential for an emergency response to natural and other unusual occurrences is ever present. Should such an event occur, the department must be able to function as a team. Each area, as a member of the team, is expected to be prepared to respond rapidly and efficiently. Response encompasses personnel management, planning documents and equipment.

To ensure that these elements are in place, I have directed Tactical Planning Section to conduct an audit of emergency response readiness in selected geographic areas. Commanding officers are expected to facilitate completion of this project so that corrections can be implemented as quickly as possible.

I had already given a special outline of instructions to Operations Headquarters Bureau at the April 10 meeting. This bureau has the primary responsibility for the department's tactical planning and liaison with other criminal justice agencies. The outline gave specific instructions to prepare the department for an anticipated UO. It covered such details as preparing a letter, in advance, for the mayor to sign to formally declare an emergency. This would allow an immediate request for the assistance of the National Guard and other military units. It asked that an early warning system be established with prosecutors and the courts to give advance notice of the likelihood of a verdict in the King case. (Although my last day in my office prior to retirement was April 24, I have been informed most or all of these instructions were followed.)

Then I called L.A. County Undersheriff Bob Edmonds and Chief Ed Gomez of the California Highway Patrol. I told them of my concern and said I had started preparations, and that our Headquarters Bureau would be our liaison with them. All the bases had been touched.

The Webster Commission later criticized the LAPD for not having any real plan to address the possibility of riots. Its report states: "The police department's 'Plan' consisted of its Tactical Manual and its 'standing plans' which together proved to be equally unspecific and non-responsive. As a result, when the violence and destruction did come, City officials and police commanders had given little specific thought to the problem of what strategies were appropriate to implement" (pp. 16-17).

The report goes on to say: "'To varying degrees, each (City and Police Depts.) has devoted modest effort to preparedness planning and training. However, the preparedness efforts of neither have resulted in anything that reasonably can be considered a 'plan' for response to an emergency. Rather, it appears to be more accurate to state that each has collected and summarized a variety of materials having to do generally with emergency powers of government and the subject of emergency response. However, neither the City nor the Police Department has produced much in the way of substantive guidance with regard to specific emergency response objectives, priorities, tasks or assignments"(p. 3).

I had met with two of the commission's attorneys and explained all the actions I took. I gave them copies of all the notes, handouts, orders, and audits I have described. The commission's brief comment about the April 10 meeting was as follows: "On April 10, 1992, Assistant Chief Vernon held a training-related meeting of Captains from the Areas. After instructing them to keep the contents of the meeting confidential in order that the meeting not cause any disturbances, Vernon told the assembled captains that they should focus their training programs on civil unrest and ensure that each officer's equipment was updated and complete" (p. 95).

During my two-hour meeting with the attorneys, I expressed my opinion that little of the information I gave them would be included in the final report, since it would not be a popular perspective. One of them said I could be right, but that he would faithfully report everything I had provided. Apparently those in charge of completing the finished document did not think my information was significant.

Shortly after being notified on February 28, 1992, that I had been eliminated as a candidate for chief of police, I announced I would be retiring by the end of the fiscal year (June 30). I wanted it on the record before the selection of the new chief from the six finalists so my departure would not be linked to the appointment of a specific person. Also, I realized that to stay on any longer would make me a lame duck, which could be harmful to the officers on the street. But before I left, I wanted plans and preparation set in motion for the riot I thought was inevitable. I had now done that. The department was ready—if only my directions were carried out.

In its analysis of what went wrong, the Webster Commission described a lack of planning and training. Their analysis is only partially correct. Certain executives did not follow the directions given them in this regard. But their reasons for not doing so are most important.

As noted earlier, I was concerned about the top leadership. We didn't seem to be a team anymore; there was so much "palace intrigue." I believe the politicization of the department encouraged this. The selection of the new chief had sent a clear message: Subjective evaluations were the new order of the day for promotions. That being the case, it was viewed as important to please the politicians rather than make decisions based on professional principles. I was worried that in the midst of a riot, some of our executives might put "political correctness" ahead of sound tactical judgment.

My worst fears were realized when the riots struck. Unfortunately, the riots were not a surprise. The department neglected to take advantage of the advance warnings. There is clear evidence that some COs of bureaus and areas had not taken the steps of preparation that had been ordered. On the other hand, some did. In certain areas of the city, the police response to the riots was swift and effective. I'll give a striking example of that in the next chapter.

Since the riot was anticipated and planning and preparation had been set in motion, why did those particular police executives fail to provide the proper leadership? What do we know about the nature of the riots and the agenda of certain politicians that may give us important insight? I've touched on those issues here; I'll develop them further in the next chapter.

15

THE NATURE
OF THE RIOTS

Members of a dangerous gang in south-central Los Angeles rushed upon the store in three separate vehicles. They had planned their actions long before the riots started, and they were ready. Although the verdict had been announced only a few hours earlier, they were well prepared to execute their destructive criminal plan.

A Korean-American store owner tells his story:

"I have owned and operated my store in south-central L.A. for more than 20 years. My family and I have worked hard to develop our business. I believe we serve our clientele well. We worked long hours to make it convenient for people in the neighborhood to purchase what they need at a fair price.

"After the Watts riots in 1965, many businesses pulled out. There were not too many grocery stores in the community. The people had to drive far to get what they needed. We were willing to try to 'make a go of it' there. We had the support of most of the community. Our customers are also our friends. We know most of the families in the neighborhood.

"Shortly after the Rodney King verdict was announced, I knew something was going to happen. There are gang members in the neighborhood. I know who they are. Some of them are the children of our customers. They were talking to other young people in the area. I could see they wanted to start something, so I closed my store early and pulled the steel protecting grates shut and padlocked them. I was not afraid of what my customers would do, but I am afraid of the gang members.

Everyone is. They carry guns and seem to have no conscience. There are not too many of them, but they are very dangerous.

"A few hours after the verdict, things began to happen. The gang members began throwing rocks and bottles at cars. Any car driven by someone who wasn't black was in danger.

"Then the gang members came to my store in three cars. The first car was a large, older station wagon. One of them drove it right into the steel grating protecting the windows and doors of my store. He just rammed right through the grating and through the window. He left the car there. He didn't care. The police later told me it was stolen.

"The second vehicle was a van. A bunch of the gang members were in it. They looted my store. They took whatever they wanted. They loaded the van with their loot. I saw them do it. I could not stop them; they are too dangerous.

"They yelled for other people in the neighborhood to come and take what they wanted. Some of them did. I didn't see any of my customers. They wouldn't do anything like that.

"Then the third vehicle came. Two or three gang members were in it. They got out and opened the trunk. They had some boxes in the trunk filled with firebombs and gasoline. They lit the bottle bombs and threw them into my store after one of them spilled gasoline all over. I yelled, but I was afraid to do anything else. I called the fire department, but they didn't come for a long while.

"Those gang members are bad people. They had it all planned. They were just waiting to do their evil job. All the cars they used were stolen before the verdict came out. The firebombs were made before the day of the verdict.

"I watched my store burn down. I cried. I am older now. I don't know if I am able to try to do it again."

Some argue the riots were a spontaneous outburst of rage. I agree that may have motivated a few of the rioters. I don't believe that's what motivated most of them, however. Many of the rioters didn't even know who Rodney King was. One reporter asked a looter, "Are you doing this for Rodney King?"

The rioter responded, "I don't follow sports that closely."

Time magazine reported in its May 1, 1992, issue the results of a survey regarding the riots. In response to questions about the motivation for the riots, the largest percentage of blacks (46 percent) said they thought looters were taking advantage of the situation. Only 15 percent of the black respondents thought the riots were justified.

I agree with those black poll respondents. A host of opportunists took advantage of a situation. For most, their participation was not an uncontrollable outburst of emotion. But there was evidence of some criminal conspiracy. My opinion is that a relatively few habitual predators were waiting for an opportunity to do with vigor what they enjoy doing. Once they started their dirty work, others, weak in character, saw their chance to join in the looting.

At about 7:00 P.M. on April 30, the second day of the rioting, two West Los Angeles Area sergeants were teamed up with six officers. That area is located in the extreme western portion of the city and takes in Bel Air, Westwood Village around UCLA, and Pacific Palisades. It is definitely not a low-income area but rather the high-rent district. The small squad was patrolling likely targets of looting, with the sergeants and two officers in the lead black and white. The remaining four officers followed in another radio car. They were moving toward what looked like some new structural fires breaking out on La Cienega Boulevard.

The two units moved east on Pico Boulevard. Just as they passed Robertson Boulevard, they observed looters moving in and out of a sporting goods store specializing in expensive workout clothing. "Let's take them," one of the sergeants barked.

They converged on the crime scene, and the looters began to scramble. The police cars skidded to a stop as nearly a dozen thieves hustled out of the broken windows and scattered.

With hardly a word, the officers jumped from their cars. But who should they chase? Several of the thieves ran toward the rear of the store, and one of the sergeants and an officer took off after them. The other sergeant backed up the second officer as he selected another looter running in the same direction. The officers' hunch was well founded: Four cars were being loaded with loot out back.

Some of the rioters went over the fence. One, already in his car, drove right at the officers as they rounded the corner of the building. They jumped out of the way to avoid being struck down, and one of the sergeants reflexively whacked the car with his nightstick as it roared past.

Another looter tried to get his car started and do the same, but he wasn't so lucky. He was arrested. In addition to loot from the sporting goods store, he had three identical microwave ovens from some unknown electronics store in his car.

A couple more thieves were also arrested. As the officers were "hooking them up" with handcuffs, one of the sergeants returned to the store. The looters were unsure if they should continue; it looked as though the cops were busy around the corner arresting others, and by then the officers had moved their cars to the lot behind the building. Some of those remaining in front of the store started to return.

The sergeant stuck his head around the corner, and the looters saw him just as they were about to go back inside. They broke away, running a short distance. Then they regrouped. They didn't want to be arrested, but they didn't want to give up the looting so easily, either. The sergeant stepped back around the corner and waited a few seconds. Then he stuck his head around the corner again. The looters were warily coming back. This time he ran a few steps in their direction, and they retreated.

"Get out of here! Beat it! Leave right now or you'll all go to jail for burglary!" the sergeant yelled.

They stood a safe distance away, knowing he probably couldn't back up his threat—not enough cops.

He played the cat-and-mouse game while his officers were impounding the cars. Every few minutes, a caravan of three to five cars would pull up in front of the store. As the looters got out of their vehicles, the sergeant would reappear, chasing them away.

Finally, when the officers were through with the confiscated cars, the sergeant left one unit to guard the store for as long as possible; an emergency call would probably pull them off in a few minutes. They had three looters in custody and three cars full of loot. They would impound the cars and hold the property in them for the victims.

Later, at the station, the officers found that the car with the three microwaves was a *rental.* The arrestee, who had payroll stubs in his wallet, had rented it in Bakersfield, where he lived. *He had driven more than 100 miles with some friends* to join in the "spontaneous outburst of rage and frustration."

———————————

Riots are a source of terror and sorrow. That's how the vast majority of the residents of south-central L.A. reacted. They were horrified and much more critical of what was happening than those who watched on TV. For example, it's estimated that well over 90 percent of the residents of South-Central did *not* participate in the riots. Many did what they could to stop them, and some were killed in the attempt. Others risked their lives to save total strangers who were being viciously attacked by gang members.

Obviously, however, there were *some* people who wanted riots. Much evidence exists to show some had planned and prepared for them, like those who looted the Korean-owned grocery store. We can understand the involvement of certain hard-core gang members. Some of them are completely amoral, dead to feelings of guilt. To them, killing and destruction provide perverted pleasure. But could it be possible that others wanted rioting as well?

There are several theories about why certain people may have wanted riots. Drug lords thrive on chaos and misery. Those parasites want any condition that may increase their business, and they know people in despair and fear often turn to drugs. Human beings who have no hope are more prone to turn to an artificial escape. The drug dealers who exploit this weakness have no guilt about making their misery worse.

I have no hard evidence that drug lords were actually involved or gave orders, but my many years of experience with them drives me to this conclusion. Moreover, many of the gang members arrested for arson and other serious crimes in the riots have police records for drug trafficking.

Hard-core criminals are another group that likes riots. Many "hardcase" burglars participated in the looting, taking advantage of circumstances that allowed them to ply their trade with relative impunity. Of course, all looters are burglars. A truly honest person can resist being "caught up in the carnival atmosphere of shopping without money or credit cards." (During the aftermath of the riots, I heard many pundits and talk-show participants explain the criminal behavior with similar statements.) But habitual criminals had bonus days during the riots.

It's no secret that several elected officials and other so-called community leaders made statements encouraging a riot. During the year preceding the King verdict, many talked of "taking it to the streets," in effect issuing a self-fulfilling prophecy. U.S. Congresswoman Maxine Waters, for instance, was quoted in the media as saying, "Riot is the voice of the unheard." A May 10, 1992, *Times* article also included this statement: "'If it took a riot . . . so be it,' Waters said. 'I would not be able to be on national television, and Bush would not be in L.A.'" Other politicians made similar statements. In my opinion, those statements gave tacit approval to such abhorrent behavior.

The desire for power and influence is another reason certain individuals may welcome social upheaval—even riots. Let me explain. Society's usual response to a serious problem is to pour in massive amounts of government money to solve it. The disbursement of that money garners power and influence. The whole process of selecting the recipients is fraught with hazards. Often decisions of this nature are made in the proverbial smoke-filled rooms, behind the scenes. I've learned that few important decisions are actually made during the public sessions of government bodies. And many politicians make those kinds of decisions based upon what return they will get out of them rather than what is right.

Additionally, during and after times of social crisis, government officials are willing to empower certain individuals who are perceived as community leaders. They want all the help they can get to look as though they are doing good for their constituents. Some local leaders therefore look forward to crises as opportunities to be empowered. True leaders don't desire situations that harm others just so they can be personally empowered. But the power hungry do.

Another group of people with a vested interest in the continuation of social problems are those involved in the industry I call the Social Dysfunction Welfare Complex (SDWC). Here again, let me explain.

Because our society's standard approach to its problems has been to throw billions of government dollars at them, a whole industry based on social dysfunction has developed. Consequently, whether intended or not, many jobs now depend on the continued existence of problems. If there are no problems, jobs in the SDWC are in jeopardy. For the SDWC to continue to expand its power and income, problems must remain—or preferably even increase. This is the receiving end of the process I just described.

Certain politicians cater to the SDWC. They do this for a number of reasons. First, as suggested above, the more money they can hand out, the more votes and power they control. Federal funds en route to the SDWC are usually channeled through state and local governments. This sets up the mechanism for the old spoils system.

One day a few years ago, I got off the Harbor Freeway at Exposition Boulevard and saw several teams of young people with political signs promoting a candidate for a city office. Some of them were waving them at cars at the off-ramp. Others were posting them on telephone poles and on sticks they were pounding into the ground. The officer with me pointed out a van from which the signs were being distributed. On its side was the logo of a youth job-training/antipoverty program funded with government monies.

A good example of how the SDWC system works in L.A. is the black charitable organization known as the Brotherhood Crusade. Danny Bakewell, a close ally of Mayor Tom Bradley, has been the executive director of that organization for a number of years. The mayor has been instrumental in getting funding for the Crusade in a number of ways. For instance, he has led the way in getting the Crusade approved for the city payroll deduction plan so city employees can have a set amount of pay taken out of each check and sent to the Crusade. He has also encouraged city workers to contribute directly to the organization. This has resulted in hundreds of thousands of dollars of funding for Bakewell's group.

Bakewell's style of leadership is not in the traditional mode of the CEO of a charitable entity. He is known as a community activist. Some of his tactics have been questionable, to say the least. For example, he was the lightning rod in a conflict between Korean store owners and their black customers, leading boycott demonstrations against some of the stores. One of the targeted stores was firebombed. I believe Bakewell's intemperate statements and actions may have incited those responsible for the outrageous crime.

Bakewell does not live in L.A., but he's active in the city whenever and wherever there's social strife. In my opinion, he wants to demonstrate that there are ongoing problems only his organization can help solve.

On the positive side, many SDWC organizations exist solely to solve problems. The Community Youth Gang Services and Youth Corps are two examples. So I'm not saying that all leaders and workers in the SDWC industry have bad motives. I know many who have altruistic motives. However, put simply and straightforwardly, I believe there were *some* who actually wanted riots to dramatically illustrate the need for continued and even greater funding for the SDWC.

As I said before, I believe the vast majority of the people in south-central L.A. did not want the riots to happen and did not participate in them. If this analysis is correct, it should have been possible to control them. So the big question is, why weren't they quickly controlled? Well, actually they were controlled in certain parts of the city. A good case in point is what happened in the Foothill area.

The Rodney King incident occurred in the Foothill area. If any portion of the city was vulnerable to a spontaneous riot, it was there. Foothill's large minority community had a strong personal interest in the outcome of the infamous case. When the verdict was announced, that community reacted with understandable anger.

Captain Tim McBride is the CO of the LAPD's Foothill area. A 27-year veteran of the department, he worked himself up through the ranks the hard way. Rather than bouncing from one inside job to another, most of his experience was on the street. His winsome smile and easygoing manner are assets both within the department and with community groups. People like Tim McBride because he sincerely likes people. Yet he has demonstrated he's able to make the tough decisions necessary to achieve the rank he has in a big-city police department.

On the day the verdicts were announced, McBride immediately went into the community, looking for opportunities to listen and respond to concerns. After Mayor Bradley's news conference—when emotions began to run high—McBride went to a black Baptist church where he had learned a meeting was underway.

When he arrived, the minister, the Reverend Dudley Chapman, introduced him to the congregation. "I knew there would be at least two people at this meeting tonight," Chapman said, "myself and the man I am about to introduce—Captain Tim

McBride."

McBride had established credibility with the community during the year following the King incident. He had maintained a grueling schedule, running a busy police precinct during the day and attending community meetings at night. He had also participated in a series of community awareness seminars; he listened and talked about the King incident, as well as any other matters of community concern. Altogether, more than thirty thousand people had been touched by his genuine desire to help improve their quality of life. He had won their trust and support. The people at the church meeting were very angry, but not with Captain McBride.

He had also attended my meeting on April 10, 1992. He had listened and then acted on the directions provided. That wasn't a change of course for him; the meeting merely added urgency to his efforts and focused attention on the probability of a riot.

After our meeting on April 10, McBride immediately began having around-the-clock roll-call training on riot-control procedures. He updated all necessary equipment. For example, he had to provide helmets and face shields to certain officers. An already scheduled training day was revised to include riot squad formation drills. When a supervisor told him they didn't have sufficient time in the schedule to include that training, he responded, "We don't have the time *not* to include it. It shall be included." It was.

McBride was at the Baptist church with the Reverend Chapman when the riots began. He was summoned back to the station at a little after 8:00 P.M. When he arrived, more than 400 demonstrators had gathered out front. Things were getting ugly. Soon a fire was started across the street from the station, and the crowd began throwing rocks and bottles.

Sergeant Sol Polen, who had been in charge of the riot training, was there as the trouble began. He took swift action, forming the officers into the formations they had practiced. They had already closed off the street when McBride arrived.

The police began to move the crowd out of the street and stop their illegal actions. First they formed a skirmish line and pushed the crowd across the street from the station. Someone in the mob fired a couple of shots into the air, and the officers had no way of knowing where the gun was pointed. They dropped to their knees, but they did not break ranks. The training paid off. They were a cool, disciplined unit.

About half a dozen arrests were necessary that night. Officers identified a handful of people who had broken the law by either throwing missiles at the police or attempting to start fires. The arrests were performed quickly and efficiently. Simultaneously, the officers moved in a skirmish line to disperse the mob. (Only three officers suffered minor injuries.) A riot in the Foothill area was averted because of quick and decisive police action.

Afterward, McBride and his staff contacted some local community leaders and asked for their help in preventing future demonstrations. The leaders said they knew who was involved, and they promised their support. They would contact the offenders. There were no further incidents at the police station.

Over the next several days of the riots, few incidents occurred in the Foothill area. Police there took a firm stand, with support from the community. They made more than 500 arrests, but there were only 15 locations where minor looting took place. No buildings were destroyed. A community-police partnership had worked.

That story should have been repeated throughout the city. Why wasn't it? If rioting was controlled in the area where the King incident took place, why wasn't it controlled elsewhere?

I have already presented facts to show that the officers on the street were ready and willing to do their job. Therefore, I believe the difference was *leadership*. In my opinion, a failure of leadership occurred for at least two basic reasons. First, the bashing of the LAPD for more than a year had taken its toll. Second, the politicization of the department had caused some leaders to compromise their professionalism.

The Christopher Commission, together with some of the media elite, had publicly pounded the LAPD. In their desire to get rid of Chief Gates and seize control, they had mounted a constant bombardment, emphasizing the failures of the department. Morale within the organization was pushed lower and lower. Naturally, many of those in leadership positions were profoundly affected. Some were stunned and paralyzed. When they were then faced with a massive crisis, they were unable to function. Some had lost their confidence. Others were afraid to be the decision makers who would, no doubt, be second-guessed later.

The political takeover of the department likewise had a predictable result. When career-minded officers know the department's top leadership must bow to political influence rather than be guided by professional standards, their behavior is often modified accordingly. It's no secret that City Councilman Mark Ridley-Thomas repeatedly cautioned police leadership in his district to not take precipitous action. At the beginning of the riots, a police commissioner stated publicly that he believed the police should allow some property damage to occur rather than force a confrontation that might result in a loss of human life. Their motives may have been good, but their logic was flawed.

To show police "restraint" at the beginning of a riot, to allow property damage, is tantamount to saying, "Allow the forest fire to burn, but only let it burn the small trees." You can't have rioting without almost certainly having serious injury and death. Swift and decisive action must be taken. It may have cost some lives to do so, but in the long run, more lives would have been saved. The Foothill experience is proof that it can be done.

I also believe some in the LAPD leadership were loathe to follow my riot-preparation plans for political and personal reasons. The ACLU-run power structure had criticized the department as being too militaristic. Some of the police executives did not want to be identified with Chief Gates and myself. I believe they purposely chose to disregard our direction. They wanted to please the new power structure. Further, some of them had been deeply involved in an unhealthy competition with me for the chief's job. As a result, they had personal antagonism for me that made them recalcitrant and rebellious toward my leadership.

Once the riots began, these leaders were not only personally unprepared, but they also didn't want to offend the politicians who were uttering rhetoric sympathetic to the rioters.

Unless the course of political leadership in L.A. is changed quickly, the LAPD will become an ineffective, second-rate, paralyzed organization. Tragically, the city, like the nation, is on a course to deterioration and failure. In the first three months of the new LAPD administration, morale is reportedly low, and crime is rising sharply. The murder rate is climbing fast. Officer-initiated arrests are down. The city's financial situation is such that even though the new chief, Willie Williams, deserves nothing but support and encouragement, he may not get the resources he needs to do an effective job.

Failure is not inevitable, however. There is hope. And understanding what causes problems is the first and most important step in solving them.

Much has been said of so-called root causes. In my opinion, most of those touted in the media are actually just surface symptoms. Poverty, racism, poor education, lack of job opportunities, and crime are very real concerns. But there are deeper problems that cause these symptoms to appear. We must probe deeply to uncover the true root causes of our society's problems. In the next five chapters, I'll try to make those deep probes, describing five vital root causes we must correct.

PART 2:
ROOT CAUSES

16

INTRODUCTION: THE NEED TO LOOK DEEPER

One day in 1968, I accompanied Esther to a Laundromat in the small village of Wilmette, Illinois. Wilmette is located on the shore of Lake Michigan, just above Chicago. It's part of what people there refer to as "The North Shore," a posh series of suburban communities that has one of the highest average incomes in the nation. I didn't understand the need for a Laundromat in such a wealthy community, but we were glad it was there. We needed it.

The LAPD had sent me to study for a full school year at the well-respected Traffic Institute of Northwestern University. The university is located in Evanston, the village between Wilmette and the northern border of Chicago. We miraculously found a rental at an affordable price. It was unfurnished, so we went to garage sales and got a few pieces of used furniture. We could not afford even a used washer and dryer, however, so we made weekly visits to the Laundromat.

Wilmette had only three or four blocks of quaint stores and other commercial buildings in the village center. The Laundromat was at the end of one of these blocks. It had no more than a dozen washers lining one wall, with four or five dryers on the other wall. Today was our third trip to do the washing, and we noticed a pattern. For some reason, a few teenagers hung around there. Maybe it was because of the rest room facilities and the Coke machine.

I hadn't paid much attention to them until I got a whiff of a familiar odor. They were smoking marijuana. I took a better look, watching them inconspicuously for several minutes. There was no doubt about it. I could see the small, hand-wrapped joint as it was passed from one teen to the other. Each would cup it in his or her hands and take the typical deep "hit," sometimes coughing but trying to hold the smoke in as long as possible. They were showing the classic symptoms of being high on grass. They were gregarious, laughing at practically every statement or action. Their eyes were red. But their actions were those of novices to the drug scene.

I was somewhat surprised. The whole drug culture had exploded in the early 1960s. I had been assigned the Juvenile Narcotics detail. We had a massive drug-abuse problem in L.A., especially in the inner city. But I really didn't expect to find it in Wilmette, Illinois—not in this bastion of tradition and high society.

Over the next few weeks, I watched groups of teenagers as I came home from school. Most of the young people did not display any actions or symptoms of drug usage. The small group at the Laundromat continued their dangerous experimentation, however. I went to the local police department.

The officers were receptive and responsive. They wanted to do the right things. They would give the Laundromat special attention and take enforcement action if possible. They also wanted me to talk to other city officials and parent groups.

Over the next few months, I did explain my observations to officials and parents. In my opinion, their community was at the same turning point that Los Angeles faced in the late 1950s and early '60s. I warned them that unless swift action was taken, drug abuse would soon be a pervasive problem.

They were polite and kind, but they did not agree with my analysis. They believed their community was different from L.A., that the problem would never rise to a dangerous level.

Five years later, my prediction had come true. The North Shore villages asked me to speak at special assemblies in both New Trier East and West high schools. Drug abuse had become a major problem, and the parents and school officials were desperate.

As stated earlier and as Wilmette's experience verifies, Los Angeles is a sort of weather vane that gives us a forecast of the nation's future. Like it or not, trends often surface in L.A. that are destined to sweep the nation. Thus, a careful analysis of social conditions and events in L.A. can give all of us a "wake-up" call. My fear is that the warning signs will be hard to believe, that many will say, like the people of Wilmette, "That may be occurring in Los Angeles, but it will never happen here." Believe me, it will.

In part 2 of this book, we turn our attention to the root causes of L.A.'s massive problems. The stories used to describe the causes are true. To many readers, they may seem bizzare, outside the norm, and in a sense they are. But we learn by examining the most blatant cases.

Observing, listening, and acting on the wake-up call will help us to avoid the continuing decline that is otherwise inevitable. Learning from the L.A. experience can provide a road map for the future. My hope is that with this map, we can change our course. We can turn away from failure and move in the direction of a bright future for ourselves and our children.

17

ROOT CAUSES: THE ABANDONMENT OF OUR CHILDREN

*When things are valued more than people,
people lose their self-esteem.*

It was twilight in south-central L.A. as three members of the Swans gang gathered in an alley. One removed the cloth wrapping from an AK-47 assault rifle, while another pushed long, brass cartridges into a magazine that held 30 rounds. When full, it was handed to the guy with the gun. He slammed it home in the receiver.

They climbed into a light-colored, four-door compact from which the plates had been removed. The car moved slowly down the alley before stopping at 110th Street. The occupants looked both ways, waited for a large, red sedan to pass, and then turned south on the first street west. When no other vehicles were in view at the next intersection, they turned west and crossed three streets. At the next alley, they turned north.

A slow drizzle fell as the compact moved carefully up the alley. The car stopped about halfway between streets, and the two passengers got out and continued north on foot. The guy on the right had the long gun. A 12-year-old girl came out the back door of a nearby house to feed a dog. Even in the dim light, she saw the gun. He really wasn't trying to hide it.

"Get back in the house, girl," he said. "We ain't looking at you. Don't you go looking at us."

She dropped the dog's dish and stepped back into the house.

As the two young men continued walking toward the next street, the car followed. They angled toward the east until they were walking right next to the double garage. The doors were closed. It was the last building on the alley before the intersection with 109th Street. A vacant lot on the corner of 109th and Figueroa extended all the way back to the alley.

An abandoned car sat just about in the middle of the lot. Its tires and wheels were gone, but otherwise it was intact. Strangely, even the windows were unbroken. Four teenage boys sat in the abandoned car, talking in low tones. The two front windows were rolled down.

The two Swans members had stopped at the edge of the garage. They both looked cautiously around the corner at the car.

"Okay, let's do it, man," one of them said.

The one with the AK-47 walked rapidly toward the abandoned car, facing the rear window. As he walked, he raised the weapon to his shoulder and squeezed the trigger. The gun jumped slightly as a ball of flame spit out of the muzzle. The rear window disintegrated. The head of the 17-year-old in the right rear jerked sickeningly forward. He never knew what happened.

The firing continued as the boy with the rifle calmly walked in a complete circle around the car. At first he fired at the windows, but as the boys inside tried to seek cover, he fired into the doors. AK-47 rounds have a cylinder of armor-piercing metal at their core. The other Swan member lifted a handgun and capped off a few rounds of his own.

It was over in less than 30 seconds. The compact slid up, the two shooters got in, and the car sped away, squealing its wheels as they turned south on Figueroa. A couple of screams from a nearby apartment pierced the air. Several dogs started barking.

I was just pulling out of the Parker Center underground parking garage when I heard the radio call. The three beeps that precede a "hotshot" got my attention.

"All units in the vicinity and 18 X 23, an ambulance shooting at the southwest corner of 109th and Figueroa. 18 X 23, code two," the dispatcher said.

"18 X 23, that's a rog."

"18 X 23, we have additional. Possible vehicle used was a beige Japanese make, left southbound on Figueroa Street. Three male black suspects in dark clothing. No further description. Multiple victims down at the scene."

"18 X 23, roger. We are approaching the scene from the north. Are there any CRASH units available? This sounds like a drive-by."

"18 X 23, checking."

"3 CRASH 6, we copied and are rolling."

Each of the city's four bureaus has a CRASH unit. CRASH is an acronym for "Community Resources Against Street Hoodlums." Each unit is composed of specially trained officers who deal with the gang problem. As the name implies, the strategy is not solely directed toward enforcement. Units mobilize community groups, meet with parents, and maintain gang information files. In recent years, gang violence has increased rapidly. Of necessity, most of the CRASH units' time is now spent in enforcement and following up on gang murders.

Now we had another drive-by with multiple victims. Although I was at least 20 minutes away, I decided to roll. I tried to get out into the field at least once a month. Often, donning my uniform, I would team up with a "partner" and work a few hours to keep in touch with what the officers at the operating level were doing and needed in terms of support. Since I was in plain clothes now, I would just observe.

I arrived 23 minutes later. The yellow tape was already up, and 109th Street was closed 100 yards from Figueroa west past the alley. The alley was completely closed between 109th and 110th. A sergeant was in charge of the scene; there were two black and whites and two plain cars. About 15 neighbors stood just outside the tape on the sidewalk. Some had umbrellas. I didn't, so I put on my trench coat and rain hat and grabbed my flashlight.

Four uniformed officers were protecting the perimeter of the scene. One plainclothes and two uniformed officers were examining the ground around the abandoned car. I later learned they were from South Bureau CRASH. They had already circled (with chalk) some expended brass casings on the alley and sidewalk and were placing white paper makeshift hoods over the casings on the dirt. The partner to the plainclothes officer protecting the casings was talking to some of the people gathered just outside the tape. He had his notebook in his hand; he was probably getting statements from witnesses. A couple of detectives I recognized from our South/East Area were just pulling up and parked behind my car.

I approached the sergeant. "What happened here, Sarge?"

"We got another drive-by, except it looks like they got out of their car to make sure everyone got hit."

"How many hit?"

"Four. One is still in the car over there. He's dead. We're waiting for the coroner. The other three have been taken to L.A. County General. One won't make it. He was dying as they left. One of the remaining two looks like he'll be okay—no torso wounds, just legs and buttocks. The other, I don't know. He was talking and looked pretty good, but he had a couple of nasty wounds. They put him in one of those pressure suits. Come on under the tape, Sir. I'll show you around."

He held up the yellow tape as I slipped under it. We walked toward the abandoned car, and he pointed out the shell casings with his flashlight. The chalk circles and white paper hoods formed an almost perfect circle with a ten-foot radius around the car. Obviously, the shooter had walked around methodically, pumping bullets into the car. The holes in the metal were easy to see, even in the darkness. The paint was blown away around the holes, making one-inch circles.

We walked carefully toward the murder scene, staying on the street and sidewalk. We didn't want to disturb any footprints or other possible evidence. The ground around the car had already been trampled by the paramedics as they tried to save lives. Some bloodied gauze pressure pads were scattered around and in the car. I flashed my light on the body in the back seat.

"He's just a kid," I said. "What a waste!"

"He was probably the oldest, Chief. The kid that was dying didn't look over 14."

We stood there for a moment. I flashed my light on one of the nearby brass casings. "Looks like either an AR-15 or an AK-47," I remarked.

"Yeah. Thirty of them. He must have emptied a banana magazine. There's also a few 9 millimeter casings here. They may not be from this shooting, though. A lot of violence around here, Sir."

One of the CRASH plainclothes officers converged with us as we walked back to the street. I looked him over. He appeared to be Hispanic, five feet ten inches tall, with a neatly trimmed mustache. From the size of his shoulders and neck and the way his arms filled out his tweed sportcoat sleeves, I guessed he pumped iron. He couldn't have been over 27 years old. He must have established a good record in patrol work or he wouldn't be part of a CRASH unit. I thought he would know the answer, so I asked the question.

"What was this shooting about?"

"Well, first of all, this is a busy corner. The kids in the car were selling rock. There were a few bags in the car. They usually just stand around on this empty lot and stash it here and there. Tonight, because of the rain, they were in that abandoned car. They walk it out to the customers who pull up to the curb. 'Narc' rips them off all the time, but there's always someone else. And the juvies rarely get any time. They're right back selling in a few hours. The young ones sell it for the older dudes. They make a couple of hundred a day. Not bad for a drop-out."

"Who shot them, and why?"

"At this point, it looks like a neighboring gang wanted the corner. They didn't take the dope or money." He shrugged his shoulders. "Hey, Chief, life is cheap to some people. You want a lucrative corner and someone is in the way—kill him. Pretty sad, huh?"

"Life is cheap." *No it's not,* I thought. *Every human life is important. Every human being is an eternal soul. The lives lost here tonight are more important than the money being made on this corner. What's happening to us in this city?*

The officer was right, of course. To some, the drug money was more important than human life. That was apparent here. I knew that in South/East, just one of the city's 18 police areas, there would probably be more than 100 murders this year. Many of them would be like these tonight—senseless slaughter of our youth.

I stuck around and watched the investigation proceed. Then, when things were wrapped up and the sergeant was about to leave, I approached him. I wanted to ride around with him for an hour or two.

We drove north on Figueroa, then turned right and crossed the freeway over to Avalon. Turning south on Avalon, I saw a group of teenagers gathered around a phone booth. A couple of them had beepers on their belts.

"Look, Sarge, some businessmen and doctors. Let's talk to them." He knew from the way I spoke that I had them pegged as dope couriers.

We pulled into a gas station adjacent to the liquor store where the pay phones were located. As I got out of the car, the kids started to walk away.

"Hey, don't split," I said. "We aren't going to arrest anyone. I just want to talk."

Two kept walking away rapidly. Three remained, looking curiously at me. The uniformed sergeant they knew, but who was this older tall guy in the trench coat? *The two that split have a gun, the dope, or both,* I thought.

"Hi, you guys. What's happening?"

"Nothin' to it. Who are you?"

"I'm one of the brass from downtown. I'm trying to learn something. Mind if I ask a couple of questions?"

"You're the police. You usually do what you want."

The one talking was the shortest of the group, but he was salty. The other two were watching sullenly. At that last reply, the fat one grinned. He looked about 13 or 14 years old.

"Look, I've worked the streets a long time. I know what you guys are up to. I know you're gang banging and pushing dope."

This time the tall one spoke: "Then why are you asking questions?"

The fat kid grinned again. He was enjoying his buddies' standing up to me. I chose my next question carefully. I didn't want them to think I was trying to build a case.

"Where is this action leading? When you're in your twenties and want a good job, it's going to haunt you. Don't you know all your arrests and gang banging will keep you from living a good life later on?"

The salty one pushed his sunglasses back on his head. "Hey, man," he answered, "I'm not going to make 21. I'll die gang banging long before then. I'm just grabbing what I can, when I can, while I'm alive."

The fat kid joined in. "Like the man say, grab what you can now. There ain't no tomorrow."

I looked into their eyes. They weren't putting me on; they believed what they were saying. There was a certain deadness about their look. They weren't innocent kids. These were human beings who didn't know their own worth. They were hard, cynical, calloused, and *hopeless.*

Valuing material things and money above people is one of the true root causes of our culture's destruction. When the material is apprized more than people, people lose self-esteem and regard for others.

Many young people today lack a healthy sense of self-worth. The intensity of the problem varies from person to person, but at the extreme end of the continuum are those who hate themselves. They see no value in themselves. Their lives are miserable. And if they're just a bunch of garbage waiting to decay, so is everyone else.

Those who have reached this extreme are very dangerous. They're angry and bitter. Life for them is a grievous, sour joke, something to dull with drugs and sex until it mercifully ends. Since that's their view, it's easy to end the "worthless" life of another. When self-respect is nonexistent, so is respect for others.

In the inner city, the overemphasis on possessions is obvious. Many young lives have been snuffed out for a leather jacket, a ghetto blaster, or a pair of Air Jordans. But is it the same in the rest of the city?

———————————————————

I had just finished addressing a high school assembly in the high-rent district. The students wore designer clothes and drove BMWs. They were predominantly white and rich. But the drug problem was there, too.

I was talking with a group of kids near the stage. One of the school officials moved in close and spoke softly in my ear: "See those two big twins over there? They want to talk to you, but they're a little shy. They need some encouragement. Don't let them walk away."

I continued answering questions from the group, but I kept my eyes on the twins. They were tall, blond, and well built. They listened at the edge of the crowd but didn't join in the dialogue.

The time slipped away. A bell rang for the next period to begin, and the group dispersed. I moved quickly toward the twins and struck up a conversation.

The school official was right. They needed help. Over the next few minutes, I could see the telltale signs. They couldn't meet my eyes with theirs. Their mannerisms were similar to those of gang bangers. They didn't like themselves. Soon we were talking about their drug abuse. They weren't the bitter, hopeless teenagers some people envision when they think of drug abusers; they were white, rich, and had opportunities most kids don't.

I found the school official and asked, "What gives with those two guys? They should have the world by the tail, but they're in bad shape. Why are they so cynical? Looks to me as if they have everything going for them."

He looked straight at me, shaking his head and tightening his jaw. "Sad story. They've got everything . . . except what they want and need the most. Come from a very wealthy family. Their estate overlooks the ocean. Their parents are busy making money and pursuing the social set. Too busy for the boys. They built the boys their own house on the property. A housekeeper tends to their needs. Now, as they're getting older, the parents want their love. The boys don't have any love to give—I guess too many years of what they saw as rejection."

Things are more important than people. That mentality is wreaking havoc here, too, I thought. Hardly a person would *say* things are more important than people. But our actions betray our stated priorities. We may say we value our children over houses, cars, and various other gadgets, but the way we behave argues otherwise.

Some say poverty causes crime and social breakdown, but I don't believe that—it wasn't true in 99 percent of the cases I saw as a police officer. (It certainly does *tempt* some people to steal, however.) If it were true, the opposite would also be true—wealth would cause goodness and family stability. We all know that's not the case.

What I *have* seen is a correlation between the *attitude* toward wealth and crime. Some of the rich won't share what they have in excess. On the contrary, they want more and will sacrifice human values to get it. For example, one reason for our lack of jobs is that wealthy factory owners and managers can find cheaper labor outside our country. So many companies have made the decision to have their manufacturing done elsewhere in order to make a bigger profit. Their personal bottom line is more important than the financial health of the nation.

At the same time, some of the poor are as much afflicted with the curse of materialism—an insatiable desire for more—as some of the rich. The cancerous passions of envy, greed, and selfishness are not bound by the size of a person's pocketbook.

On the other hand, there are many moral, loving, and healthy families in the inner-city ghettos, just as there are in suburbia. The issue isn't wealth or the lack thereof. It's the priority we place on material things as demonstrated by our behavior.

An overemphasis on the material is a terrible evil, a subtle, deadly diversion from the people in our lives and their needs. A common denominator I've seen in the lives of dysfunctional families is this plague of materialism. Children observe the role models around them. When they see their parents value material things over them, they don't feel good about themselves.

I pulled out of the police academy parking lot one day and headed down Academy Road. I had just enjoyed a good workout and steam and had that good tired feeling. It was a little after 7:00 P.M. I had called Esther from the locker room and told her I was on the way home. I turned on my police radio.

"Any Northeast unit. 11 A 21 is requesting a backup. They are pulling over a blue pickup truck with six possible gang members. 11 A 21 is requesting a backup at Fletcher Drive and San Fernando Road."

I was just turning onto Stadium Way, which runs into San Fernando Road about two miles north. Fletcher Drive is another mile. I listened for a response to the request, but none came.

Then I heard a sergeant broadcast, "11 L 20, I don't believe there are any Northeast units available. Show me handling the backup on San Fernando Road."

I had my 48-channel Rover switched to the Northeast/Rampart frequency. I picked up the mike and said, "11 L 20, this is Staff 2. I copied. I'll assist you with the backup. My ETA is about 3 minutes."

"Staff 2, that's a roger, Sir . . . and thanks."

When I rolled up on the scene, the sergeant was getting out of his black and white. The patrol car had all six of the occupants out of the truck and on the sidewalk, their hands clasped behind their heads. They were "dressed down"—definitely gang bangers. Four of them had blue bandannas hanging out of their rear pockets—Crips.

The officers were waiting for their backup before they started their search. Gang members in L.A. are often armed and dangerous. The search revealed no guns, but the young lady in the front seat had a few rocks of cocaine in her purse. The driver of the truck was wanted on a felony warrant for armed robbery. The two of them were hooked up and put in the back of the patrol car.

The four who had been riding in the bed of the truck were "wanna be's." None of them was carrying anything except their colors. They admitted to being eastside Crips.

The situation was stabilized. Two were going to jail, and the others would be released and put on a bus for home. I got in my car and continued on home. And as I drove, I thought about what had happened.

The four released were all under 16. One was only 12 years old. If I were a parent of one of those young men, I would want to know about this encounter. Here they were in the back of a pickup, flying their colors, being driven by an older gang banger wanted for armed robbery and probably his girlfriend, who was holding the dope.

When I got into my office the next day, I told my staff that we were starting a new program. It would be called "Jeopardy." We would devise a system where we would notify the parents of "wanna be's" observed in a dangerous but legal situation.

An order was cut. Officers observing neophyte gang bangers in potentially dangerous situations would conduct a field interview (FI), prepare an FI card, and mark it with a red J for Jeopardy. Station personnel would then file the J cards in a special folder, and specially trained CRASH or Juvenile officers would schedule occasional Jeopardy notification nights. The officers would go to the residence of a subject at the dinner hour, hoping to establish contact with the parent(s).

Two weeks later, I decided to monitor how the program was going. Our 77th Street area was having its first notification night. I grabbed a fast bite of dinner and drove to the station, where Captain Scott LaChasse was talking to some officers in the parking lot. He waved me over. As I approached, he greeted me and then gave me the news.

"We've got a problem with our Jeopardy notifications, Sir."

I wondered what he was going to tell me. Perhaps the parents were irate. Maybe they were angry we had identified their children as potential gang members. Or perhaps they were telling us to mind our own business. After all, the Jeopardy candidates had not been arrested.

"All right, what's the problem, Scotty?" I asked.

"Well, we've got several teams and quite a few cards to follow up on. We had scheduled 20 minutes per notification. That way we could finish the cards we have. But it's taking a lot longer than that. The parents or guardians want us to come in and sit down. They're very interested. They want a lot more than just a notification. They want some help."

"Scotty, that's not a problem. That's good news. Can I tag along with one of the units?"

Soon we were knocking on the door of a small, well-kept house. The neighborhood looked to be about 1920s vintage. Most of the houses had wood siding and front porches. This one had a beautiful flower garden.

An elderly black lady opened the door. One of the Juvenile officers said, "We are police officers, Ma'am. We are here as friends to leave a message. We're not here to arrest anyone."

"Thank you, officers. Now tell me what this is about."

"Are you the parent or guardian of James Gentry?"

"I am his grandmother. Why, has he done something wrong?"

"No, Ma'am, that's not why we're here. You see, James was stopped twice in the last two weeks in the company of some older, known gang members. We aren't here to threaten you or him about arresting him. We just thought you would want to know that. As dangerous as it is these days, if he keeps hanging around with those gang members, he's probably going to end up getting shot."

"Officers, would you please come in? We need to talk." Turning into the house, she called, "James!"

After she called a couple of times, James came into the room. He was 12 years old. She had him sit down also. He was very uncomfortable. The officers described the circumstances surrounding the contact with him and offered suggestions for how to pull him back from his gang associations. The woman asked the officers some questions, then turned to her grandson.

"James, you know I took you in here because your mother doesn't want you."

I was watching the lad's face. When she said that, he winced as if he'd been stabbed with a knife.

"She's too busy with her life. With her working and running around with men, she's got no time for you.

"Your father never did want you. Always running around, chasing women. Now he's in and out of jail. He don't want you."

He recoiled again. His head went down, and he stared at the floor. If despair can be seen, that was it.

"James, this is serious," she continued. "I won't have you doin' that gang-banging stuff. If you won't do what these officers say, you can't stay here, either."

That was it. The end of the road. This lad had suffered rejection by parents on their own trajectory.

Our visit with James and his grandmother was typical of the calls made that night. They all had one thing in common: The kids had experienced rejection—some overt, some more subtle. They needed acceptance. And in its perverted way, a gang is a family—a support group.

Most readers of this book may not identify with the precise circumstances of James's story. But the basic principles touch a majority of American families today.

We rationalize the shameful practice of putting possessions before our children. The phrase "standard of living" is used a lot. We say, "To maintain our standard of living, we both must work." That's a euphemism for saying cars, VCRs, microwaves, CD players, nice houses, and the latest fashions are more important than our children. I know there are many single parents who have to work outside the home. But I believe that in many cases, the argument that both parents in a two-parent home need outside work is only a rationalization. They may truly need more income to pay for the standard of living they've adopted—by choice. Their monthly bills may exceed the income of one wage earner. But my thesis is that many of those bills are discretionary and not true necessities.

If American parents could clearly see the choice before them, I believe most would choose the best interests of their children. There is massive, subtle deception on this issue. Many forces have clouded their vision. Advertising, for instance, is intended to convince consumers they have a need to buy something new, and it's powerfully effective. Much of our economy is based on the assumption that both parents are working.

Additionally, those who have suffered failure with their children due to materialism inadvertently rationalize and justify their choice. Their egos have jaded their judgment. They want to feel good about their wrong choices. In hindsight, their guilt is too hard to face. So they work hard at selling others on the rightness of their life-style. Consequently, the prevailing opinion on this issue supports the "need" and moral justification for both parents' working outside the home.

As a result, many of our children come home to empty houses. They either cope with profound loneliness or share their burden with other lonely kids. Still other children share a house with parents who subconsciously see them as distractions and diversions from their main goals.

I realize my analysis sounds harsh, but my 38 years of dealing with society's problems demand candor, even facing the probability of ridicule and rejection.

Children need supportive families. They need lasting relationships with people who have journeyed through life before them. They need to feel they belong to a group that will encourage, guide, and protect them. All of this takes time. All of this is a demonstration of what human beings want above all else. All of this is love.

> *Hold back the unruly,*
> *Encourage the timid,*
> *Support the weak,*
> *Be patient with all.*
>
> Paul, the apostle, circa A.D. 30

18

ROOT CAUSES: HEDONISM

When pleasure is pursued at all costs,
lasting fulfillment is lost.

During the 1960s, I worked the Juvenile Narcotics Detail and saw the drug problem explode. At first it was just a few kids at a few high schools. Then the numbers grew to 10 to 15 percent at practically every high school. Soon, the only way to have some semblance of control on the campuses was to send in undercover cops.

We took a few young-looking officers out of each academy class, cut their hair in the latest fashion, and dressed them appropriately. They actually enrolled in school, attended classes, and did homework. Even the teachers didn't know they were cops.

Our officers would observe who was selling drugs on campus and make buys from each active pusher. We usually covered from six to ten schools each semester. After about three months, we would round up all the pushers, usually on the same day, and surface the officers. We would then call a press conference to announce the results of the operation, hoping the open, widespread coverage would act as a deterrent to others.

A high school student-body president echoed my feelings about these operations when a TV reporter interviewed him. On camera, the reporter asked, "Tell me, how do you, as student-body president, feel about having an undercover cop on your campus?"

The student frowned and answered, "I don't like it. I don't like it at all."

Then he paused, frowned again, sighed, and continued, "But there's one thing I like even less. I don't like dope dealers on our campus, either. I guess if I have to choose . . . I'll go with the cop."

The big increases in drug usage in the 1960s leveled off somewhat in the '70s. The fad of sniffing cocaine started to spread in the latter part of the decade. Then crack, or rock, cocaine entered the scene in the 1980s. Drug abuse took off again. Smoking rock spread throughout society, crossing all ethnic, economic, and geographic lines. In Los Angeles, the "rock house" phenomenon emerged.

When I worked the streets as a dope cop, forcing entry into these distribution centers was relatively simple. If we had a warrant to serve and were not granted entrance, we would merely kick in the door. A healthy kick or two, just a few inches from the latch, would usually do the trick. On the more sturdy doors, we would take "the key to the city."

The "key" was a battering ram that took several men to pick up and carry. The problem with using it was that we often had trouble stopping once we were through the door. The whole pack of officers might stumble several feet into the building. We used to joke, "Watch out or we'll end up in the bathroom."

In response, crack dealers began barricading their distribution points. At the early rock houses, buyers would put their money in a slot and receive the cocaine out of the same slot. The houses had steel bars over the windows and steel plate or screen doors, with steel-reinforced latches. The "key" became obsolete.

Then we started using a pull cable and a four-by-four truck to yank the bars off the windows. But most of the rock houses had heavily armed guards, so we also found it necessary to begin using diversionary concussion grenades. The "flash-bangs," as we began calling them, will immobilize an armed suspect for a few seconds—just enough time for us to make a rapid entry and possibly disarm the guards rather than having to shoot.

In this ever-escalating battle, the dealers next began building metal cages inside the door. If we were successful in battering down the door, we would find ourselves in an inner cage, vulnerable to gunfire. They also reinforced the bars on the windows across at least two studs in the wall. We damaged a good truck the first time we went up against that.

We needed another tool, so we acquired an armored personnel carrier from the military. It looks like a tank, but in place of a cannon, we installed a 15-foot, heavy pipe battering ram with an 18-inch square plate on the end. It became known as the LAPD ram. With that tool we could make our own entry point, and did. It worked like a charm.

But once again, the dealers made adjustments. Soon they would barricade a room in the center of the house. Sometimes they would stack cars around the house on the lawn to make it difficult or impossible to use the ram.

Then our bomb squad devised linear-shaped charges. With a small amount of plastic explosives pushed into a steel angle iron, we could focus the force surgically. I've seen blown entry points that looked like the work of a band saw. Of course, the use of these extreme measures was carefully controlled and done only with the approval of the chief of police.

One afternoon, the paperwork for the approval of one such "extraordinary entry" came across my desk. The lieutenant from the SWAT team serving the warrant was hand carrying the approval form through the chain of command. They were working against time: The entry would be attempted that night at 8:00.

This one was unusual. The LAPD ram could not be used. The distribution building was a reinforced garage facing a narrow alley. We couldn't get the ram down the alley and negotiate the tight turn that would be necessary. I asked what plans had been developed. The lieutenant had a couple of sergeants with him. They laid out a diagram on the conference table in my office, and the lieutenant explained.

"Well, Sir, we can't use the ram, and explosives would be ineffective." He paused a moment and brought his eyes up from the diagram to meet mine. "They're always trying to keep one step ahead of us." Then he grinned and said, "That will be the day, Sir. Tonight we've got a secret weapon. They think they're really smart. They've built a wall inside the outer wall." He pointed to a cross-section drawing of the structure of the garage double wall.

I was puzzled, so I asked, "Why did they do that?"

"That, Sir, is to neutralize our plastic explosive shaped charge. They have filled this three-foot space between the walls with old car tires. Our explosives would cut a nice entry point through the outer wall, but not through three feet of tires and another wall. The size of the charge to get through both would be too dangerous to anyone inside. By the time we worked our way through the tires and breached the second wall, the dope would be down the flush system connected to the sewer line."

I shook my head and replied, "Lieutenant, our job is changing, isn't it? Tanks, explosives, and concussion grenades. And we're up against AK-47s and battlements like this." I looked over the photos taken from our helicopter and asked, "Okay, what's the secret weapon?"

He took a manila envelope from the table, pulled out another photo, and handed it to me.

I looked it over and said, "It looks like a big spear, with some weird device just behind the point. Back near the end of the thing is some type of lever . . . or something."

"You're close. This thing works like a giant Molly screw. The entry team will sneak down the alley. Grady here will hold the thing at the proper place against the outer wall. Big Dave will drive the thing through both walls with a big sledgehammer. Once it's in there, we pull back the lever, and those four steel shanks open up inside the inner wall."

"Then what?"

"See this big ring welded on near the end of the device? That's where we attach it to the cable on Pete's heavy-duty tow truck. When he puts it in compound and presses the pedal to the metal, we got ourselves a nice entry hole. In the meantime, our boys in the front will have dropped in a flash-bang to get their attention."

"Where's your roll call, and at what time? I've got to see this."

The roll call was held at South/West station on Martin Luther King Boulevard. I saw the new device up close. It was about 7 feet long and must have weighed at least 100 pounds. It would take a guy like Grady to hold it in place. Big Dave had his huge sledge. They were all in their SWAT turn-out fatigues. Their appearance alone should cause most crooks to throw in the towel. They wear black fatigues, black boots, black knit face covers with black goggles, and each has a Heckler and Koch MP-5 submachine gun hanging across his chest on a sling.

The large diagram of the scene was taped to the blackboard at the front of the room. The various enlarged pictures of the area were also displayed. Each man was given his assignment. The radio communications system was tested. Every officer had an earplug receiver and a small mike positioned against his mouth. Once activated, they would be in constant communication with each other.

We rendezvoused two blocks from the location on 43rd Street at Budlong. I would go with the team to the front of the location. We had an observation point (OP) down two houses and across the street from the location. It was a small delivery truck with an appropriate ad on the side; it was equipped with covert visual monitoring devices, plus a complete communications package. The men in the truck kept us informed of the activities around the location. From the traffic going in and out, it looked as if they were well stocked with drugs. We would send in an undercover officer (UC) to make sure, just before entry.

Sitting in a plain car with the lieutenant, I could hear the radio communication.

"R 50 David to 20 David, this looks like a busy night. Why don't you go ahead and send in the UC?"

"R 20 David to 50, that's a rog. He'll be coming eastbound on 43rd Street. He's wearing a long, black coat. The 'friendly' with him has on a leather jacket and a green baseball cap."

Several minutes went by. Then we heard, "R 50 David, we see the UC and his 'friendly.' They're approaching the location."

Again there was dead time on the radio. Then 50 came in again. "R 20 David, the UC just came back out. He's giving the go signal. He's made a buy."

The lieutenant keyed his mike and said, "All units stand by. Give me your affirmative. 22 David, are you ready?"

"22 David, roger."

The lieutenant went down his list of units participating in the operation. Each was in place and ready. "R 10 David to all units. It's a go. Let's move in. Go! Go! Go!"

We fired up our car and followed one of the units going to the front of the garage. Two teams were assigned to secure the house. We would go down a walkway alongside the front house, behind one of the entry teams. Even though I was an observer and would not go in until the location was secured, my adrenaline was pumping. I was wearing my bulletproof vest and had put my "raid jacket" over it. The word *POLICE* was emblazoned on both the front and back of the navy blue coat.

The lieutenant stopped the car 100 feet or so west of the location. We jumped out. The entry teams were moving quietly, double time, between the houses. We followed about 50 feet behind. Then I heard some officers shouting "Police officers!" The first flash-bang exploded. Again I heard, "Police officers! Get your hands in the air!"

Moments later, a SWAT member came running around the garage and approached the lieutenant. "Okay, Sir, clear," he said. "You guys can come in now. We're opening the front entry with our cutting torch."

He led us to the front of the garage, where the man with the torch had just finished his job. The acrid smell of burnt metal and explosives was in the air. We pushed past the smoldering metal door. One of the officers was holding a young man who looked about 14 or 15 years old. My eyes scanned the room. The south wall had a gaping hole in it. I pointed my flashlight into the hole and could see through to a second wall that had a similar hole. Tires were strewn around. The secret weapon had worked.

I turned and walked over to where the officer had the young man. "Look who they had on the slot, Chief," the cop said. "He's just a kid."

My eyes turned to the seller. He was still shaking from the impact of the entry. The flash-bang followed by the entry of SWAT officers usually has that effect on people of all ages. No one was hurt. Large quantities of both dope and money were seized.

I waited for the kid to gather his composure. Then I asked, "What were you doing here?"

"You know what I was doin'. I'm selling rock."

I noticed a TV set on a table. It was positioned next to a desk-type arrangement someone had built just inside the slot in the metal door.

"What's the TV for?" I supposed it was some type of closed-circuit monitoring system such as many rock houses have.

"That's for my video games," the kid said. "That's part of the deal. I work a few hours a day. I get to play my games between customers, and I take home over a hundred a shift."

"What are you doing with all that money?"

"I keep a little. I give most of it to my mom."

"Doesn't your mom wonder about where and how you're getting that kind of money?"

He squirmed a bit before he answered, "She knows."

That young man's mother *did* know, but she had only imitated many in our society. She rationalized her son's involvement in the drug culture as tolerable because she needed the money. The "recreational" use of drugs is widespread. "Everyone" is doing it. If it makes people happy, why not supply the demand?

Drug abuse is a major problem in our society today, but it's a surface issue. The underlying problem is the widespread acceptance of the philosophy of hedonism. That philosophy leads not only to the establishment of a drug trafficking enterprise, but also to many other practices that are destroying our culture. The smugglers and sellers of drugs are simply supplying what many people want. I'm not justifying the actions of drug dealers, of course. Rather, I'm trying to emphasize the pervasive acceptance of the "recreational" use of mind-altering chemicals. It's just one surface manifestation of a pleasure-bent culture.

This devotion to hedonism, the pursuit of sensual pleasure above all else, is a second major root cause of the sickness in our society. It substitutes a quick feeling (often artificial) for real and lasting fulfillment. When feeling good becomes our top priority, complex human beings are reduced to self-centered castoffs at the level of simple animals. The depravity of "pleasure at all costs" is destroying our families and society.

Webster's Collegiate Dictionary (5th ed.) defines hedonism as follows: "The doctrine that pleasure is the sole or chief good in life, and that moral duty is fulfilled in the gratification of pleasure-seeking instincts and dispositions."

One historic test of a culture's priorities is to examine its rewards. Who makes the most money? Rather than listen to rhetoric from leaders or pundits about a culture's values, look at who's paid the best.

In our society, the people with the highest incomes are entertainers—people who sing for us, play games for us, and make us laugh. Madonna, the Rolling Stones, Bill Cosby, Bobby Bonilla, Jose Canseco, Kevin Costner, and Barbra Streisand are all in that category.

I don't see anything evil about playing a game. I *am* concerned about the content of some song lyrics and movies, but that's not my point here. The issue is that our priorities, as expressed by our reward system, are pleasure, entertainment, and feeling good.

The doctors or lab technicians who develop a vaccine or serum to prevent or cure AIDS will probably get a plaque and some certificates of recognition. They will continue to draw their annual salaries of well under $100,000. That seems twisted to me. Someone who entertains us gets several million dollars a year, but a person who saves millions of lives gets a plaque.

Some social observers have referred to this society as having a "me first" mentality. More than in previous generations, the attitude seems to be to "look out for number one." A whole movement has been built on self-fulfillment. Seminars are offered and books are written to pander to this egocentrism. The trend has penetrated every part of our culture, including the family.

The Old English word for family was *teme*, from which we get the modern word *team*. A team is a group of people who subordinate their personal interests to the welfare of the group. Those involved in organized sports understand the importance of that principle. A team on which each member is looking out for his or her own interests does not win the championship. Likewise, a family does not work when its members, especially the parents, want their desires met above all else.

In years past, parents who sacrificed for their children were looked upon as noble and honorable. Today, a person who follows that pattern is often looked upon as foolish and out of touch. I've heard counselors advise parents not to subordinate their interests for their families. They are warned that the children will soon be gone, and they're encouraged to think of themselves. That is precisely what many are doing. They bail out of marriages that seem not to fully satisfy them. They put careers first, relegating their children to child-care centers.

Many parents clearly see that it's wrong to choose material things over their children, but they end up with the same results from a different motivation because they've been seduced by the pervasive hedonism of our day. This devotion to self-gratification above all else is wreaking havoc on our families.

Children do best when they have the lifetime commitment of both parents. Urie Bronfenbrenner, professor of human development, family studies, and psychology at Cornell University, says:

Children growing up in such [single-parent] households are at greater risk for experiencing a variety of behavioral and educational problems, including extremes of hyperactivity or withdrawal, lack of attentiveness in the classroom, difficulty in deferring gratification, impaired academic achievement, school misbehavior, absenteeism, dropping out, involvement in socially alienated peer groups, and especially, the so-called "teenage syndrome" of behavior that tend to hang together—smoking, drinking, early and frequent sexual experience, a cynical attitude toward work, adolescent pregnancy and, in the more extreme cases, drugs, suicide, vandalism, violence, and criminal acts. ("What Do Families Do?" *Family Affairs*, 4, no. 1-2, winter/spring 1991: 1-6)

I see the results of hedonism and the connected egocentrism in the gang bangers of Los Angeles, the runaways (or, more accurately, throwaways) of Hollywood Boulevard, and the punk rockers of Beverly Hills. The young people who run into trouble at school and eventually with the police have one thing in common: They come from dysfunctional families, usually broken or single-parent homes. Most of the time, these are situations where someone has put his or her personal gratification first.

Drug abuse is an obvious example of the pursuit of hedonism, but other behaviors are just as destructive. An extramarital affair or a social life-style that excludes the children is also corrosive to family life. Pursuing an ego-satisfying career rather than fulfilling one's most important role—parenthood—is less offensive to society, but it's just as harmful to a child.

Children see this behavior pattern in their parents and adopt the same values. They, too, look out for themselves. They, too, pursue instant gratification at all costs.

The sad part is that when the bluebird of happiness is pursued this way, it's never grasped. Hedonism brings some immediate, short-lived thrills and gratification. But all the pleasure and achievement pale when people are estranged from their own flesh and blood. We all want happiness that's real and lasting. Family relationships are meant to endure and provide that fulfillment for a lifetime.

He whose passion is pleasure
will become impoverished of all else.

19

ROOT CAUSES: LOSS OF CONSCIENCE

When rebelling is a badge of honor,
peace and security vanish.

One of the sergeants from my administrative staff tapped on the open door and walked into my office. "Sir," he said, "there's been a bad shooting in Newton area. Some gang banger shot up several of the princesses in the Jefferson High School homecoming parade. Sounds pretty tragic. I thought you might want to roll."

"Shot up princesses in a homecoming celebration? Why would anyone want to do that?"

"That's what I wondered, Sir. I guess there's a lot of confusion going on right now. It just happened."

"Okay, Sergeant, I'll be going. Get my car. I'll meet you at the back door."

We drove quickly toward Newton Street Police Station. On the way over, we checked by radio and determined there wasn't much more to be done at the scene. The victims had been removed to the hospital, the witnesses to the station. They had a line on a suspect.

Going south on Central Avenue, we passed the headquarters for the Coca Cola Bottling Company in Los Angeles. The building looks like a large cruise ship and takes up an entire block of frontage. I continue to be amazed at the way the company maintains the superb appearance of the structure in a tough part of the city. We continued south one more block, then turned left on Newton. They call Newton Street Police Area "Shootin' Newton." That day, unfortunately, it again deserved the handle.

We pulled into the station's parking lot. Several officers were unloading arrestees from a couple of black and whites by the back door to the detective squad room. They greeted us as we walked past them to the other back door, by the watch commander's office. I made it my practice to check in with the watch commander upon arrival at a station.

The watch commander was busier than the proverbial one-armed paper hanger. He had a phone screwed into his ear, and at least two sergeants and four officers were waiting for his attention. As he held the phone against his shoulder with his head, he removed his "Sam Brown" gunbelt. I later learned he had just returned from supervising the crime scene. That's my kind of watch commander, ready and willing to be where it's happening and make the tough decisions.

When his eyes caught mine, I could tell what he was thinking: *All I need right now is for a chief to show up.* He finished the phone conversation and hung up.

"Hello, Sir," he said. "I guess you'll want a briefing?"

I tried to remember what it was like to be in his shoes. He was in charge of that station's operations for 8 hours, serving more than 100,000 people, with all the problems they can concoct. And that afternoon, he had just under 20 uniformed officers to try to keep some semblance of order.

"Lieutenant," I answered, "I suspect you've got plenty to do without briefing me. Give me a sergeant who knows a little of what happened, and you take care of business. When you get your head above water, we can talk. Where's your captain?"

"He's down in the detective squad room. We've got a suspect. Sergeant Rocket here can give you the story."

I motioned for Rocket to follow me out into the hall. I remembered him. One night when a shooter high in a multistory building had pinned down one of our officers, Rocket had led me down a dark alley toward the action. We had started zigzagging to get closer to the building when our own helicopter lit us up with its light. That was a nervous moment or two. Rocket takes some ribbing about his name, but not from too many; he's a no-nonsense veteran who has paid his dues.

"What have we got, Sergeant?" I asked.

He consulted his notebook and told me, "About 40 minutes ago now, Jefferson High School was having its homecoming celebration. I guess they had some sort of parade. Several of the homecoming princesses or queens were on a car or float. This guy came out of the crowd and just started shooting. Three of the girls were hit, one badly. She may not make it."

"Have we figured out the motive?"

He frowned and shook his head. "No, we haven't. It doesn't make any sense. You should go talk to the detectives. We rounded up anyone who knows anything about it. They're talking to the 'wits.' They have some guy they suspect in custody."

I thanked Rocket and walked down the hall toward the detective bureau. About 35 detectives worked out of this station. Their tables and desks were crammed into 1 squad room about 25 by 50 feet, with a few in an overflow room. If stacked reports and mug books are any indication of work, those guys had more than their share.

I walked over to where I saw the captain and several detectives talking. As we approached, the captain turned and said, "Hello, Chief. We've sure got a senseless one here."

"Yeah, I heard."

"The good news is we've got the shooter. Several eyeball wits put the jacket right on him. He's in that interrogation room." He gestured toward one of the closet-sized rooms off the squad room.

"The guys from SID [Scientific Investigation Division] are doing the gunshot residue test on his hands right now. As soon as they're through, Jerry will do the interview." The captain indicated Jerry Ferrin, one of the best interrogators around. If anyone could get the suspect talking, it was Ferrin.

"Jerry," I said, "when you start the interview, I'd like to sit in. Will that cause you any problems or interfere with establishing rapport?"

Ferrin shrugged his shoulders. "No, I don't think so. I'll tell him who you are. I know this guy. He'll probably get a charge talking with the big brass. It might even make the job easier."

Several minutes later, we were sitting in the room. Our interview rooms almost always come from the same cookie cutter—five feet by seven feet in size; Armstrong tile on the ceiling and floors (the kind with random tiny holes all over); usually painted light green; furnished with a plain table and three plain wooden chairs.

We sat on one side of the table. "Cool Aid," the street name by which he preferred to be called, sat on the other.

Ferrin went through some small talk with the suspect. He knows how to treat people warmly, even the bad guys. Soon Cool Aid was talking freely. Ferrin got him a cigarette and lit it for him. Within a few minutes, he was talking about the shooting, which he admitted doing.

"Cool Aid," Ferrin asked, "why did you shoot them? What's the story?"

Cool Aid was looking at the table. He quickly glanced up and took a long drag from the cigarette. "There's no story, man," he answered, "I just need a name. You know—a rep."

"A reputation?"

"Yeah. I'll be known as the enforcer."

Ferrin did a good job of concealing his feelings as he said, "You've got to know something, man. One or more of those girls may die. You may be facing a murder charge. Do you understand that?"

"Yeah, I kind of figured that might happen. But it's no big deal. I'm a 'juvie.' I won't do more than three years. You guys know that as well as I do. I need to do some time anyhow. I've got a few teeth that need filling, I may have a dose of the clap, and I need to get in shape—you know, get buffed out on weights. I need some jail time. Then when I come out, I'll have a rep."

In a few more minutes, Ferrin had the location where Cool Aid had dumped the gun. A team of detectives was sent to pick it up. The case was a "wrap." But what a perverted sense of logic! Several girls were shot, one was near death or paralysis, and for what? A reputation. Evil as a badge of honor.

Most of us will agree that Cool Aid's logic is sick. Something is wrong when a human being looks upon an act of violence as a proud achievement. But believe it or not, Cool Aid has a lot of company in that way of thinking.

In my lengthy law-enforcement career, I've seen a shift in the way our culture views selfish antisocial acts. None of us is perfect. We've all taken actions that later caused us shame. But in the past, when people broke a social taboo, they generally felt some guilt and remorse. They knew they had violated the moral consensus, and they wanted to hide the transgression, not flaunt it. But that's changing.

The story of Cool Aid, although true, is an extreme. Being proud of a deadly, senseless assault is the epitome of the problem I'm trying to describe. But sometimes the best way to see a problem is when the circumstances are obvious and flagrant.

What we see so clearly in Cool Aid's case is the third major root problem destroying our society and families: the loss of conscience. The trend is to no longer be ashamed of our darker side. This shocking trend is ravaging our culture. It's becoming a badge of honor to not only violate social norms, but even to flaunt that behavior, like the bumper sticker that announces, "So many men; so little time."

The significant change is not in the acts we perform. As Solomon wisely said nearly 2,500 years ago, "That which has been is that which will be, and that which has been done is that which will be done. So, there is nothing new under the sun" (Ecclesiastes 1:9).

The behaviors have always been there, even those we've recognized as harmful to society. The significant change is in how we react to those actions. Today it's not uncommon to literally applaud a person who discloses what in the past has been looked upon as a weakness. The "Phil Donahue Show" is an obvious example of this trend. People get on nationwide TV, admit to breaking their marriage vows, and boast of a determination to continue the practice. Others talk of purposely bringing a baby into the world with no family to support it. Some flaunt the lies and deception that have brought them wealth, and many brag about cheating the government on their tax returns. Usually the audience cheers the speaker's "courage" in publicly going against the social norms.

The change has happened gradually and with great subtlety. The first step was to encourage the noble trait of acceptance. It was recognized that people who err need help, not rejection. This position is not without good foundation. Jesus Christ did not condemn the woman caught in adultery. He didn't reject her. But neither did He accept the act: He condemned it and told her to do it no more. I call that the Jesus principle. He hated the sin, but He loved the sinner. That's an important principle that has been muddied over the years.

In the name of acceptance and tolerance, we've become confused. We now accept not only the person, but the antisocial conduct as well—the weakness.

As a student at Claremont Graduate School, I was forced to read, study, and report my knowledge of the Federalist Papers. Those essays were written after the drafting of the U.S. Constitution to "sell" it to the American people. During the ratification of that great document, Alexander Hamilton, James Madison, and John Jay wrote the essays to give the electorate an understanding of the principles behind it. They're the best insight we have into the thinking of the people who established our great heritage.

In those essays we see a consensus about some basic principles. One of them dealt with the nature of mankind. The writers recognized our bent to go the way of least resistance. So, they explained, the framers of the Constitution took steps to restrain our weaknesses rather than give free rein to them. In Federalist Paper number 6, Alexander Hamilton wrote:

> To presume a want of motives for frequent and violent contests with each other . . . would be to forget that men are ambitious, vindictive and rapacious. To look for a continuation of harmony between a number of independent, unconnected sovereignties in the same neighborhood would be to disregard the uniform course of human events and to get at defiance the accumulated experience of the ages.

That statement could be used to explain such current problems as the gang warfare that plagues our city neighborhoods. Our early leaders recognized that the nature of humanity is flawed, that checks and balances are needed to counter our bent toward harmful behavior. They wisely understood that our darker side should not be encouraged; that rebellion should not be praised. Somewhere along the line, however, that realistic approach was lost.

For example, the Los Angeles City School District, in May 1992, designated the month of June each year as "gay pride month." I don't know all the implications of that action. I assume it means the children will be taught that *gay* means "homosexual." It appears the school board is placing a badge of honor on people who choose to commit homosexual acts.

I don't presume to judge for anyone other than myself the morality of those acts. But whether immoral or not, they clearly are not natural. Any doctor will admit that the act of sodomy is harmful to the body. The body parts were not made to accomplish that act. Therefore, the act is unnatural.

Consider a parallel: I am writing this book with an Apple Powerbook 140, a laptop computer. I could use this wonderful device in another way, adopting a preferred life-style of using it as a hammer to pound nails. That act would not be immoral. But no one could argue logically that it wouldn't be a deviation from the machine's intended use. The computer was not made to pound nails; I would be perverting its use to do so.

The spirit of rebellion is present in all of us. We all have the potential to give in to our weaknesses. Thus, we all need encouragement to exercise discipline, not dissipation. Historically, when a culture has taken the giant step of encouraging behavior that erodes important institutions like the family, it has crumbled.

Our society should be inclusive, not exclusive. It's noble and right to accept all people. But it's destructive to endorse all behavior. There's a big difference between the two.

When there is no shame for wrong,
violence, perversion, and abuse abound.

20

ROOT CAUSES:
NEGLECT OF PRINCIPLES

When wrong is defended,
when right is attacked,
the pillars of social structure
crumble and fall.

The three beeps indicating a "hotshot" interrupted the conversation of Officers Dave Tyrie and Al Jost as they drove slowly south on Lincoln Boulevard, approaching Manchester. They were both outdoorsmen and were planning a duck-hunting trip. Now they paused, waiting for the broadcast.

"All units in the vicinity and 14 A 23. 14 A 23, a 211 in progress, shots fired, at the liquor store at Culver and Centinela. Handle the call code 3."

A 211 indicated an armed robbery. Code 3 means red lights and siren.

Tyrie and Jost were working 14 A 56 and in position to assist. Jost was driving. Tyrie told him, "Al, let's try covering the south end. If they go that way, they'll probably either get on the 405 or use Sepulveda."

Jost increased his speed a bit and turned east on Manchester.

"All units, additional on the 211 at Culver and Centinela. The suspects are described as two male blacks; both in their mid-20s, average height, wearing dark clothing. They left the scene in a dark green, possible MG sports car, canvas top, southbound on Centinela. They took approximately $700 in miscellaneous bills. Use caution. Shots were fired; they are armed."

"Hot dog, they're coming south," Tyrie said. "Let's take Sepulveda. The CHP can handle the freeway. If they live in South-Central, they'll be going across the city on either Century or Imperial. I'm betting Imperial."

Jost nodded his head in agreement.

Tyrie keyed his mike. "14 A 56, we are going code 100 on Sepulveda, between Century and Imperial. Requesting the CHP be notified to handle the 405 southbound."

"14 A 56, roger, showing you code 100 on Sepulveda, between Century and Imperial."

It was after 11:00 P.M., and traffic was light. Jost accelerated past a couple of slow-moving vehicles. As they approached Sepulveda, the light turned red. Jost braked for a stop, looked northbound, and, seeing no close traffic, slid through the signal, turning right (south). The rear tires broke loose a bit but caught traction again as he hit the accelerator.

"Dave, am I seeing things or is that an MG about a block ahead of us?"

Tyrie squinted, straining his eyes to see past the two cars immediately in front of them. "Could be, Al. Let's boogie around these cars and get a closer look. Don't make it too obvious. Let's get in nice and easy."

Jost carefully eased past the first car, passing on the left. The second car was in the center lane. Jost would have to pass on the right or blink him over with his high beams. He didn't want to do that, so he waited patiently until he had plenty of clearance and then passed on the right. He accelerated slowly, gradually gaining on the car in question.

Tyrie was leaning forward as if that would help him see better. The car passed under a street light. It was now less than half a block ahead of them.

"Bingo, Al. It's an MG all right. Green, too. We've got the turkeys. Don't hit the reds until we're right on them."

"You got it, Partner."

Tyrie keyed the mike. "14 A 56, we are following a green MG southbound on Sepulveda, approaching Imperial. Possible suspects in the 211 at Culver and Centinela. Do you have a plate number on the suspects' vehicle?"

"14 A 56, negative on the plate. Do you need a backup?"

"14 A 56, roger. Get one unit rolling this way. We are going to attempt a stop on

Imperial, east of Sepulveda."

Turning to Jost, Tyrie said, "Okay, Partner, let's get right on their tail and 'light them up.'" He talked a little quicker than usual; the adrenaline was starting to flow.

Jost flipped the switch for the red lights. He also activated the system that turned his horn pressure point on the steering wheel into a siren. Tyrie picked up the hand-held spotlight and began flashing it into the rear window of the car as Jost activated the siren. The sports car quickly accelerated rather than pull over, turning onto Imperial. The chase was on.

"14 A 56, we're in pursuit. We are following a green MG sports car, canvas top, eastbound on Imperial Highway. Possible suspects in the 211 at Culver and Centinela. We've got a partial plate of King, Henry, Henry. Notify 77th Area, we're heading their way."

"All units on all frequencies, stand by. 14 A 56 is in pursuit of a green MG sports car. Partial license number King, Henry, Henry; eastbound on Imperial Highway. 14 A 56, your location."

Tyrie was taking the shotgun out of the rack when Jost spoke. "Watch it, Partner. The passenger is putting his arm out the window. He may be going to shoot."

"No, he's throwing something out." Paper fluttered into the air, scattering a trail behind the fast-moving car. "My gosh, it's money!" Tyrie said. "They're getting rid of the money!"

Tyrie keyed the mike. "14 A 56, the vehicle we are pursuing is throwing paper currency out of the window. We've got the suspects all right."

The MG took a sharp right turn onto Prairie Boulevard. Jost was hanging close as Tyrie tried to confuse the driver by flashing his blinding spotlight into the rear plastic window of the canvas top.

The pursuit continued. Tyrie read off the streets as they flashed by. Soon they were in the city of Hawthorne. The MG had turned onto a side street and nearly hit a couple of other cars.

Tyrie shouted over the siren, "Partner, we've hit that moment of truth. These guys are going to kill somebody. We either terminate this chase or we stop them. I'm going to stop them. Get me as close as you dare."

Jost punched the big V8 forward. Tyrie was leaning out the window with the Ithaca 12-gauge shotgun. He sighted quickly and squeezed the trigger. A large ball of flame belched from the huge muzzle, temporarily blinding him, as the gun slammed against his shoulder with a roar.

The MG swerved, seemed to hesitate, and then leaped forward again.

"I think you hit the deck," Jost yelled.

"I know I hit the deck lid. See the holes on the right? Just where I had my sight pattern. Get up close again. I'll give them another warning."

The patrol car closed the gap. Tyrie's skill with a shotgun struck again. This time, 15 32-caliber pellets from a magnum load struck the left side of the deck lid. The occupants couldn't have missed the loud blast of the gun or the rattle of the pellets penetrating the metal of the car. But they continued their escape attempt.

"Okay, this one is for real. I'm putting this one through the plastic window on that ragtop."

Once again the large gun bellowed. Tyrie's aim was higher. The MG continued forward a few seconds and then skidded to a stop.

My phone rang a few minutes before midnight. I jumped out of bed, moving as fast as I could to the hallway. It had to be the office that late.

"Captain Vernon, this is Charlie Strupkow from DHD [Detective Headquarters Division]. A couple of your men have been involved in a shooting."

I got the sketchy details, threw on some clothes, and drove to the scene. By the time I arrived, the only personnel left were the Officer Involved Shooting (OIS) team from Robbery/Homicide. The head of the OIS team gave me the briefing.

The third shotgun blast had gone through the center of the MG's plastic rear window. Fourteen pellets had exited the windshield; one hadn't. The passenger had slid down in his seat for protection when he heard the first two blasts hit the car. His knees were high. The fifteenth pellet had struck his left knee, nearly removing the cap completely. It was a painful wound, but he would make it to trial a few weeks later. Some of the loot remained in the car, and a gun lay on the floor.

The officers were back at the station. The OIS team would get complete statements from them after they questioned all the other witnesses. I called out our Law Enforcement Explorer Scouts (young people who were part of an LAPD program designed to acquaint them with police work) to help search for the scattered money. Believe it or not, much of it was recovered.

Several weeks later, I had the completed OIS report on my desk. I had gone over it thoroughly. Officers Dave Tyrie and Al Jost had been successful, but they had violated a departmental rule against shooting at a moving vehicle. I called them in for an interview prior to submitting my final recommendations to the shooting review board.

They were both sitting in front of my desk in the old Venice station. I told them I had reviewed the investigation and offered Tyrie the chance to explain why he had violated our no-shoot rule. He was eager to respond.

"Sir, the way I understand our shooting policy, I believe I can justify my actions. Our reason for not shooting at moving vehicles is based on a few important principles. First and foremost, we have a respect for life and must do all we can to protect it."

So far he was right on. I could see he had put a lot of thought into his presentation.

Tyrie continued: "Based on that basic principle, generally we don't shoot at cars for three reasons. Number one, the chances of hitting a moving car from another moving car are slight. Generally I agree with that. Not, however, in this case. That MG was no match for our Plymouth Fury Interceptor. We were right on their tail. Added to that is the fact that I'm good with a shotgun. I shoot skeet and trap all the time. I'm a bird hunter. I knew I could put those pellets right where I wanted to."

"Okay, Tyrie, I'll buy that," I said. "But there are other factors involved."

"I know, Sir. The second reason we don't generally shoot is that even if our bullets hit, they are usually ineffective. Most of the time they will just ricochet off the vehicle and hit somewhere, or worse yet, someone else. On that score, I've got two thoughts. First, I was using a shotgun, not my pistol. No one was on the side street we were on when I shot. And a ricocheting shotgun pellet is not going to penetrate a house like a rifled bullet will. Second, they were in a ragtop. I knew I could be effective."

He was making some sense. I would hear him out.

"Finally, we don't shoot because if we are effective, we have a driverless car that is going to crash."

I wondered how he would handle that one.

"They were already a moving missile, endangering people's lives. Chances were that would continue even if we broke the pursuit. These were dangerous men. They were armed bandits who had used their gun. In the public interest, we had to stop them if we could do it safely.

"Sir, I know you went to the scene that night. You had to see that the neighborhood was filled with apartments. There was inadequate off-street parking. The curbs were lined with parked cars. I knew that if the car went out of control where I took that final shot, it would just crash into a parked car. I firmly believe my decision to shoot was a good one. I think it is in accordance with the principles I have been taught by you. It was either allow the danger to continue or do what I did."

In my opinion, his logic was good. I later presented his case to the shooting review board. The deputy chiefs listened carefully to all the facts and logic as I argued for an exception to the rule. After a thoughtful debate, the majority of the panel voted to classify it as an out-of-policy shooting, but they recommended no discipline or corrective action due to the mitigating circumstances.

That event illustrates the important difference between rules and principles. Rules are essential and usually have good reasons behind them. But without the foundation of guiding principles, rules can become meaningless. They can actually lead us to the wrong action. Standing by themselves, rules can also breed contempt and rebellion. When a rule doesn't make sense, it is questioned and often rejected.

A bedrock of guiding principles, however, is supportive to rules. When we understand the reasons behind the rules, we're more apt to keep them. Principles also give needed flexibility when rules don't apply. They provide true guidance rather than thoughtless, rote procedures and regulations. They make it possible to carry out the spirit of the rule maker and not just be in technical compliance. If we understand a principle, it is sometimes necessary to go beyond the rule to fulfill the spirit of the principle.

Neglect of principles is the fourth root cause of the problems destroying our society and families. Our culture is in deep trouble because, generally, we have done a poor job of passing on the Judeo-Christian principles on which this nation was founded.

My examination of historic American documents and literature reveals the founders had an obvious knowledge of principles. They wrote about them, discussed them, taught from them, and believed them. They went past the surface of clichés, pronouncements, and rules. They were deep thinkers and true intellectuals.

They discussed principles like the importance of lifetime family commitment; submission to authority; respect for the property of others; patriotism and loyalty to country; honesty and integrity in both business and personal living; the moral connection between love, marriage, and sex; and the recognition of and accountability to a higher power (in my family, God).

For several decades, the many logical reasons behind a lifetime monogamous sexual relationship between husband and wife have been neglected. As a result, children are entering the world without two parents committed to their normal development. Also, sexually transmitted diseases are epidemic, and the murder of unwanted, unborn babies is creating a holocaust.

Neglecting the principles pertaining to integrity, diligence, loyalty, and authority has also affected America's work force. We now have difficulty competing with the rest of the world in terms of product quality.

It takes time and communication skills to pass on principles. Determination and patience are also required. Our busy lives and personal agendas have pulled us away from meaningful communication. But it's far more effective to provide guidance through understandable principles.

When I was a boy, we had few choices to make regarding our free time (which we had more of, because there were fewer demands on our lives). The alternatives were meager. Often we sat around and did something that's rarely done today, even in family settings: We talked. Yes, my parents set some rules and followed them up with discipline, but they undergirded the rules with principles. They gave me true guidance.

Dealing with principles requires thought, energy, and time. It's much easier to declare an order, speak a taboo, or prepare a regulation. The rules and mandates were passed from one generation to the next, but somewhere along the line, we stopped instilling the principles held dear by our founders. Our lives became too cluttered with a surfeit of activities and roles. Various alternatives emerged to fill our lives, including TV, other electronic gadgets, long commutes, and various leisure activities.

Our culture survived in that mode for a generation or two. Then children began to question the rules and challenge the taboos. They asked questions like "Why not have sex outside of marriage?" Many parents and other authorities could not provide thoughtful answers. And soon the rules were rejected. A social revolution was under way.

Today we live in a world of confusion. The guiding plumb line has vanished. Relativism has replaced time-tested principles and become the religion of the day. Its basic doctrine states that there are no absolutes and there is no real truth. Relativism and its cousin "openness" declare that circumstances and context have more to say about right and wrong than any absolute code of morality. Professor Allan Bloom, in his classic book, *The Closing of the American Mind,* commented on this phenomenon:

> The danger they [today's college students] have been taught to fear from absolutism is not error, but intolerance. Relativism is necessary to openness, and this is the virtue, the only virtue . . . it is the great insight of our time. The point is not to correct mistakes and really be right, rather it is not to think you are right at all.

During the last several decades, we have not only turned with a vengeance away from God, but we have seemingly set about to excise any and all of His principles from our culture. Now we have no guiding absolutes. We are adrift.

Democracy does not work without a moral consensus. America was an incredible success story when we had that consensus. When we departed from absolutes expressed in principles, we lost it. Now we're not only floundering, but our thinking has become so perverse that we often reverse right and wrong. Consider these examples:

> It is right to hand out condoms in our schools.
> It is wrong to criticize having babies out of wedlock.
>
> It is right to investigate someone's religious beliefs.
> It is wrong to investigate subversion.

It is right to murder innocent babies in the womb.
It is wrong to execute convicted murderers.

It is right to use political correctness as a litmus test in evaluating a person's career.
It is wrong to use an applicant's criminal record.

A looter was stopped by a TV reporter as he left a toy store in south-central L.A. with both hands full of toys. The reporter asked him, on camera, what he was going to do with the toys.

He replied that he would give them to his children.

The reporter then asked, "You are going to give stolen toys to your children?"

"They're not stolen," the man rationalized. "I just took them from this store. Everyone is doing it." He smiled and continued on his way.

> *Woe to those who call evil good, and good evil;*
> *who substitute darkness for light and light for darkness;*
> *who substitute bitter for sweet, and sweet for bitter!*
>
> *Isaiah, circa 700 B.C.*

21

ROOT CAUSES: ARROGANT ELITISM

When the arrogant elite rule,
the eye of history is blind.

I saw more than my share of murders in almost four decades of police work, and I saw gray hair come quickly to a lot of guys working homicide. But two killings in particular stuck in my mind and convinced me we had to do more to *prevent* crime rather than just reacting after the fact.

One night, I was called to a gruesome crime scene. The victims were two innocent girls. The older girl had recently finished high school, and her parents had given her a bright red car as a graduation gift. Proud, happy, and full of life, she had offered to take her little cousin for a spin in her new "toy."

Shortly after they left home, as they drove through a nice, quiet neighborhood, two men forced them to the side of the street, got out of their own vehicle, and calmly pumped multiple shots into the red car. The girls never had a chance. It was an execution, plain and simple.

The girls had no gang connections, no enemies we could find. Nor had they been robbed. On the surface, the brutal killings seemed to be without motive. Later the same night, however, the story came out. Two men who had been ripped off in a drug deal had decided to get revenge by blowing away the girlfriend of the man who had cheated them. They had staked out the area where the woman lived, waiting and watching for her red car. When the car they thought was hers appeared, they had acted quickly and ruthlessly.

The killers had hit the wrong people. Two wonderful young women had been murdered for nothing. And to make matters even worse, when the suspects were told of their mistake, they looked at one another and laughed. At that point, my sympathy for the grieving families turned to intense anger toward the assassins.

Because of seeing so many murders, I knew what others were feeling that night. The profound grief, the sense of loss, the irreparable deep hurt were just beginning for scores of friends and family touched by this heinous act. Their tears even now were flowing and would continue until none were left. And that was just the beginning. This was wrong. This was evil.

Later, on my way home from the crime scene, the tragedy I had just witnessed weighed heavily on my mind. I thought of the grieving family members. How would I react if one of my loved ones were murdered? How would I feel toward a human being who laughed about stealing my beloved's life? The statistics coming across my desk concerned me. But seeing, hearing, and feeling a tragedy as I had that night reminded me of the misery and deep grief that accompany each statistic. We cannot become dulled to the impact of such events.

I also thought of the murderers. How do human beings become so brutal, their consciences seared to the point of having no remorse, pity, or guilt? What is happening in our culture that spawns such people? They have gone beyond the point of immorality to being moral flatliners, dead to thoughts of right and wrong.

I felt helpless. Our job was to protect the people of L.A., yet more and more of this violence was occurring. We were doing our best; the men who pulled the triggers on this horrible crime would probably be convicted. But the carnage would continue. We had to do more. Traditional investigation and enforcement must continue, but additional measures to prevent this type of thing were needed.

Shortly after the murder of the two young women, I shared my frustration with my staff. The killings were increasing, and nearly half of the drive-by victims were innocent bystanders. We had to try something different. I asked for ideas.

Now here is where the story ties in to the societal problem I want to address in this chapter. We did come up with an idea to reduce crime, an excellent idea that worked well (so well that I think it should serve as a model for cities across the country). But when we reported the positive results of the program to a group of so-called community leaders, we met with strong resistance. The reasons for their opposition are a clear example of the arrogant, elitist attitude that's doing so much damage today. But let me go back and tell this part of the story from the beginning.

In response to my request for ideas, Lieutenant Sergio Robleto called my attention to some recent experiences in one of our Valley Bureau areas. Certain streets had been blocked off, restricting traffic to residents only. The results were amazing. The area, previously infected with gang activity, drug sales, and graffiti, made a dramatic reversal. The small neighborhood was reclaimed. Sergio wondered if that approach would work in a larger area—perhaps the most dangerous neighborhood in the city.

I asked him and his staff to research our crime data and find the single census tract in L.A. that had the highest number of drive-by shootings. He identified our Reporting District number 1345, which comprises 40 square blocks of an inner-city neighborhood in our Newton Area. The population was dense; more than five thousand residents lived in less than seven hundred dwellings. In the year prior, this small area had reported 34 drive-by shootings. It also ranked among the top 5 most-crime-ridden districts overall. More than 150 assaults and street robberies were reported during the same time. Many residents admitted crime was underreported. One lady said there was so much crime, she felt it was useless to continue reporting it

The district also faced other challenges. It had recently undergone rapid ethnic transition. In 1988, approximately 95 percent of the residents were black. Now nearly 60 percent were Hispanics, many of them newly arrived immigrants.

I liked the choice of RD 1345 as a target. The people needed help desperately, and if innovative alternatives worked there, they would probably work anywhere.

For help with the project, I met with Dr. James R. Lasley, associate professor of criminal justice at California State University, Fullerton. I had worked with him on another project and found him to be energetic, curious, brilliant, and open to new ways of doing things. I explained the crude plans I had developed with my staff. He was interested and agreed to provide counsel, guide us in forming the conceptual framework, and conduct the outside evaluation of the project.

We also brought in Captain Gordon Harrison, Newton Area CO. He liked the idea and wanted the chance to be the leader to make it go. In turn, he selected a young, energetic sergeant to take this as his personal project. Sergeant George Gascon would become the glue that brought all the factors together. He developed a passion for the experiment and became the driving force behind it.

What we needed to do was to help create a sense of community in RD 1345. Young people need parents to nourish and guide them, but they also need the support of other social institutions—the backing of a community. In large cities like L.A., however, neighborhoods usually have an "identity crisis."

Herbert J. Gans, an authority on social organization, defines a community as "an aggregate of people who occupy a common and bounded territory in which they establish and participate in shared institutions." According to that definition, few areas in L.A. can qualify as communities. Certainly RD 1345 could not. It had experienced such rapid changes that it had no identity. Its geographic, demographic, and institutional boundaries were nebulous. Its residents shared no common social bonds.

This presented a problem if we were going to help improve life in RD 1345, because we needed community approval, support, and participation. We were convinced that crime control is best achieved through informal, citizen-based control networks—that crime is ultimately controlled by the public and not the police. Therefore, we needed to establish a police-community partnership. But there was no community. Somehow a sense of community had to be established, so that's where we decided to start.

We went to Al Howenstein, director of the state's Office of Criminal Justice Planning, for some seed money to get the program off the ground. He caught the vision and approved a grant. We were on our way.

To kick things off, a public meeting was held at Jefferson High School announcing our desire to help the community develop an identity and form a partnership. It was attended by several hundred residents. Interest was high.

We also went directly to the people. All seven hundred houses were canvassed. Since the district had no natural boundaries—it was just part of the massive grid of streets of south-central L.A.—we asked if the residents approved of the construction of some type of boundaries in order to create a physical sense of community. We found that more than 94 percent did, even if it meant closing certain streets.

With that support, we moved ahead. Initially, temporary cement road dividers were used to block off several streets. The idea was to form a type of cul-de-sac neighborhood. Later, the barricades were replaced with wrought-iron gates and large cement planters holding trees and shrubs. We wanted to discourage nonresidents, intent on criminal activity, from entering a maze of streets with limited exits. Additionally, the gates formed an obvious boundary, physically identifying the community.

Streets with a history of frequent drive-by shootings or drug traffic were selected for closure. The gates were locked to all traffic. Only emergency services agencies were given keys to allow entry for their equipment. All residents could get to their houses, but they experienced some inconvenience in having to pass through limited entry points.

Once the external symbols of community were in place, work began on the internal community structure. Initially, 15 police officers were assigned to the area. They walked foot patrols and rode bicycles. Their primary mission was to establish a friendly partnership with the community. Arrests and citations were not their measure of success. Rather, the absence of crime and an improved relationship with the people was their goal. Later, once the community mobilization took hold, it was possible to reduce the number of cops.

The officers also coordinated various city services to improve the environment. Crews were brought in to remove garbage from streets and alleys. Graffiti were painted over. The neighborhood began to look good.

Next, the officers organized a picnic at a local playground to celebrate the rediscovery of the sense of community. We arranged for funds to hire school teachers on an overtime basis to tutor students needing extra attention. Block clubs were started as a forum for the officers and community members to communicate their specific needs to each other.

Within a few months, it became apparent the experiment was a resounding success. Dr. Lasley performed a before-and-after survey of the residents. A solid 82 percent felt that placement of the barricades around their neighborhoods created a stronger sense of community. An amazing 93 percent said they had become personally acquainted with more of their neighbors. While crime was increasing in the rest of the city, it had dropped in the experimental area. Part one crimes (an FBI classification of those most reliably reported, like murder, robbery, rape, and burglary) were 15 percent lower than in the previous year. Nor was crime simply being displaced to adjoining patrol sectors; part one crime in those areas was also down—about 9 percent on average.

Most dramatically, *drive-by shootings dropped 70 percent in the district.* No doubt this was one of the primary reasons residents became less afraid. Approximately 65 percent more of them were willing to walk in their neighborhoods at night.

Confidence in the police improved as well. Prior to the test, 49 percent of the residents gave the police a highest possible rating of "very helpful." Six months into the program, the rating increased to 63 percent. And after one year, this rating climbed to 78 percent.

Interestingly, the last rating was taken *following* the highly publicized Rodney King incident. When the residents were asked why they still held the police in high regard, the response heard most often was, "The police we have gotten to know are different. They would never do anything like that."

Perhaps the most unexpected effect of the program was experienced at Jefferson High School. About two months after the program began, the principal, Phillip Saldivar, called Captain Gordon Harrison to report a problem. He said his cafeteria director reported running short of food. When they checked into what was causing this shortage, *they discovered the average daily attendance had leaped by more than two hundred.* Truants were coming back to school. When they were asked why they had decided to return, they answered candidly, "It's now safe to come to school."

My stereotype of a truant was shattered. Apparently many young people do not attend school because of fear. When that fear is removed, they willingly attend.

That's the kind of success we were able to achieve in reducing crime and improving quality of life. We had a program of demonstrated worth that deserved to be implemented throughout the city. But then arrogant elitism reared its ugly head.

Chief Gates called one of his regular meetings with some of the leaders of south-central Los Angeles. He wanted me to brief them on the progress of several programs the department had going. "Operation Cul-de-Sac," as our experiment was now being called, was on the agenda. We were approximately a year into the program. I would give an overview, and Sergeant Gascon would fill in the details. Gascon and I were up in spirits. It's fun and rewarding to be able to report good news once in a while.

I started the overview with a map display and handouts describing the program. As I made the presentation, I observed the group. Something was wrong. The body language and other nonverbal messages clearly said the people didn't like what they were hearing. I didn't get it. The news was good. The operation was working.

Some of them began to ask questions. They were concerned about the possibility of bad perceptions. Wouldn't the gates and barriers make the area look like a war zone? Could it be perceived that the gates and barriers were intended to restrict people's freedom to move about? Weren't we fencing people in like in a concentration camp? And why hadn't we come to them first to get permission to begin the experiment?

I answered their questions calmly, with as much control as I could muster. I believe some were honest expressions of legitimate concern. But after those were answered, the resistance continued on the part of some. It became clear that they had a hidden agenda.

I described the comprehensive surveying of the residents in the involved neighborhoods, explaining that over 90 percent were in favor of the program. One of the leaders interrupted, saying that people don't always know what's best for them and that this group of leaders should decide on such programs for the people.

Gascon's face began to flush. He was personally involved. He had been there daily, on the streets, talking to the officers and people. He saw the great improvements in the community. He knew the program was a success. He knew it could be just as successful elsewhere if it had the support of this influential group. Then he erupted.

"Which one of you actually lives in the experimental community?" he demanded.

No one spoke. His voice increased in volume.

"I asked if any of you lives in the Cul-de-Sac area!"

Again silence.

"I didn't think so. We have just told you that 94 percent of the people who live there want it—desperately need it—are crying out for it—and you have the gall to sit here in this air-conditioned room and try to shoot it down. You are trying to take it away from them for some petty political reason that I—"

Chief Gates broke in. He thanked the sergeant for his part in the presentation and told him he was excused.

After Gascon left, Gates took on the group who had attacked the program. Not all of them did. One, a local college professor, spoke in support of Sergeant Gascon and the experiment. But some remained rigid in their opposition. A clue to their resistance came when someone said ideas like this should not come from the police department; they should come from their organizations or from the politicians. I was stunned.

We needed their political support. The program had some costs above the normal police budget, and the funds received from the state were only start-up money. The city would have to continue the financial support: one hundred fifty thousand dollars a year. That amount, however, was a small fraction of the costs of the usual social programs.

But this important group of leaders had an unexplained, peculiar resistance to a strategy that was accomplishing our common goals. Lives were being saved, the quality of life was improving, and perhaps most importantly, a community was being rebuilt. Support systems for the family were being shored up. Maybe over the long haul there would be fewer moral flatliners, fewer people who kill and then laugh.

No wonder Gascon lost it.

I later got some insight into the motivation of those community leaders from a deputy to one of the city council members. The issue, he said, was money and power. When programs like Operation Cul-de-Sac are funded through special community groups, patronage jobs are available. Our program had practically no administrative cost. The money went directly to the program, so no porkbarrel jobs were available. The power brokers got no opportunity to make people indebted to them. Instead, the police were the good guys in this program.

Operation Cul-de-Sac was still working well when I retired. Crime was still dropping, school attendance was high, and community reaction was positive. I had an architect prepare drawings for making the neighborhood cul-de-sacs more cosmetically appealing by having the temporary gates transformed into attractive boundaries and small playgrounds.

Unfortunately, due to the lack of political support from the power brokers, I fear for the program's continued success. The councilwoman representing that district reportedly asked that the gates be removed. Sergeant Gascon told me as I was finishing this book that the program will soon be all but dead.

This story happened in Los Angeles, but it's representative of what is happening across the nation. I believe that a spirit of arrogant elitism like that shown by those community leaders is the fifth root cause of the breakdown in our families and society.

Unfortunately, many in our country look with disdain on "the common people." They view themselves as society's intelligentsia. They know what's best for us. They are members of Congress, of the judiciary, and of the executive branch. They are also college professors and political action committees (PACs). They're members, too, of the most powerful force in our country today—the news and entertainment media.

The elitists among the groups I've mentioned all share one attitude: They're not interested in or impressed by the desires, values, or ideas of us ordinary people. They are not true learners. They think they already have the corner on knowledge. They have closed their minds to anything that doesn't fit their view of the world.

The elitists patronize an open mind, but they behave with intolerance. They advocate what they call a "plurality of thinking," yet they crush and ridicule those who dare oppose their positions. The arrogant elitists created the concept of being "politically correct."

The most dangerous attribute of the elitists, however, is their blindness to the obvious. They disregard the lessons of history. Oh, they know of the historic failure of some behavior patterns. They're aware of the harmful effects of certain social adaptations. They realize other cultures have been destroyed by the very values they accept and promote. But they actually believe they are superior to those who have tried such things before and failed. Somehow, now, here in our enlightened state, they believe they will break the mold. They think our society can walk the same path that has led others to oblivion and yet not pay the terrible toll. The elitists are intoxicated with their intellect and power.

The elitists can't wield power, however, without a constituency. They are a small, deluded, but passionate band; their remarkable success requires a following. Their strength lies in the mass of people who blindly go along with their deception. Thus, those who buy into the line of the elitists face a terrible accountability. They haven't challenged their corrupt leadership. They are either apathetic or in agreement with the perverse elitist mentality.

We all need to react individually and collectively when we see this elitist attitude. We must express our opinions in a variety of ways—for example, in the voting booth and as we decide what products to buy and which media to support. I'll say more about this in the final chapter.

Another clear example of the way this arrogant elitism works is found in the way the L.A. city charter was changed after the Rodney King incident. The charter reform of the late 1930s corrected an abuse of power. It recognized the truth that power corrupts and that absolute power corrupts absolutely. That's why the chief of police was insulated from the influence of political power brokers with civil service protection.

The post-Rodney-King "reformers" were successful, however, in duping the public, convincing them to reverse that earlier, wise measure. They claim the city no longer needs the checks and balances it provided. Their "eye of history" is blinded to the lessons of the corrupt 1930s, or else they are purposely seizing power. Either way, L.A. is now on course to repeat the painful mistakes of the past, and it almost certainly will.

> *Woe to those . . . who justify the wicked for a bribe,*
> *and take away the rights of the ones who are in the right!*
> *Isaiah, circa 700 B.C.*

22

WHAT WE
MUST DO NOW

I have described what I believe to be the deep root causes of our social problems. Those insights are based on nearly 38 years of dealing with the surface symptoms every day. It would be much easier to focus on the superficial symptoms, to recommend some step-by-step programs for dealing with them and ignore the deeper issues. But providing temporary relief from the symptoms is not enough. We have to get beyond the fever and treat its cause.

This means dealing with basic values and attitudes. It isn't easy to change attitudes. Commitment, personal sacrifice, and a spirit of humility will be required. Just as every individual—including me—finds it difficult to admit to going down the wrong track, so do we collectively as a society. But we *are* going down the wrong track, and the first step to changing that is to admit it to ourselves.

I don't pretend to know all the answers. But I do believe I know where to focus our attention.

That's not to say we should ignore the symptoms, however. Many actions need to be taken to address some pressing surface problems. We learned from the 1992 Los Angeles riots that police executives need to be insulated from political pressure. Everyone knows that our criminal justice system needs an overhaul; that we must improve our job training in certain communities; that many of our schools are failing in their mission; and that our children should be protected from blatant pornography. We have an abundance of problems that need immediate first aid, and

I don't mean to make light of them.

The purpose of this book, however, is to address what I think is the most urgent root cause of our cultural breakdown. I want to focus on the family.

Every social problem we're experiencing is related to the disintegration of our families. The August 1992 issue of *Fortune* magazine was devoted to the plight of the American family. The lead article stated that the problems of our families are affecting the "entire American social order." One of the articles said that the most reliable predictor of criminal behavior is growing up in a fatherless family. That claim came from data supplied by the National Center for Health Statistics: Compared to children from two-parent homes, children from single-parent homes are 100 percent to 200 percent more likely to experience emotional behavior problems, and 50 percent more likely to experience learning problems. Seventy-five percent of single-parent children will sink into poverty.

If we can bring all our attention to bear on this true root cause of our dilemma, we will change the course of our history. We'll get off our downward spiral to destruction and oblivion. Dysfunctional families breed all sorts of problems and unhappiness—alcoholism, drug abuse, criminal behavior, mental illness, incest, violence.

The American dream should not be a few people living together in a luxury house with two cars in the driveway, a collection of electronic gadgets, and a ski boat—but the father is an alcoholic, the kids are druggies, and the mother is involved in an affair. We must have a fundamental shift in our values. People, rather than things, must be our first priority. To move in that direction, I offer the following seven imperatives.

1. The family must be protected and strengthened.

Some tough decisions need to be made, followed by actions. It's easy to agree that our culture's most important institution must be preserved, but it will be hard to do it. Children deserve to have two people committed to them, and to one another, for life. A broken family causes great anxiety, insecurity, and anger for all concerned, but especially the children. The ideal situation is for children to grow up in warm, supportive, and stable families where they are loved.

Unfortunately, this is often not the case anymore. The traditional family is becoming an exception to the rule. Broken families and children born out of wedlock may soon make up a majority of domestic arrangements. But that should not make us back away from the ideal of the two-parent family, as some suggest.

Using the logic of those who say we should abandon the ideal could lead to this scenario: A man breaks his leg in several places, causing it to bend unnaturally. Paramedics arrive on the scene, and they administer first aid to prevent additional complications and begin preparing him for transport to the hospital. But someone at the scene argues, "Don't worry about treating the leg. It's broken—that's reality. We have to accept it and not try to fix it. Just make him feel good. Don't even call attention to the fact that he's seriously injured. That will just make him feel worse. Give him some drugs."

That logic is as flawed as the thinking of those who say, "Face reality: The family is broken. Don't try to fix it. Don't say things that point to an ideal relationship— that just makes people feel bad. Make them feel good by telling them that their arrangement is normal and acceptable."

Although the job is difficult, broken legs are repaired. We do not retreat from that ideal. Neither should we abandon the model of the two-parent family.

We need some ideals to aspire to. There's nothing wrong in offering people a challenge. Of course hurting people need some first aid. But they also need to see a doctor. I believe the American family needs to see the Doctor.

To strengthen and protect the family, I specifically recommend the appointment of a federal family czar who, like the drug czar, would report directly to the president. None of the other issues faced by our government will matter if our families continue to deteriorate. All else pales in importance.

Furthermore, this czar must be given the right mission. He or she must be charged with supporting the ideal, and statistics like those in the *Fortune* magazine articles show that the traditional family is still the ideal. That doesn't mean that the mass of families that don't match the ideal are ignored or denigrated. It must mean, however, that we don't throw in the towel on what we know is best for our children.

A family czar would bring national leadership to this issue. We need to more clearly define public policy on the family. This czar should be charged with ensuring that policies throughout government are "family friendly." To make this position work, the czar must either have appropriations from Congress or the power to influence them. The lack of such power has been the weakness of similar positions in the past. A czar must do more than just articulate policy; he or she must have direct influence over the money that will ensure implementation of those policies.

The czar could also use the position as a bully pulpit to honor healthy families and hold them up as models, as well as to condemn behavior destructive to the family. This goes a step beyond simply stating the ideal, recognizing that people are more powerfully guided by seeing what is rewarded and what's condemned than they are by mere rhetoric.

We should not shy away from condemning dysfunctional behavior. That is how a culture moves toward the ideal. Behavior can be rejected without rejecting the individual involved. Once again, I am not recommending forcing a prescribed morality upon all. People performing antisocial acts need help and encouragement. But often the first step of help is to let them know their behavior is harming them and others.

Our welfare systems also need to be changed to become more supportive of the family. Right now they tend to be completely at odds with this posture. They actually reward sexual promiscuity and punish responsible work efforts. This has got to stop. We can tell welfare recipients that we want to see responsible behavior from them. But if we continue to reward irresponsible acts and punish responsible ones, most of them will follow our actions, not our talk.

For example, fathers must be made to support their offspring. The lack of action to hold fathers accountable is disgraceful. Those who accept their responsibility should be rewarded; those who don't must be punished.

Another idea is to begin requiring family impact reports on proposed legislation and other governmental actions in the same way environmental impact reports are already required. As things stand now, decisions are often made that adversely affect families, yet that impact is never considered carefully beforehand. If we're serious about helping family relationships improve, that has to change. Before setting public policy or passing legislation, a study should be required to assess the impact on the family. And all proposed measures should have to pass the test of being "friendly" to the traditional family and an encouragement to parenting.

Let's look again at our broken welfare systems. Experts from both political parties agree they actually destroy rather than support families. A program like Aid to Families with Dependent Children (AFDC), for example, encourages out-of-wedlock births, because the mother gets more money for each child born, yet benefits can be canceled or reduced if she marries. Getting a job can likewise result in having benefits cut or eliminated altogether.

In our inner cities, where welfare is most prevalent, its effects are obvious. For example, in 1960, more than 75 percent of black families were intact, with both parents nurturing the children. By 1985, that figure had dropped dramatically to just 50 percent. More recently, in its May 18, 1992, issue, *Newsweek* reported that two-thirds of the nation's black children are born out of wedlock.

The whole welfare system needs to be rebuilt. Some people legitimately need the government's help and will never be able to live without it. However, the system should feature incentives to direct most recipients toward marriage or work and, eventually, financial independence.

The government should also do more to help two-parent families make the choice to have one parent stay at home with the children. It takes time to communicate properly, teach values, and provide meaningful guidance. With both parents working outside the home full-time, these things become extremely difficult. "Latch-key kids" suffer neglect. Moreover, the best of child-care centers cannot meet all the needs of a young, developing human being.

How can government help? One possibility is a federal earned income tax credit (EITC) for two-parent families that have one parent at home. An EITC would be more desirable than an income tax deduction, since it rewards work. The more income earned, the more credit is allowed. Some may argue this would result in lower overall tax revenue, but the operative principle is the one used to advertise car parts: "Pay me now, or pay me later." Offering tax incentives for parenting could dramatically reduce the cost of picking up the pieces of poor parenting in terms of police, courts, mental health care, jails, and other corrective measures. An ounce of prevention could be worth more than a pound of cure.

On the other hand, there should be no government assistance for child care when both parents work by choice rather than out of necessity. Some families desperately need and deserve government help, especially single-parent families. But government policy should not encourage two-parent families to abdicate their responsibilities to their children.

If the federal government had tried to force us a few years ago to allow someone of its choosing to take our babies from us, we would have resisted with all our might. Most parents want to give their own kids the love and guidance they need. They want to implant in them their beliefs and values. Yet somehow, because government-regulated child care frees parents to increase their standard of living—"for their families"—it is now acceptable and even demanded by many. We have deceived ourselves.

Our commitment to value our children over material things must be translated into action. Our expectations for prosperity have risen sharply during the last several decades. Our poor are rich in comparison with most of the world. We must turn our expectations around. It won't be easy, and it won't be done overnight. It will involve discipline and sacrifice. But all parents must ask themselves, "What can I do to fix my family?" The first steps may include a parent's choosing to stay home, even if it means reducing the family's material standard of living.

If you asked our two grown children which year stands out in their memories as a great Vernon family year, they would both mention our time in the Chicago area. Without doubt, that was our poorest year financially. We were paying our mortgage in California, rent in Chicago, my school costs, plus many other unusual expenses. We ate a lot of macaroni and cheese, sitting on chairs someone else had dumped. All we really had, other than the absolute necessities, was one another. But there was a lot of love, and we talked, played, laughed, and cried . . . together.

I am meeting more and more young couples who have made the difficult decision to lower their standard of living in favor of their children. Our children and their spouses are two of those couples. Our son's wife works full-time in the home, nurturing their two sons. Our daughter works almost full-time in the home, raising her five children. (As an RN, she works one day a week at the hospital to keep up her skills and qualifications.) Her husband is a police officer. Both families must pinch their pennies. They have less than most of their peers materially, but they're rich in happiness and love.

We need to realize that when we give up the responsibility of parenting our children to someone else, we're choosing something above our kids. If this fact is understood, I believe most Americans will choose their children. We have deceived ourselves on this issue. We *can't* have everything. On this most important issue, a choice must be made. Career and money issues are in direct conflict with parenting responsibilities. A balance is needed. When the choice is to put the highest priority on careers and material wealth—when both parents work full-time outside the home—family life *will* suffer. It's that simple.

2. The media must hold up self-discipline as a model rather than dissipation.

In today's world, the media are powerful opinion makers. The pen has always been more powerful than the sword. Now, the media have not only the pen, but also many other highly sophisticated tools to help communicate ideas and values. Radio, TV, videos, and movies have made the media one of the most powerful forces in our world community. Like it or not, they mold our thinking and shape our values.

Dr. James Q. Wilson, a noted professor in the field of criminal justice, identified four probable contributing factors to our radical rise in crime and violence in recent years. One of them is "a change in the popular culture which emphasized self-indulgence or self-expression as opposed to self-control." I believe Dr. Wilson is right on target.

People who achieve greatness and cultures that pursue excellence have one thing in common—discipline. The loss of self-control brings mediocrity, unhappiness, and eventually low self-esteem. Without discipline, we become takers rather than givers. There is no easy road to excellence, but taking its hard, steep path pays off.

We must all develop and exercise self-control. We can't blame the media entirely for our decline in this area. However, the media have played a big role in this regard. Our children constantly see models of self-indulgence glorified in the media, along with behavior destructive to the family. This is doing our culture great harm.

The media can be influenced without resorting to censorship. Our real position on this issue is measured in our willingness to accept their product and even pay for it. We must choose carefully what books we buy, which videos we rent, and what movies we go to see. When we're offended by a TV program, we should write to the sponsors. If we're not satisfied with the sponsors' reaction, we should stop buying their products. I have already stopped buying certain things, even though I like them, because I'm offended by the antifamily positions of the parent corporations. The media can be held accountable by their customers—you and I.

3. We must develop anew a moral, ethical consensus.

This is the most difficult recommendation to implement. I don't have all the answers on how it should be done, but I'm convinced it is an absolute necessity. Democracy does not work over the long haul without a moral consensus. A free society depends on voluntary compliance with a core of standards and norms. When the percentage of individuals deviating from those norms goes above a certain point, the social systems begin to break down. That's what has happened in America.

Our criminal justice systems are in shambles. Our police can no longer respond in a timely manner to the increasing calls for service. Our prosecutors are forced to plea bargain cases rather than go to trial since they and the courts would otherwise be overwhelmed. Our probation systems do not work because our probation officers likewise have unrealistic caseloads. Our prisons and jails are full, forcing the early release of dangerous criminals to make room for incoming inmates. We are a civilization in crisis.

In these ways and more, we are reaping the results of abandoning moral and ethical absolutes. As Dr. Allan Bloom observed in his landmark book, *The Closing of the American Mind,* we have closed our minds to absolutes. The religion of openness and relativism has created a monster. Taken to an extreme, openness ironically prohibits our being open to the possibility of ultimate truth. Genuine openness should recognize that real truth may exist out there—that there is the possibility of moral and ethical absolutes.

Dr. Bloom pointed out that "the old view was that, by recognizing and accepting man's natural rights, men found a fundamental basis of unity and sameness." But now, he said, "the recent education of openness has rejected all that. . . . It is open to all kinds of men, all kinds of life-styles, all ideologies. There is no enemy other than the man who is not open to everything. But when there are no shared goals or vision of the public good, is the social contract any longer possible?"

As a society, we have growing intolerance for anyone who believes something—anything. As William F. Buckley has stated, abuse of the word *judgmental* by the relativists has made it impossible to oppose a given position based on morality. The growing bigotry toward people who hold to moral absolutes is founded in the notion that if someone believes profoundly in a set of morals, he or she will undoubtedly try to force those values on others. But in most cases, that assumption is just not true.

I recognize that true morality cannot be legislated. That's not what I'm recommending. However, our forefathers were able to build a moral, ethical consensus. They may not have all lived according to that consensus at all times, but they acknowledged that when they didn't live by it, they were immoral. They didn't try to justify their actions by calling them "right," and they didn't demand that everyone agree they were in the right.

A moral, ethical consensus, even if it's not followed by all, is the first step toward eliminating moral flatliners. When a society agrees upon pursuing noble goals, the process is begun. Many will change their actions. Therefore, we need a few basic goals of desirable behavior—not mandates, but goals.

The Ten Commandments would be a good place to begin. A strong majority of Americans already agree that those basic statements of right and wrong are worth pursuing. Let's post them in our schools and allow their standards to be used as ideals again. Let's include their principles in the stories in our children's reading primers. It's hard to understand why we allow books that many consider pornographic in our schools but prohibit using those time-tested morals.

I believe that establishing a moral consensus will, of necessity, involve the recognition of a higher power. That in turn leads to accountability, and accountability ultimately demands the acceptance of the concepts of right and wrong.

In their book *Lessons from History,* Will and Ariel Durant observed, "There is no significant example in history, before our time, of a society successfully maintaining moral life without the aid of religion."

Our first president, George Washington, also recognized this need when he said, "Let us with caution indulge the supposition that morality can be maintained without religion. Whatever may be conceded to the influence of refined education on minds of peculiar structure, reason and experience both forbid us to expect that national morality can prevail in exclusion of religious principle."

Building a moral consensus would help us find our lost conscience.

245

4. We must rebuild our cities to support the family.

Many of our large cities are hostile to the family, whereas smaller communities seem to be more supportive. Various theories attempt to explain this phenomenon, but there is little debate that it's so. Our experiment with Operation Cul-de-Sac (see chap. 21) proved that even the most dangerous section of Los Angeles could become a better environment when it was changed into a small community. Therefore, we should take steps to break down our large cities into many identifiable neighborhoods.

The cost of making the structural adjustments would be a one-time expense. The savings in criminal justice expenses alone would pay for it. But more importantly, the change would benefit the family. Most of our newer suburbs feature planned cul-de-sac neighborhoods. The advantages of limited access and community identification have been demonstrated. The generally poorer families of our inner cities deserve those same advantages.

Other strategies to rebuild our cities must be tried as well. For example, urban enterprise zones to attract businesses and jobs to the inner city seem to have great potential. So does occupant ownership of public housing. Job training provided by privately supported ministries like Dr. Keith Phillips's "World Impact" is another necessity.

5. We should adopt a school voucher system.

All our experience shows that children learn better when their parents are involved in and supportive of their schools. Today, however, parents are not supportive for many reasons. For some, the school is too distant—their children are being bused out of their community. Others view the schools as teaching things they do not believe, competing with them for the minds and souls of their children. Adopting a voucher system would set the stage for more parental involvement and support.

Such a system would distribute tax dollars to schools that parents believe in. All parents—rich and poor—would be able to choose the schools for their children. Those who so desired could pick schools that include religious training. In short, parents could choose schools that support their value systems and reinforce what they are teaching in the home.

There will always be some schools, however, that enjoy little or no parental involvement. We all have a responsibility to support the children who find themselves in such schools. Churches and civic groups should consider "adopting" such schools. Several service clubs in the Los Angeles area have taken such action.

The L.A. #5 Rotary Club, for example, provided several hundred thousand dollars during the last few years to fund the DARE (Drug Abuse Resistance Education) program in schools that couldn't afford it. The Lake Avenue Congregational Church in Pasadena, California, offers a tutoring service to children in its neighborhood. Other service clubs provide scholarship money to children who remain in school and desire to go on to college.

6. We must form family political action committees.

Elected officials understand that political action committees (PACs) are a major source of political power. Those leaders may not like the agenda of a given PAC, but they listen to its representatives anyway. PACs can bring blocks of voters together to concentrate their power. They're also a big source of campaign funding.

My suggestion is that people across the country form profamily PACs in their neighborhoods, cities, and states. As individuals unite to promote family-building public policy, their collective impact can be great.

To find out what may already be happening in your state in this area, as well as what issues to consider getting involved in, I recommend you take a look at *Citizen* magazine. (For subscription information, write to Focus on the Family, Colorado Springs, CO 80995.)

7. We must each be willing to take the first steps.

The soul, the essence, of America is not in its land. It isn't even in its matchless Constitution. The real heart of America is in its people—you and me. If America is going to survive—if it is going to change its destructive course—we must change . . . individually.

Don't wait for someone else to make the first move. You and I must make the first moves, take the first steps. If we don't get involved, America won't change. We *are* America.

History is abundant with obvious examples of behavior and attitudes that led to the collapse of nations. We must not close our eyes to those examples; rather, we should learn from them. We do not have superior qualities that make us immune to the results of conduct that destroyed cultures before us. To truly learn the lessons of history, we must be willing to admit to ourselves that we do not know it all. In other words, we need a profound national humility that often seems to be missing today.

But again, *we* are the nation, so the humbling process has to start with each of us. A true story from inner-city L.A. will show how genuine humility is the beginning point in developing hope and purpose in people of any age and in any place. Without such humility, we have no lasting hope. But with it, our nation can surely be restored.

Eric, age 12, was living with his grandfather in the Jordan Downs housing project when the riots began. He was scared, but his grandpa had showed him how to slump down on the couch, below the level of the windows, while watching TV. The brick construction of the building ought to stop a bullet. Eric had learned to live with gunfire, which is common in that part of town.

Eric's situation is all too familiar. His mother, Darlene, had him when she was 15 years old. Her first pregnancy occurred earlier; that baby was aborted. Another pregnancy ended with a stillborn delivery, probably due to her drug abuse. (An adult started her using drugs when she was just 12.) She was still a child with severe problems when Eric came along, and she had reasons not to trust people. After Eric, she had two girls and two more boys, though she never married.

When the riots began, many boys Eric's age joined in the burning, looting, and shooting. In a strange, sad way, 12 years old is older in the projects than it is in other parts of town. But Eric did not get involved in the riots, because 4 years earlier, he had found some hope.

Eric was on his bicycle when he first saw her that summer day. A lady had set up her "classroom" out in the sun, near the wall of one of the housing project buildings. The temperature was nearly 90 degrees. Broken glass littered the ground.

A group of 25 to 30 children, mostly black, was gathered to hear the lady tell stories from the Bible about Moses, King David, and Jesus. Her stories illustrated important principles like loyalty, respect for others, self-discipline, sacrifice, and love.

Eric was interested. The lady had a flash-card book with pictures that she used to illustrate her stories. He wanted to listen, but he was cautious. He cut tight circles around the group with his bike. Then he just sat on his bike.

The lady saw him and said, "Why don't you come over and sit on the blankets on the grass with the others? You sure are welcome to do so. Come on over."

Eric didn't answer. He just started pedaling around again, trying to look uninterested but still listening.

That was the beginning.

Nancy Thomason, the lady who reached out to Eric and the other children, lives with her husband in a middle-class suburb of Los Angeles. But more than most people, she cares about what goes on around her. She cares about others.

She knew Eric was interested, even though he tried to look otherwise. He was eight years old that summer, and he was black, angry, and suspicious, especially of white people. Nancy Thomason is white.

Most white, middle-aged women are afraid to venture into Jordan Downs, and with good reason. That part of the city is very dangerous. Nancy Thomason knows that, but she's compelled to go anyway. She wants to give hope to the children growing up there.

Eric eventually started joining the other kids as they gathered each week to hear Nancy. His two sisters were regular attendees as well. Eventually his grandfather invited Nancy to use his apartment for the Good News Club meetings.

Later in the summer, Nancy secured some scholarships to a summer camp. Eric was the only one of his brothers and sisters old enough to attend, and he was offered the chance to go. For him it was a dream come true. His grandfather approved. Eric could hardly wait.

The day for camp departure arrived. When Nancy Thomason drove over to pick up Eric, however, she found his mother waiting. Nancy could see anger and hostility in Darlene's eyes as she introduced herself.

"Hello, I'm Nancy Thomason," she said. "I teach your children Bible stories every week."

"I know," Darlene replied. "What do you want now?"

"I've come to pick up your son Eric and take him to the bus that will take him to summer camp."

"He ain't going," said Darlene matter-of-factly. She threw her head to one side and stared challengingly at Nancy, daring her to disagree.

Nancy didn't know what to do, but she knew Eric would be devastated if he couldn't go. So she decided to try playing the same assertiveness game. "His grandfather already gave his permission. Eric, take your things to the car."

"Eric, stay here." Darlene took a step toward Nancy, planted her feet, and stuck both hands on her hips. "Look, woman, this is my child. There is no way—no how— he's going with you. His grandfather can't be giving his permission over my child."

Nancy could see she was not going to push this mother into something she didn't accept. She saw more than anger and hostility in Darlene's eyes; she also saw fear and the protective love of a mother.

"Darlene," she said, "I can see you love your children. You really love them, don't you?"

Nancy paused, waiting for some response. Darlene continued to stare at Nancy, a strong frown furrowing her brow. Then some moisture appeared. She seemed determined not to let it happen, but a tear formed and crept down one cheek, then the other. Darlene broke her stare and wiped away the tears, almost in anger. Her eyes flashed back to Nancy's.

"Yes, I love my babies, and I don't want to lose them." She grabbed her five-year-old daughter, April, and pointed to a scar on her neck. "Here is where they shot my baby when she was only three years old. I was standing next to her when it happened. They weren't shooting at her, but she nearly died. I don't want anything happening to Eric."

"Neither do I, Darlene. I love your babies. That's why I come over here every week."

Darlene looked at her, but this time it was not in challenge. It was a searching look.

Nancy began to understand. She invited Darlene to accompany her to the local church where a bus would pick up the children. She could meet some of the leaders and have her questions answered. Darlene went and looked things over. Then Nancy drove her back to the projects. As they arrived, Darlene turned and looked at her. For the first time, Nancy could see her eyes softening.

"I guess I have to learn to start trusting somebody—sometime," Darlene said. She gave her permission for Eric to go.

Eric had a great camping experience. He had fun with the games, the crafts, and the campfires. He also enjoyed the Bible stories. He learned important principles in those stories. He also learned of God's love and that God had a plan for his life. He learned to pray. Eric began to have hope.

Today, Eric continues to attend the Good News Club. He has memorized portions of the Bible and has chosen to respond to the love he has learned of and experienced. He saw in the life, death, and resurrection of Jesus Christ a model of love and power he had not witnessed on the streets of L.A., and he committed his life to Him.

Darlene is now being affected by the faith of her children. Her two daughters have also begun a personal relationship with God. Danielle, her ten-year-old, recently plead with her in a letter she sent from her foster home: "Mommy, I want you to please pray this every night, 'Dear Lord Jesus, please help me, so me and my children can come together and be a family.' Mommy, please pray that every night . . . please."

Darlene reported to Nancy, "I know God. I believe in Him. I know He can help me." At the time of this writing, Darlene is several months into a drug treatment program. She's not "out of the woods" yet, but I believe her prayers and those of her children will some day be answered.

The Sunday after the riots started, Nancy Thomason met with Eric, his sisters, and their grandfather. She wanted to know how they were faring. They were saddened and disappointed by the riots. Their neighborhood stores were burned down. The grandfather reported that he must now travel all the way to Wilmington (several miles) to shop. When asked why he didn't join others in the looting, Eric said, "Because it is bad." When asked why it's bad, he replied, "God does not want us to do that."

Some say the faith of a child is meaningless. Some say that efforts like those of Nancy Thomason are wasted. Some believe that even sincere steps of faith by the young are not fully understood and therefore have no lasting effect. I have to disagree. I began my own personal relationship with God in a Good News Club.

In spite of the decay, gang warfare, and despair surrounding Eric and his family, I believe they have real hope. I believe their future is brighter than their past. And I believe they and others like them in their community will have a positive impact for years to come. Their faith and moral convictions are L.A.'s greatest hope for a better tomorrow.

The same is true for our nation as a whole. President Abraham Lincoln recognized this in an earlier time of great national peril. His words, now more than one hundred years old, are just as relevant today—maybe even more so:

> We have been the recipients of the choicest bounties of heaven. We have grown in numbers, wealth, and power, as no other nation has ever grown. But we have forgotten God. We have forgotten the gracious hand which preserved us in peace and which multiplied, and enriched, and strengthened us, and we have vainly imagined in the deceitfulness of our hearts, that all these blessings were produced by some superior wisdom and virtue of our own. Intoxicated with unbroken success, we have become too self-sufficient to feel the necessity of redeeming and preserving grace, too proud to pray to the God that made us.

Fortunately, a growing number of people realize that treating the surface symptoms, although necessary, is not enough. They understand that our troubles are deep and fundamental. But more important than that, they're willing to do whatever is necessary to change their attitudes and actions—even if that means humbling themselves before God.

Fortunately as well, God has promised to respond when we turn to Him in humility. As He said through the prophet Jeremiah, "And you will seek me and find me, when you search for me with all your heart."

EPILOGUE

A sergeant with more than ten years on the LAPD called me when he heard I was writing this book. He gave me the following statement:

"On the first day of the riots, I worked through the night. The total experience was unreal. It seemed as if the whole city was on fire. Fire Chief Manning's staff car arrived at the scene of one of the bigger fires. We were trying to protect the firefighters from sniper fire. Someone called to my attention that the Fire Chief had arrived. I turned to look. There, protruding out of the windshield of his car, was a bottle of champagne. The whole scene was bizarre.

"When I got home the following morning, I turned on the TV for a few minutes. I saw the various recorded videos of the riot. I watched with horror and sorrow. I was exhausted and weary. When they replayed the beating of Mr. Denny, I wept. I am not easily given to tears, but I wept. In the past, we had always responded to people who needed help. I watched as a man, in my city, was nearly beaten to death—and no police were there to help."

Webster's Collegiate Dictionary (5th ed.), defines *justice* as "the virtue which consists in giving to every one what is his due; practical conformity to the laws and to the principles of rectitude in the dealings of men with each other." *Rectitude* is defined as "undeviating adherence to moral standards; uprightness." In other words, *justice* means conforming with undeviating adherence to *moral* standards in our social interaction.

The Los Angeles experience has provided a valuable glimpse into the future of America. Today, since we have gone through a purging of moral standards, there's not much justice in L.A. But we have a chance to change things for the better for all our citizens. The questions before us are these: Do we have enough resolve to act? And do we have enough humility to ask for help?

Made in the USA
Charleston, SC
31 January 2012